AGATHOS Kalos
EXCELLENCE IN CHRISTIAN PUBLISHING

# UNQUENCHABLE FIRE
Teresa Eklund

# UNQUENCHABLE FIRE
Teresa Eklund

AGATHOS *Kalos*
EXCELLENCE IN CHRISTIAN PUBLISHING

WASHINGTON, D.C.

Unquenchable Fire

Copyright 2006 Teresa Eklund

Published by

Agathos Kalos

*"Excellence in Christian Publishing"*

6601 Lawndale Drive

Falls Church, Virginia 22042

ISBN - 13: 978-0-9785186-0-8

All rights reserved. No part of this publication may be reproduced or transmitted in any form or by any means, electronic or mechanical, including photocopy, recording, or any information storage and retreieval system, without the prior written permission of the publisher.

Book design by Harriet R.T. Lewis

Cover design by underpindesign (www.underpindesign.com)

Printed in the United States of America

# DEDICATION

*This book is dedicated to my incredible
husband. Steve, I love you!
You have been a living demonstration to me, over and
over again, of my loving heavenly Bridegroom. If our
earthly marriage is just a small taste of what marriage
to the Lamb will be, its wonder and
beauty defy my imagination, and my heart cries out all
the more "Come, Lord Jesus, Come!"*

# TABLE OF CONTENTS

Prelude……………………………………….......i
Introduction ………………………………..............iii

1st Movement – The Symphony …………....…..…....…1
   Chapter 1 – Heaven's Song …..…………………..5
   *Song of Solomon 1:1*

2nd Movement – Awakening ……………………17
   Chapter 2 – Awakening Sleeping Beauty ……....21
   *Song of Solomon 1:2-1:4*

3rd Movement – Desire ……………….…………..33
   Chapter 3 – Dark but Lovely …………………39
   *Song of Solomon 1:5-1:11*

4th Movement – Rest ……………….…………….63
   Chapter 4 – Feasting on the Lord ………….......67
   *Song of Solomon 1:12- 1:14*

5th Movement – Romance...……………...……....85
   Chapter 5 – Romance of the King……….….......89
   *Song of Solomon 1:15-2:7*

6th Movement – The Sign of Spring ……………..107
    Chapter 6 – The Call …..……………………......111
    *Song of Solomon 2:8-2:17*

7th Movement – Turning …………………….…...131
    Chapter 7 – Divine Discipline …………….…....137
    *Song of Solomon 3:1-3:5*

8th Movement – Who is This? …………….……...153
    Chapter 8 – The Desert ………………….….....155
    *Song of Solomon 3:6*

9th Movement – Picture of Destiny …………….177
    Chapter 9 – Bridal Carriage; Funeral Pyre ….181
    *Song of Solomon 3:7-3:11*

10th Movement – I Will Go! ……………......…..199
    Chapter 10 – Answering the Call ..…………..203
    *Song of Solomon 4:1-5:1*

11th Movement – The Midnight Hour ………...221
    Chapter 11 – Dark Night of the Soul ……....227
    *Song of Solomon 5:2-5:8*

12th Movement – Beauty of the King ……….....245

Chapter 12 – The Gospel of Love ……….……....249
   *Song of Solomon 5:9-6:9*

13th Movement – The Vision Unfolds ……….….....267
   Chapter 13 – The Dance ……….......………......271
   *Song of Solomon 6:10-8:4*

Finale – Blazing Love ……………...…………….......285
   Chapter 14 – Unquenchable Fire …...…….........289
   *Song of Solomon 8:5-8:14*

Postlude – High and Lofty Wall …………….....…..303

Endnotes..................................................................307

About the Author ..................…………………......321

# UNQUENCHABLE FIRE
Teresa Eklund

*Prelude*
# Song of Creation

*Listen to the song of creation
A symphony of never-ending praise
Patiently waiting My redemption
Longing for the Desire of the Days*

*Can you not see?
Do you not understand?
The wind is My breath
The song is My hand*

*Let the music touch you
Let it reach your inner core
For there is none like Me
From now and evermore*

*Listen to the song of My creation
A symphony of never-ending praise
Patiently waiting My redemption
Longing for the Desire of the Days*

## Introduction: The Journey

I invite you to come with me on one of the most exciting journeys of your life, a journey designed to touch every one of your senses and evoke every emotion within your heart. This is a journey filled with adventure, danger, and love. This journey will take you into the very heart of God.

Often as we enter into our walks with God we experience triumphs and tragedies that completely confuse us. Much of the confusion stems from the fact that we really don't understand how much God likes us. I have come to realize that God is indeed crazy about the crowning jewel in His creation – mankind.

For me this journey really started one week in 1991, when God totally surprised me. I was attending a worship conference with a friend who was the worship leader at our church. Her husband didn't want her to drive the six-hour trip by herself so she asked me to go with her. Because I am not a worship leader or musician, I thought that I was just going along for the ride. But God had much bigger plans in store. I soon discovered that this trip was as much for me and my destiny as it was for my friend. It was here that God began to open my heart wider.

The theme for the weekend was intimacy. Although I had been a Christian for several years at this point in my life, I don't remember hearing people talk about God in the way these speakers were. They spoke on the love of God and His ravished heart for us. They spoke on covenant and being the Bride of Christ. I was in awe!

One of the speakers at the conference was Mike Bickle, senior pastor of a large church attended by several of my friends. He stood before us sharing about the believer's journey into the heart of God through a book of the Bible, Song of Solomon. I was riveted. Something within me came alive as I heard from the very Word of God of the journey into Jesus' heart. Mike was explaining that within the Bible there is a description of the progression of spiritual growth for each individual believer, and it is contained in this little-known book sandwiched between Ecclesiastes and Isaiah.

God created us to be passionate beings. But because that was foreign in my church experience, I often found my expressions for passion coming out in sinful ways. But here I was sitting in a church listening to men of God tell me that God Himself is passionate and that everything He has done on this earth is for one purpose – to express that passion to mankind.

At that time a friend of mine worked for Mike Bickle and was also at the conference. As I shared with her how touched I was by Mike's teaching, she agreed to send me her notes from the class she attended that Mike had taught on the Song of Solomon. Within a few weeks of that conference I received those notes in the mail. That week at the conference and the notes from Mike Bickle's class launched me on a lifelong study into this magnificent book. It has literally changed my life: the way I read Scripture, the way I see God and the way that I embrace life's circumstances. And, perhaps most importantly, it has given me the freedom to express the passion within my heart to God, purely and righteously.

So I invite you, once again, to join me on this journey into the heart of God through the Song of Solomon.

## Introduction

### The Song of Solomon

As we begin to look at the Song of Solomon we must realize that there are several ways that this book has been interpreted over time: 1) the perspective of a natural husband and wife, 2) Israel and God, 3) the church and Jesus, and 4) the individual believer and Jesus. All of these views are valid. God's word is so deep that it can have many applications without deviating from the truth. The way we will be looking at it is from the viewpoint of Christ and the individual believer.

I have found as I study the Scriptures that the words of the English language tend to be less descriptive than their original Greek or Hebrew meaning. As we walk through this book together I will note when I have learned something from going to the Greek or Hebrew word in Bible concordances. We also must keep in mind that this book is highly symbolic because it is the lyrics to a song. (We will discuss this more at length in the next chapter.) Looking into the word as a symbol can also shed much light into the deeper meaning.

### The Characters

As we begin to go through the song together we will see that this song is written like a duet accompanied by a choir. Throughout you will hear three voices expressed.

1. <u>The daughters of Jerusalem.</u> Throughout the study the daughters of Jerusalem will be referred to as "friends." The daughters of Jerusalem represent other believers in the body of Christ. *Jerusalem* means *double peace*. It is by seeing the meaning of their title, *daughters of double peace*, that we are shown that they are part of the body of believers.

2. <u>King Solomon.</u> Solomon will be referred to as "Lord" or "Bridegroom." The name *Solomon* means *peace is His*, and he represents Christ. For we know Christ is the Prince of Peace, and all true peace is only found in knowing Him.

3. <u>The Shulamite maiden.</u> The Shulamite will be referred to as "believer" or "bride." The Shulamite maiden, who is the object of affection in this book, represents the corporate Bride of Christ and also the individual believer. As stated earlier, we will be looking at the Song of Solomon from the perspective of Christ and the individual. We will see how in the life of the Shulamite our own lives and relationship with the Lord are represented. *Shulamite* means *perfected in peace*, for as we walk out our lives in Jesus then we become perfected in Him.

## Tools for the Journey

As I have put together this book you will begin to see that each chapter has 5 distinct sections. These are here to help us better grasp within our hearts the reality of God's love for us.

The Song of Solomon is a song of love. Love cannot be intellectualized; it must be felt. Just as there are several different ways that we learn intellectually, there are several different ways we learn with the heart. Teachers say that there are three different types of learners and several combinations of those learning styles. There is auditory – we learn by hearing; visual – we learn by seeing; and kinetic – we learn by doing. The way the heart learns is really not that different than the head, but the medium that brings the message usually is. The head learns through facts, but the heart learns through feeling. Often feelings are expressed through the visual arts, music and poetry.

# Introduction

Somehow art, music and poetry open our hearts to grasp things in different ways. So it is with this in mind that I have attempted to utilize as many of the learning styles as possible to touch both your heart and your head.

The first section within every chapter is what I affectionately call "The Symphony." It is within this section that I have taken artistic license with the actual Song of Solomon and written it out more fully by using less symbolic language and giving examples as to how the actual story could be played out.

Next you will find the bulk of the writing. These parts of the chapters contain the commentary. Here I will share with you revelation and insights that will help to bring understanding to this often-confusing book. Here we will look at those strange descriptions that are used and dissect their meaning, phrases like "You are a mare among the chariots of pharaoh" (Song of Solomon 1:9). Although, because of space, I have not gone through each and every line of the scripture, that I hope to do in a follow-up study. (See www.unquenchablefire.com)

Between both the symphony and after the commentary you will find a section called Selah. *Selah* is a Hebrew word that means *to pause and reflect*. The first Selah is just for you to breathe and allow the allegory of the symphony to sink in. The second Selah has a paragraph of questions to think on. I have put them into paragraph form because they are not necessarily meant to be answered, but rather to help you to think. They are to be used as thinking and writing prompts. Questions to help bring it to a more personal level and apply it to your life.

Previously I mentioned the different learning styles; the last Selahs are intended to help you with the next section, which

vii

utilizes the kinetic learning style. After the last Selah, get out a notebook and write. Some of you may say that you don't like writing. I never thought I did. I hated anything to do with reading and writing. Now I love them both. Much of what you will read in this book comes out of my journals.

I discovered something within myself when I began to journal – sometimes good things, sometimes ugly things that needed to be cleaned out. I also discovered that I often hear God as I write. I encourage you as you begin each journaling section to write at least 2-3 pages, even if you don't feel like writing. If you don't know what to write, write that. Even that will help to unlock some of the things that are deep within. Also don't feel like you need to like everything I have to say. If you disagree or get angry, write about it. Use this time to allow the Spirit of God to bubble up and out.

Lastly you will find a list of books that have been of great impact to me. Over the years these books have touched me and drawn me closer to the Lord.

So let's begin our journey into the heart of God.

## 1st Movement
# The Symphony

This is it, the night that you have been looking forward to for months! All the preparations have been made and the tickets bought. Your first symphony! It is the unveiling of what is touted to be the best symphony ever, with the orchestra beyond compare. This is something you've only ever heard about, and now you get to experience it first hand. There is a little apprehension, as this is unfamiliar music to you and unfamiliar surroundings. But you've read all the previews, you've heard people talk, and now you felt it was time to experience it yourself.

You enter the grand hall. It truly is more spectacular than you imagined: red carpet, golden walls and beautiful chandeliers. The patrons are all decked in their finest; women shine like jewels with a beauty that seems unmatched. The tuxedo-clad usher leads you down the aisle. There is an energy in the air that is almost tangible. A sense of romance sweeps over you, almost bringing a tear to your eye. Pushing it aside as "silly," you find your seat and settle in.

The lights lower in the auditorium. A hush falls over the crowd. The conductor walks to center stage. Excitement wells up within you. The conductor turns to the audience and makes a sweeping bow. The applause of a full house reverberates to the ceiling. The conductor turns to the orchestra, and, tapping his baton on the music stand, calls the musicians to attention.

You can hear the audience holding their breath in anticipation.

UNQUENCHABLE FIRE

Suddenly the cymbals clang, the trumpets blare and everything begins with a flurry. The melody instantly and surprisingly catapults you into the midst of the music. There has been no introduction, no overture – just "boom" and you're in the midst of a new sound. It is so startling, so sudden, that it nearly takes your breath away, and you are unsure of what will follow. The music is so new and so honest that you are unsure of how you feel.

You strain to listen to the movements of the song again. It begins to warm you and touch something deep within. Honestly, there is something within you that says, "I am not sure I like this; it is not at all what I was expecting." Yet something in the music draws you in. It is as if the music is calling to you. It seems to be speaking to the deepest places of your heart, places that you didn't even know were there. It arouses you and comforts you all at the same time. It causes fear and joy to intermingle within.

As the strains continue to ebb, a deep rest begins to come over you, like resting from the journey you've been on all your life. The music seems to paint a picture, yet the picture is not stagnant. Scenes of serene mountain lakes reflecting the grandeur of snow-covered summits begin to drift through your mind. Images of sheep grazing in blossoming alpine pastures bring a comfort to your heart. The music is so alive that it is as if you can feel a gentle breeze blowing and smell the fresh scents of spring being carried on it. The music is so vivid that the images within seem almost to be a memory from some distant past you can't seem to put your mind around. Maybe it is a desire for what life could be.

"Ah, that must be it, desire," you conclude. That's what the music speaks to you, your desire and someone else's – but who? This desire is so passionate and so strong you want to run, but it is as if you are held in place by unseen hands. As the resonating sounds echo deep within, you find your desire to run diminishes, and the desire to feel whatever the music is awakening grows. It grows until you find yourself hoping this night will never end. Enjoying, for what seems like the first time in your life, feeling.

You begin to look around the room. Do others feel this? Are you the only one it's touching? But seeing the looks on the faces, you know that this music is causing hearts to stir in many different and profound ways. Some are very uncomfortable. Some seem angry. There are others enraptured, like you, and still others so comfortable in this place that they seem to know the song; they seem to be humming along with it.

Still searching for some explanation to the obvious emotions arousing in the audience, you turn to your program. Here you find a synopsis of the symphony. Here you begin to understand.

**Shir-Hashirim**
*A provocative new symphony by Shlomo.*
*A critic's preview on the front cover reads,* **"In the score of Shir-Hashirim pulses the heartbeat of a wild lover. The strains reveal the desire of this lover with vivid expression that words alone could not capture."** *That's it – "The heartbeat of a wild lover."*
*Selah*

*chapter one*
# HEAVEN'S SONG

Song 1:1

Can you imagine life without music? Even those who are deaf will move to the vibrations of the music, "hearing" it within their bodies. Music is used in every culture, from the most primitive to the most sophisticated. It is used in every cult and religion. It affects us body, soul and spirit.

> From the first cry of life to the last sigh of death, from the beating of our hearts to the soaring of our imaginations, we are enveloped by sound and vibration every moment of our lives. It is the primal breath of creation itself, the speech of angels and atoms, the stuff of which life and dreams, worlds and stars are ultimately fashioned.[1]

We use music to help with memory: most of us were taught the alphabet to song; many of us can remember jingles from TV and radio because they were put to song or rhythm. There are those who hypothesize that to let a baby listen to the classics while in the womb will help to calm them and aid in the formation of their brain, giving them a higher IQ.

Researchers have found that if you take your DNA and unwind it so that it lays out flat, it will actually give you the notes to your own personal song. Music is also used in healing the body and as an alternative to pain medication. In the Bible, David used songs to bring relief to King Saul whenever an evil spirit tormented him.

Music can go below the radar of our intellect and unlock our hearts like no other medium. It can make us laugh or cry, fearful or happy, calm us or energize us.

> Nothing can do for me what music does. It bathes otherwise arid ideas in refreshing waters. It empowers my wandering mind to concentrate with energetic intensity. It stirs my heart to tell the Lord just how much I love him, again and again and again, without the slightest tinge of repetitive boredom.[2]

What is it about music that moves us? What connection does it have with the spirit? Why does it touch us so deeply? I believe because within it lies the heartbeat of God Himself.

### The Rhythm of His Voice

The Bible tells us that "in the beginning was the Word."[3] The Greek word *logos* means not only *word* but also *sound*. Ray Hughes, a musician and teacher, contends that the echo of God's voice from the first day of creation is still reverberating today and continuing to create the galaxies that scientists are now finding. The Word spoke,[4] and all we know was created and is still being held together by the sound of His voice.

C.S. Lewis gives us an incredible picture of the creative power of music in his book, *The Magician's Nephew*. He writes,
> In the darkness something was beginning to happen at last. A voice had begun to sing. It was very far away and Digory found it hard to decide from what direction it was coming.

Sometimes it seemed to come from all directions at once. Sometimes he almost thought it was coming out of the earth beneath them, its lower notes were deep enough to be the voice of the earth herself. There were no words. There was hardly even a tune. But it was beyond comparison, the most beautiful noise he had ever heard. It was so beautiful he could hardly bear it.... Then two wonders happened at the same moment. One was that the voice was suddenly joined by other voices; more voices than you could possibly count. They were in harmony with it, but far higher up the scale: cold, tingling, silvery voices. The second wonder was that the blackness overhead, all at once, was blazing with stars. They didn't come out gently one by one, as they do on a summer evening. One moment there had been nothing but darkness; the next moment a thousand, thousand points of light leaped out – single stars, constellations, and planets, brighter and bigger than any in our world. There were no clouds. The new stars and the new voices began exactly at the same time. If you had seen and heard it, as Digory did, you would have felt quite certain that it was the stars themselves who were singing, and that it was the First Voice, the deep one, which had made them appear and made them sing[5]

Scientists have begun to discover what C.S. Lewis so poignantly writes about to be not fiction, but to be fact. Reportedly, some scientists put a microphone into space to record its sounds. They found the sounds of the planets rotating around the sun performed a heavenly symphony, each planet having its own song. Physicists in the area of non-linear studies are studying the effects of sound vibrations (music) on matter and living things; they have found that different tones will produce different effects on different matter. Vibrations are found in all physical matter, down to the smallest atom. One scientist said that he has seen the formation of mountains before his very eyes as he experimented with sound and matter.

The Scripture is also full of songs: the song of Moses, the songs of David and Miriam and Deborah, and the Song of the Lamb in the book of Revelations, not to mention the entire book of Psalms. In fact, all of the scripture itself is a song. In ancient settings the Bible was always sung in public, never spoken. If you were to see the Old Testament written in Hebrew you would see musical notations above and below the words and phrases throughout. In *The Music of The Bible Revealed,* Suzanne Haik-Vantoura puts forth her research on those notations, showing how all the musical styles we have today are contained within these notations. She contends that a possible reason that the original Hebrew text has no punctuation is because it was sung, and the singing itself added the natural pauses and stops.

### God's Song

The trees clap their hands, the hills break forth in song[6] and God rejoices over you with singing.[7]  Creation is moving to the rhythm of God's voice. But the best song of all is the one the Lord is singing and that song is over you, the crowning jewel of His creation. How incredible! The Holy Father sings over us. The word for singing in Zephaniah 3:17 is *rinnah,* and it means *shout, gladness, joy, proclamation, triumph, cause to sing aloud for joy, a time that demands loud singing.* The Lord doesn't quietly sing over you – **He loudly rejoices over you!**

Could it be that the pull that music has on us is because we were created by a God who sings? Could it be that in the sounds of music something speaks to our very spirits and reveals a God of love and beauty, a God of deep emotion? Music can touch us like no other medium. Ken Gire shares an experience he had at a conference in his book *Divine Embrace*:

> By the third chorus or so, the words, "Jesus, I love you" sent tears streaming down my face. And I found myself standing with a taste of heaven on my lips, wishing the song would never end.... What I experienced that day, as I reflect on it, was not simply a great song, or a talented worship leader, or a heady mix of crowd dynamics that frothed up a moment of mass spiritual intoxication. I believe that brief moment of ecstasy, where my longing for Jesus grew more and more intense, was a lifting of the bridal veil, so to speak, when I saw in His eyes the longing for me for all my life. And everything within me ached to embrace Him.[8]

Without words music speaks to the person we truly are and awakens us to what we are made to be – worshipers and lovers.

## The Language of Love

As you begin to read this book on the Song of Solomon you will see that I talk about the bride of Christ a lot. To many this is a new concept, but throughout scripture the Church and individual believers are called the bride.

Isaiah 62:5 says, *"The Lord rejoices over us like a bridegroom over his bride."* And Revelation 19:7 says, *"Let us rejoice and be glad and give Him glory! For the wedding of the Lamb has come, and the bride has made herself ready."*

If you are a man this may be a hard one for you. But, being the bride of Christ is not about gender, it's about position. It is about ruling and reigning with Him in heavenly places, and it's about knowing the God of the universe intimately, as a husband and a wife know each other.

The Lord uses the poetic medium of a song to hold a key to His heart's desire for us, His bride. We are given a glimpse into the heart of God through the most excellent of all songs recorded in the Scripture. In this song we will hear the calling forth of the bride of Christ. These beautiful refrains reveal the passionate heart of God, a lover captivated by the heart of His people. We will see the growth of the believer as the Holy Spirit puts a desire for the deep things of God into her heart. How does the bride prepare herself for the coming of Christ and the wedding supper? How do we become the pure and spotless bride? How do we put the first commandment first, *"to Love the Lord your God with all your heart and with all your soul and with all your strength?"*[9] I believe that the Song of Solomon gives us a glimpse into that process that every believer must go through to grow in intimacy with Jesus.

> In [the Song of Solomon] lies the heartbeat of Jesus our Savior, for within [it] is revealed the desire on the part of Jesus to make Himself known to those who love Him and obey Him – those whom He calls His friends. Jesus is seeking those with whom He can share His heart, His purpose and His plans. He earnestly desires those with whom He can enter into a mature relationship – those that will share His life, His power and His throne. In short, He is seeking a bride – those who will become one spirit with Him. He is not looking for someone who is concerned with his own life

and blessing or even for one who is determined to do great things for God. Rather, He is looking for those who desire to enter into intimate union with Him.[10]

## Poetry

The Song of Solomon is written in a poetic language. Why? Why would God choose to communicate the Love in His heart in poetic language that is hard for the reader to understand on initial contact? Could it be that it is in poetry and song that the feelings of the heart, which there are often few words for, are able to be expressed in ways that truly can convince us of God's love? Brennan Manning says, "Words without poetry lack passion; words without passion lack persuasion; words without persuasion lack power."[11] Somehow, speaking to us in this way, actually singing to us as God does, "infuses words with a dynamic energy that merely speaking them could never do."[12]

Like all poetry the Song contains symbolism. The use of symbolism adds more to a statement than meets the eye. It can be difficult to read without taking time to consider almost every word. For those who disagree that the Bible is at all symbolic, let me mention a few Scriptures where the Bible itself interprets the symbolism.

In Revelation 5:8 gold bowls of incense are said to stand for the prayers of the saints. In Zechariah 4 we are told that the two olive trees represent two witnesses. And Jesus used parables – symbolic stories – to bring understanding of the ways of God. A.W. Tozer says in his book *The Knowledge of the Holy*, "In its struggle to free itself from the tyranny of the natural world, the human heart must learn to translate upward the language the spirit uses to instruct us." In the Song of Solomon we see that the language the Lord uses to translate us upward and instructus is symbolic poetry.

I have found that reading the Song of Solomon is very much like watching a Shakespeare play – it takes ten minutes or more into the play before you begin to understand and flow with the language. Here, too, it takes time to learn to flow in this symbolic love-language. There are many books available that can give you understanding of types and symbols in Scripture. (See book list at end of chapter.) You might find it helpful to have one or more of these on hand as you journey through this study.

## The Pathway Up

This song, I believe, poetically shares the progression that we as believers go through in attaining spiritual maturity. It is important to remember that the believer in the beginning of this song is not a mature Christian but desiring to become one. The Lord takes delight in this young fervent believer and continues throughout the song to call her onward. Maturity is the work of the Holy Spirit; it is nothing that we can do in and of ourselves. All we can do is say "yes" and cooperate with the Holy Spirit. Can the vine do anything more than stay grafted to the root to produce fruit?[13] It is most important to realize that the Lord loves and delights in us regardless of our level of maturity. Maturity is coming to utter dependence on the Lord, and having nothing in and of ourselves. Maturity is becoming Christ-like, becoming wholly the Lord's.

The Song begins with a startling explosion – a heart-cry from a believer who is finally being honest with her desires, a believer who has come to a place of recognizing that there has to be more in this life than she has been living. (It matters not how long you have been a Christian; if you are seeking God you will one day reach this point, even if it is subtle.) In fact she will come to this place over and over again in her journey. Some have said that this song is the progression of spiritual growth for all believers. And indeed I believe this to be true. However, I don't believe it to be a straight line that once you pass one point you will never see it again. Rather, I see it as a spiral pathway going up a mountain.

Paths up mountainsides circle and hairpin, often bringing you in close proximity to where you just were, often making you feel as though you haven't made any progress. Growing up, I did a lot of camping and hiking in the Rocky Mountains. Going up the steep mountain slopes, the trails are full of switch-backs, or hairpin turns. I have often thought as I stood to catch my breath on one of those turns, looking back down to where I just was, that it would have been so much faster had I just gone straight up. But if I had done that I would find that I was dirty and much more tired than if I had stuck to the trail marked out for me. In the same way as a mountain switchback trail, as you travel up the road to the heart of God you have moments where you look at where you are and where you have come from; the progress doesn't seem very significant, but in reality you are in a very different place.

## The Song of Songs

As you begin to read the Song of Solomon you will find some

startling words and phrases that you aren't even sure should be in the Bible. As you read these words, allow the Holy Spirit to mysteriously open your heart to hear the heavenly symphony and create within you only those things that the vibrations of THE WORD can create. Persevere through the first jarring sounds. As you do, the discord of the world will begin to die away and you will begin to hear the beauty of the heavenly choir. You will begin to hear the heartbeat of God Himself. It is important to remember to read this word with the heart of love – the heart of one who loves another so much that he wants to spend the rest of eternity in the other's loving embrace. It is my prayer that all believers see the reality of who they are in the Lord's eyes.

*"I pray that you, being rooted and established in love, may have power, together with all the saints, to grasp how wide and long and high and deep is the love of Christ, and to know this love that surpasses knowledge – that you may be filled to the measure of all the fullness of God."*[14] That you could grasp the fact that you are so loved that Jesus died for you and is coming back to take you home to be in His arms forever!

## Selah

How has music affected you? What would your life be like without music? How would your life be affected if the Lord himself were to sing a love song over you? Have you ever thought that the Lord would delight over you? How about Him quieting you with His love? Have you overlooked certain passage of scripture because they were symbolic? How do you feel about poetry? Are you willing to ask God, right now, to bring down any walls that you have against symbolic language so that you can hear what God is saying to you?

## Further Reading
*The Divine Embrace* by Ken Gire

*The Singing God* by Sam Storms

*Symphony of Heaven, Sounds of Earth* by Ray Hughes

*A Kiss a Day* by Jamie Lash

*Preparation for the Bride* by Bob and Rose Weiner

*Song of Songs* by Watchman Nee

*Symbols and Types* by Kevin Conner

*Dictionary of Biblical Imagery* by Leland Ryken, Jim Wilhoit, Tremper Longman, and Colin Duriez

## 2nd Movement
# Awakening

As you are sitting in the lush surroundings of the concert hall, your attention once again goes to the program in your hands. In the dim light you read the poetry that ignited the spark for the composer. And understanding begins.

**Love's Awakening**
Listen in your heart – the beginning of love's awakening.

Long ago and far away a transformation took place
Love seized upon a poor broken spirit and enthroned
it on high.
Can you hear the song?
Can you see the dance?
Can you hear your heart rising and falling to the melody of
Love?

Listen in your soul – let the chrysalis form.

Today, in this hour, the transformation may once again occur.
You have ravished my heart. Your beauty is rare,
beyond compare.
Can you hear the song?
Can you see the dance?
Can you hear your heart rising and falling to the melody
of Love?

## UNQUENCHABLE FIRE

> Listen in your spirit – love does not fail.
>
> Place me like a seal over your heart – love is stronger than the grave
> burning, blazing, unquenchable flame.
> Sing the song!
> Dance the dance!
> Let your heart rise on wings, join Me in the melody
> of Love!

Putting down the program, you let the beautiful melody cascade over your heart; as you listen the images begin to return. Softly a song begins to rise from within, putting words to the music that seems to beat with your very heartbeat. Images of alpine pastures grow within your mind; you can see the foothills covered with vineyards. The images within begin to focus more, and you picture a young maiden working the vineyards. She stops in the warmth of the sun, wiping the sweat from her brow....

"Meeting the King was wonderful!" she says with a sigh.
"I wonder if there is possibly more than just mere introductions? What if there is more to His kingdom than mere civility? There are those who say we can be as close to Him as we want. That we can even live in Him, and Him in us. What if the words He spoke of love are true? For I have heard that He is passionate. That He even knows each of His own intimately. But who am I? I am a nobody; I am poor and dirty."

*For just a moment she allows her mind to dream, "But it is said that He cannot lie, His words must be true! Oh, how I long to believe in Him. How I long to believe He is passionate. How I long to look into His eyes. How I long to feel the touch of His lips to mine. To feel my very being enraptured in His embrace. To be His queen and reign on the throne with Him, the One whom my heart loves. How I long to release this passion within me. At times it wells up within me so strongly that I feel as though it would burst forth like a geyser spouting up to the sky. Even now the force of these feelings of love are too much. I don't think I can hold them in. I will not hold them back any longer!"*

*She throws her arms open, looks skyward and cries, "Oh, My King, come and kiss me! Oh, how delightful is your love! Nothing in this world can compare with you. Oh, the smell of your presence is intoxicating. I feel giddy, as if I've drunk the best wine. When You touch me it sends my senses reeling. Is it any wonder You are the desire of the nations? Is it any wonder that all fall at Your feet in worship?"*

*Selah*

*chapter two*
# AWAKENING SLEEPING BEAUTY

Song 1:2-1:4

As we begin reading the Song of Solomon we see that Solomon holds nothing back here. He gives no introduction, no warning, just words that hit you between the eyes and rattle you to your very core. *"Let him kiss me...."* You will find this is not the only time this song takes a startling turn. It is almost as if the Lord knows that the beauty and peace of the music, the warmth of the atmosphere and the serenity felt as you listen to His words of love, can cause your eyes to become sleepy. So He throws in loud sounds and clanging cymbals to shake us out of our sleep, words that jar and shake us to our inner being.

Many have come away from these first words so startled that they cannot go on. They close the book and say, "God could not sound like that." Others believe that God could indeed speak so graphically, after all intimacy – kissing – was His invention.

But, they reason, "He would never speak to *us* like this. He would never speak to *me* like this. God could not possibly long for *me* in this way." So they push the song away as strictly "human love," saying, "This is only the song of the love between husband and wife."

Oh how we limit God! Ephesians 5:32 tells us that we have

a God of great mystery, and that one of the greatest mysteries of all is that we are His bride. God so desired intimate relationship with mankind that He gave up His crown and royal robes, He gave up his power and limited Himself to a human body: a body in need of food and rest, a body in need of touch and affection. Yet we need to remember that His coming in bodily form was just a different form of the same being – now limited. His needs were now physical, His desires now on our level, but He was still God. We were created in that very same image. That image is one that longs for and desires intimacy. Not just physical intimacy, but more importantly, spiritual intimacy.

In this day and age when intimacy is so closely related to sexual expression, it is probably necessary to define the word intimacy. Webster's 1828 Dictionary defines *intimacy* as *near; close; close in friendship or acquaintance; familiar. A familiar friend or associate; one to whom the thoughts of another are entrusted without reserve.*

Passion is closely related to intimacy, another word that we don't like to use much in religious settings because of its sexual connotations. Webster's defines *passion* as *the feelings of the mind, as desire, fear, hope, joy, grief, love, hatred, zeal; ardor; vehement desire, love.*

## Breaking the Boxes

There is no holding back here. The song comes on with a strong statement from the very beginning that almost knocks the wind out of you, especially when we remember that we are reading this in the Bible. It seems obvious that the believer has some relationship already with the Lord for her to be requesting such a thing as a kiss. It is hard to say how long she has known the Lord, and it really doesn't matter because these emotions seem to just come bursting out of her heart. The same is true for us. There seems to come a time and place in our walks with God that we find ourselves saying, "There's got to be more!" Some simply stop there, barely willing to acknowledge that being a Christian can have its moments of boredom, as if acknowledging boredom is somehow blasphemous. Others, as I myself have experienced, find an undeniable cry from within that screams, "This is the God of the universe, the God who formed the mountains, the God who walked as a man turning the known world upside down. I know that there is more. There has got to be more!" And with this cry we begin to search for the deeper experiences of God. As we go through our life these cries turn up again and again, daring us forward into realms unknown.

Throughout His life on earth, Jesus constantly said things to shake the religious boxes. Even from the beginning He wanted a bride that would go the distance and walk out of the restrictions of religious legalism and out of the confines of the natural comfort zone. One of the things you will need to wrestle with if you are a man is being called "the bride of Christ," just as women need to wrestle with being "sons of God." Being the bride of Christ is not about gender, *but about position*. We were created to rule and reign with Christ as a co-heir, whether male or female. (For ease in this study we will refer to the believer in the feminine, similar to the usage of a ship.)

## The Kiss

The song starts with a kiss, or at least a desire for one. When we look at this from the perspective of our relationship with the Lord, this imagery is very unsettling for most of us. And maybe that is the whole point. We do not serve a passionless God who sits in Heaven indifferent to us little people below. We serve a God who gave His very life for us, who bled and died for us. Why can we not see a God who would long to kiss us?

There are skeptics out there who throw cold water on the idea that this beautiful song could be the heart of God for His people. They claim that it is merely human love portrayed. Oh, but who invented human love? Who invented romance? You cannot invent something that has no place in your heart. Writers write what is in their hearts; musicians play and sing from the life within; painters paint with an eye outwardly of what they perceive through the colored lenses of what they believe inside. We look at life through the glasses of our hearts. I believe that God created love and romance and beauty and physical love from the heartbeat within Him. What other image could startle us and give us such a vivid picture of a God who is love and wants to draw close? A kiss seems to be the perfect metaphor.

In ancient rabbinical teaching, a kiss from God is a word directly spoken to your heart – the living word of God. A kiss is direct contact with the creator. This could be a prophetic word, a scripture highlighted as you read, or a quickening in your heart of truth. Mike Bickle calls it "a touch of God that enlarges the capacity of your heart." I see it like the classic

Christmas cartoon, *The Grinch Who Stole Christmas*. As the Grinch suddenly received a revelation of truth that Christmas is far different than he had thought, his heart grew three sizes. This is what the kisses of God do to our hearts. Revelation comes, and our heart's capacity to love grows.

The Hebrew word for kiss is *nashaq* (from the root *nasaq*). It means *to touch, to equip, to catch fire, fasten upon, conquer, delight, cling to*. There is nothing tame about these meanings. They are words that are filled with passion and emotion, words that very much describe the heart of God and His actions toward us and our actions toward Him. One of the Greek words for worship, *proskuneo*, means to kiss. When we worship the Lord we fasten upon Him, cling to Him and delight in Him. When we do this, His spirit touches us, and our hearts catch fire, equipping us for life and conquering the dark places within us. This is what was happening to Ken Gire in the experience I quoted earlier when he was worshiping and found himself "in that brief moment of ecstasy, where my longing for Jesus grew more and more intense, was a lifting of the bridal veil, so to speak, when I saw in His eyes the longing for me for all my life. And everything within me ached to embrace Him."[1]

That is a kiss from God!

Why a kiss? I have heard it said that the single most arousing act in intimacy is the kiss. What is it about this action that the believer longs for? Christianity is a different religion than all the others of the world in several ways, but the most startling is that it is about a relationship with a loving God, not about appeasing an angry deity. Could it be that the Lord is trying to arouse our spirits, trying to awaken something within us, so He puts in His written word the example of a believer crying out for a kiss from God?

## Invading Our Senses

Beyond just the meanings of the word kiss, the act itself can reveal insights to us. There are many kinds of kisses: the kiss on the cheek of a friend, the kiss on the head of a parent or the kiss on the lips of intimacy. The believer specifically asks for the kisses of His mouth. When you kiss someone on the mouth, it is a very intimate kiss, one in which you use all your senses. We are told that we are to "love the Lord our God with all our heart, soul and strength."[2] We are told to love the Lord with everything.

The kiss of intimacy, or lovers, is not a kiss from a distance; it is very up close and personal and involves all five senses. You are so close that all you can smell is that person: their cologne, their personal fragrance and even their very breath. When you are close enough to kiss, all you can see is the person you are kissing, and you can't even see all of them, all you can see is their eyes. What you hear the loudest is their voice, which is usually in a whisper, their breathing, and their heartbeat. And what do you taste, but the person you are kissing – what they are made up of, and what they've been eating. When we allow God to come close enough to us to touch our hearts intimately, our senses become filled with God.

The believer, although not fully understanding, is asking for this type of experience. Within the first nine verses of the Song of Solomon, all five of the senses are mentioned. In verse 1:2, the believer is calling out for the kisses (touch). She compares

His love to wine (taste) and extols the fragrance of His presence (smell) in 1:3. She feels His eyes looking upon her in 1:6 (sight), and in 1:9 she hears Him speaking to her (hearing).

When God touches us it is like this kind of kiss. We can smell Him, we can hear His very heartbeat and we can taste of His goodness. We serve a Lord who doesn't want us to just know about Him, but to know HIM up close and personal. It is a God-given desire and one that the Lord longs to answer. For He says, "Draw near to me and I will draw near to you."[3] Once the believer prays this prayer all the boredom is about to be displaced, and a romance that is beyond anything ever hoped for is about to sweep this believer off her feet. The Lord is about to "wine and dine" her.

## Better Than Wine

The believer tells the Lord, "Kiss me because Your love is better than wine" (1:2). Again the poet chooses an analogy that helps to capture all the components of love. What does wine have to do with love? Wine is cultivated, aged, treasured and intoxicating. When tasting wine you don't just drink it down. You smell its bouquet, you look at its color and then you taste its flavor. The believer cries out for His kisses, to smell His fragrance and to taste His goodness. And she finds it intoxicating.

There is an intoxication in natural love. There is an even greater intoxication that happens when the Lord touches us. After the Spirit fell on Pentecost, *"Some [in the crowd], however, made fun of them and said, 'They have had too much wine.'"*[4] The disciples were acting intoxicated, people thought they were drunk. In reality they had been kissed with "tongues of fire."[5]

They were intoxicated with the Holy Spirit. Paul tells us, *"Do not get drunk on wine, which leads to debauchery. Instead, be filled with the Spirit."*[6] The human soul is ever reaching to be intoxicated as only the Holy Spirit can do.

What passion the believer is releasing to the Lord! How often have we felt these emotions but not felt they were appropriate to say to the Lord? But here it is in Scripture. We have permission to be passionate and to pour out our heart's desire unto the King of Kings. She wants it all, and at the moment she is so enraptured that she feels no regret in saying it. "Take me! Let's run together! I want to go into the inner chambers where only the most intimate go. Your love is amazing!" (paraphrase of Song 1:2)

She has been ruined for anything less than all of God. She knows that it is only by His spirit and the grace of the Lord Jesus that she can be drawn deeper. She is so desperate for more that she is impatient. She wants to be with the Lord NOW. Although she is still young and immature she has seen enough of the world to long for more of God and is beginning her quest to find Him. She wants to live her life in Him, to run in service to Him, to be used of Him, to find her meaning through Him.

In the first stanza of Solomon's song the Lord throws away all pretenses and rips away any guards that would keep us from Him. In essence He says, "If you will persevere through your fears, through the startling realization of the words of affection and intimacy, then your heart will become one with mine."

## Drawing Close

She goes on to pray that He take her into His chamber. What is this chamber that she is wanting to experience? It is the place of intimacy. In the Old Testament it would be the Holy of Holies, the place where the Ark of the Covenant rested and where the Lord met with His people above the Mercy Seat. Under the New Covenant, that chamber is the depths of our hearts where the Lord takes up residency.

You may have had many "chamber experiences" already, although you may not know it. They are those times that you have had with the Lord that have changed your life. The first time you came to Him was a chamber experience. When He brings fresh insight from His word or from His Spirit, these are chamber experiences. We receive these revelations as we spend time studying Scripture and praying. Prayer is not just talking to God; prayer is also quieting our hearts and minds before the Lord and hearing Him speak to us. No one else can experience these chamber times for you. They come directly from the heart of God. (This is not to say that people cannot be the ones to speak the words of God into your lives.) The kisses of God come in the chamber times. They enlarge the capacity of your heart to receive more of God and to live as He lived.

> There remains an incomprehensible vastness in God for those who will seek His fullness. There is a depth of relationship in fellowship with Him that only those who have a burning passion for Him will ever experience. He wants us to run after Him. He does not want us to be content or satisfied with what we have or what we've experienced.

There is a place of shelter, a relationship, a reality of the spiritual presence of God that is for our experience in this life that will only be attained as we press into Him with all our hearts, with all our strength. We too easily forget there is a vastness and limitlessness that God has for us. It is His manifest presence and it is there for all who respond – and keep on responding – to God's call in their lives.[7]

It is in these times of intimacy that we are changed. Many Christians are frustrated because nothing ever seems to change. Their lives seem powerless. But until you allow Jesus to take you, to kiss you, to have His way with you in the inner chambers of your heart – you will not see change. The maiden has come to the place of desiring change – she wants to go deeper. "It is the revelation of Jesus, given by the Spirit, of His beauty and magnificent glory that draws us to Himself."[8]

## Selah

Have you ever been kissed by God? How do you think His kiss might affect you? Which of your senses have never been touched by God? Would it change your life, the way you see the Lord, or the way you see yourself? Would it intoxicate you? What will it take for you to want His kiss? Will you ask Him to kiss you today?

## Further Reading

*Song of the Beloved* by Jeanne Guyon

*Experiencing the Depths of Jesus Christ* by Jeanne Guyon

*Union with God* by Jeanne Guyon

*His Manifest Presence* by Don Nori

*Moving into the Holy of Holies* by David Swan

*Song of Songs* by Watchman Nee

## 3rd Movement
# Desire

*The music of the symphony is flowing over you as you contemplate the poetry that the composer has brought to life. The rhythm and the cadence have become part of your very heart and mind. As you listen, you begin to be able to distinguish the voice of the instruments representing the characters and the emotions they are portraying.*

Once again your mind is on the young Maiden pouring out her heart to the broad expanse above her. As her love and adoration flow from her lips, she feels her spirit rise like an eagle on the wind soaring into the heavens. You see her shut her eyes and relax into the feelings, enjoying the release for which she had waited so long. She finally opens her heart and allows the truth of her love for the King to flow out.

As her feelings begin to calm down she opens her eyes. To her surprise she is now in the courtyard of the King's palace. The cry of love within her heart for the King brought her to Him. For in this enchanted land, the wishes of true love are granted upon request. But just like any enchanted land, the answers sometimes come in unexpected ways. The King's response to her flow of love is to bring her close to Him, for this too is the desire of His heart.

As she opens her eyes in disbelief, you watch as she begins to look around at her surroundings. The courtyard is indeed magnificent. The castle is nestled high on a mountaintop. Even the sun seems brighter here. It is clearer and more radiant than she had ever believed possible. She thinks it must be due to the height of the mountain on which the castle was standing. Tall thick walls surround it with watchtowers on each corner. The walls look as if they are made of pure gold and precious stones.

The entrance to the courtyard is at the east end. Very ancient gates guard the way. As the Maiden looks at the gates she understands why they named the gates "beautiful," for indeed they are one of the most impressive things she has ever seen. They look as if they were made out of pearls and carved with palm trees and beautiful heavenly creatures with two faces, one of a lion and one of a man. She had seen this before on the shields of the King's soldiers: this is the King's emblem."If these gates could speak, what stories they could tell. They look as if they hold secrets from ages long past," she thinks out loud.

The Maiden can just imagine the proclamation being shouted from the watchtower as the watchmen spot the King returning from one of His journeys. She can see the watchmen on the towers raise the long, beautiful ram's horn to their lips and trumpet forth the majestic song of the King. Then the shout would ring out: "Lift up your heads, you ancient gates! Be lifted up, you everlasting doors, that the King of glory can come in!"She walks from the gates looking around the courtyard. Just through the east gate there is a fire burning bright and clear. It is a large fire, unlike anything the maiden had ever seen before. The flames are almost transparent, and within the flames are every color imaginable. There are even some she had never seen before. The fire is captivating, and she feels drawn to it, as a moth is unexplainably drawn to the light of a flame.

## Dark but Lovely

*As she looks at the flame she begins to feel a stirring deep within. "This fire," she thinks, "is so different – so captivating – yet frightening at the same time. Its heat is affecting me differently. I don't feel any warmer on the outside but rather on the inside, in my heart."*

She leans closer and cannot resist temptation to touch the flame. First, cautiously, she reaches her hand in, only to discover it does not burn her, but instead her hand begins to glow as if the light were inside her hand. It tingles as if an electrical current were racing through her arm. Startled, she pulls it back. She is reaching for the flame again when she hears the voice of the King close behind her.

She looks about quickly and sees Him nearing the fire. Her heart begins to leap within her at the sight of Him. Then, all too suddenly, she remembers her appearance. She has not bathed or changed her clothes. She looks as she had while working in the vineyards that very day. She tries to escape His notice, looking about frantically for a place to hide. But it is no use. He sees her and walks straight toward her. As He stands in front of her, she bows low in His presence. Before He can speak one word, she begins,

"O my King, please do not look at me. Do not look at me with those eyes of love. I have heard it said that You find all your subjects beautiful, but me? I am a mess; I am filthy and unwashed. The inside of my heart is as dirty as the outside. Please, look away." She continues in nervous prattle. "I was unprepared for You bringing me here. You see, I have these brothers. They are very angry with me. They have not allowed me to take care of the things You have entrusted to me, but insist that I truly have not met You and cannot possibly have heard from You. They cause me to doubt. They cause me to think that they know better than I do what I need to put my hand to. Oh, my King, I am sorry! But, my King, I have been so busy with their work (those angry subjects of yours....)"

She pauses for a moment, but there is no response from the King. Without lifting her eyes up, she continues."I feel lost. Can you tell me how to find the place we first met? It was so peaceful there. It was like being beside quiet waters on a warm afternoon, like lying on a blanket in the shade eating and resting through the day."

A light of remembrance seems to go on somewhere in the back of her mind. Then anger and sorrow mixed begin to boil within her, "They told me to forget about You, to pretend I had never met You. They said that someone like me couldn't truly be changed by You. Oh, why must I hide my desires for You? Why must I pretend I don't know You when You are near?" She lifts her eyes, pleading with Him, "Please, my King, help me, help me find our trysting place again."

"O, fair Maiden," the King says as He walks to her and takes her hand, drawing her close to Him. What a feeling being in His arms! Could there possibly be any place better? It reminds her of how her father would comfort her during the night when she was a girl. That time seems so long ago, and the world is now so unsafe.

His fragrance begins to engulf her, myrrh, aloes and cassia. It is an intoxicating fragrance causing warmth, trust and desire to block all doubts away. After a moment the King speaks:

*"The pathway is still there. It has been traveled by my faithful ones through the generations. It is hidden from view of those who don't want to see. For there are those who are content to be part of My kingdom, enjoying its benefits, but prefer to go on as they did in their other lands. But there are others who long to know the secrets of My kingdom. Look for their tracks. Let them teach you the way to go. To those who truly are seeking, the way has not been hidden."*

*"Look also to the ones whom you know are faithful to Me, and look to the shepherds they will protect you. They hold the truth, they know the way, and it will set you free. They will help you, for their desire is for all that love Me to follow the paths and be with Me. Seek them out, for they will help you."*

*Selah*

*chapter three*
# DARK BUT LOVELY

Song 1:5-11

At this point the believer faces a spiritual crisis of sorts. She has just been crying out for more of God, for His kisses and the chamber experiences. Yet as she draws near to Him she sees the stark realities of who she is and who God is. Suddenly reality hits like a cold shower. The voice of the enemy comes in, screaming the half-truths and bringing shame and condemnation to her soul. The battle of the mind and the battle of the true heart's belief ensues. "You're dark – the King can't take you to the holy place. He is holy, and only the holy and anointed can enter there." The counter-thoughts come, "But He loves me; I am washed clean by His blood." On and on the battle goes.

As we begin to grow in our relationship with the Lord we must realize that we have a very real enemy who would like nothing better than for us to keep it on a surface level. God wants a relationship with a friend, not a slave. The enemy has made a lot of pitfalls to trap a new believer. If we begin to get involved in religious activity, I don't think the enemy gets too worried about that. This type of activity is a religious structure with nothing more than a lot of lists of do's and don'ts. It is activity that keeps us busy and spinning our wheels, never really moving toward God, and often brings a lot of condemnation with it. When relationship really starts and it isn't about religion anymore but about the person of Jesus Christ, then the real battle ensues. The battle always starts in the gray matter between our ears – our minds. It is a battle over our souls, which will result in how we live our lives.

As the reality of the believer's life begins to dawn on her, she begins to realize that she has gone about things the wrong way. She has been striving to work for the Lord, following the do's and don'ts of a religious system instead of getting to know the Lover of her soul.

## Gazing

The story of Mary and Martha is the classic story given about the differences of how we come to Jesus. Jesus is visiting the home of these sisters for dinner. Martha is so busy preparing the meal that she becomes agitated with Mary. Mary has welcomed Jesus into their home, but instead of doing the normal womanly chores of the house she is sitting at the feet of Jesus enthralled by His every word. Mary was gazing in rapt attention; Martha was working to get His attention.

When Martha realized that Mary was getting His attention from doing nothing, she became indignant. She came to Him and asked, *"Lord, don't you care that my sister has left me to do the work by myself? Tell her to help me!"*

*"Martha, Martha,"* the Lord answered, *"you are worried and upset about many things, but only one thing is needed. Mary has chosen what is better, and it will not be taken away from her."*[1]

It is not that Martha was doing something bad. It was that she had things out of order. There is always time for everything that needs to get done when we spend time with God first.  In the very beginning of this Song the believer asked that the Lord would draw her; the cry of David is echoing through the heart of the believer:

*"One thing I ask of the LORD, this is what I seek: that I may dwell in the house of the LORD all the days of my life,* **to gaze upon the beauty** *of the LORD and to seek Him in His temple."*[2]

Jesus told Martha, "Only one thing is needed."  David described that one thing as "gazing upon the Lord and His beauty."  To *gaze* means *to fix the eyes and look steadily and earnestly; to look with eagerness or curiosity; as in admiration, astonishment, or in study.*[3]  Can't you just see it?  That is exactly what Mary is doing: sitting at the feet of Jesus, gazing upon Him, drinking in every word.  And the things spoken to her can never be taken away.  Mary is forever changed.

The believer is about to realize the incomparable beauty of God and the transforming power of fixing her eyes and looking steadily, earnestly, with eagerness in admiration upon the Lord.  But she doesn't know what she is asking.  It sounds really harmless "to gaze upon the beauty of the Lord."  But something happens that is unsettling when we begin to gaze.  **GOD GAZES BACK!**

As the believer's cry ascends to the throne in verse 1:4, suddenly the Lord sits up taller in His throne; His ears hear the cry of a lover and He begins to turn.  "I heard that.  Where is she?  Where is the one who called out for more?  Ah there, there is the one whose heart cries after me."  Then He looks with eyes that blaze with fiery love into the eyes of this one who would yearn for Him, never saying a word.  **You see you just can't**

**look at Jesus and He not look back.** He doesn't want to be some beautiful museum piece set on a pedestal under glass that you walk in occasionally look at and admire, then walk away having your senses tantalized. You leave talking about how beautiful He was to look at but never touching Him or Him touching you.

The religions of man are good at the museum-gazing. Setting God up as some delicate object, looking at Him behind the invisible security lines guarded by religious spirits that say "stand back please, don't touch." It is as if religion is scared that somehow humanity could mar the vestige of Jesus. But we fail so often to realize it is His humanity that enables us to come close to Him in the first place.

If our weak fragile humanity could mar the personhood of Jesus, why did He Himself don the attire of flesh and blood? No, God is not afraid of our humanity; He is not afraid of us tarnishing His image. If Scripture can record the patriarchs, the men and women of renown and the disciples in their humanity – both good and bad – then we need not fear touching God with ours. The reality is that we don't change God when we touch Him, but rather we are changed into His likeness and image.

In the Old Testament we are shown that the wages of sin is death and defilement. It is the cause and effect of mankind going their own way. In the Old Testament the things you touched could make you dirty, unclean and unable to go before God. If you had leprosy or another disease you had to walk through the streets declaring, "Unclean!" so that people wouldn't come near you. But the New Testament shows us that Jesus makes all things new. Jesus constantly touched and was touched by the unclean. This did not cause Him to become unclean as the law stated; rather, the person He touched became clean and whole. So it is today.

> *Therefore, since we have a great high priest who has gone through the heavens, Jesus the Son of God, let us hold firmly to the faith we profess. For we do not have a high priest who is unable to sympathize with our weaknesses, but we have one who has been tempted in every way, just as we are—yet was without sin. Let us then approach the throne of grace with confidence, so that we may receive mercy and find grace to help us in our time of need.*[4]

Jesus doesn't want a religious system that keeps us at a distance taunting us and shaming us into thinking that if we come close enough to touch Him we will pollute Him. He wants us to come boldly before the throne of grace, allowing Him to touch us and cleanse us from all unrighteousness.

### I Am Dark

Isaiah shares his experience of gazing in the sixth chapter of his book, verses 1- 6:

> *In the year that King Uzziah died, I saw the Lord seated on a throne, high and exalted, and the train of his robe filled the temple.... "Woe to me!" I cried. "I am ruined! For I am a man of unclean lips, and I live among a people of unclean lips, and **my eyes have seen the King**, the Lord Almighty.*

Isaiah declared, "I am ruined."[5] Other versions translate it, "I am undone."[6]

As the believer dares to approach the Lord, her internal struggle continues. You see, the closer we get to God the more our hearts are exposed and we discover how righteous Jesus is and how unrighteous we are. And we cry out like Isaiah, *"Woe to me!"* The believer is recognizing that her personal life with the Lord isn't what it should be. She has come face to face with God and recognizes her own nature. Here she expresses that she feels like all eyes are on her; everyone else can see what a facade her life has been. Her walk has only been at face value. The believer is having a hard time comprehending the truth that the Lord has just spoken over her.

Startled by the drawing of His attention, the believer begins to get nervous. She says, "Do not look at me, I am dark." Isaiah said it this way: "I am undone." The believer compares herself to the nomadic tribes of the Kedar. These were a people-group who were descendants of Ishmael, Abraham's son, who was born out of Abraham's attempt to bring fruition to the promises of God.[7] The Kedar homes were tents of black goat hair. The Kedar were a war-like people who were enemies of Israel. They were also a nomadic people, a people without a homeland. The name *Kedar* itself means *dark*.

She has cried out with great desire to gaze upon God, but in answer to that cry she finds that He is gazing back. As they begin to gaze upon each other, she begins to see herself in His light and realizes she is not quite where she thought she was, who she thought she was, for light exposes the things that we cannot see in the darkness. As we walk through life in the world we are "under the sun." (See the book of Ecclesiastes.) Just as the natural sun causes our skin to darken and can even cause damage, so living in the world can darken and cause damage to our hearts. The believer begins to feel shame and embarrassment that she has been damaged living life under the sun. She asks the Lord to turn His gaze from her, and she asks that others would not scrutinize.

Our enemy, Satan, is so cunning. The truth is we are not worthy on our own merit, and so it is with half-truths that the enemy comes at us. He whispers into our ears, "You are dark; you are blemished; you are unworthy to go before the King. For He is holy and nothing unholy can stand before Him." He begins to repeat lies about our character based on our old nature, who we were before we came to know Jesus. *"You are dark of heart – dark like the tents of Kedar. You are constantly warring against God."* And in our weakness, as Satan repeats the lies so often, we believe them and begin to rehearse them to ourselves.

Ephesians 4:22-24 says, *"You were taught, with regard to your former way of life, to put off your old self, which is being corrupted by its deceitful desires; to be made new in the attitude of your minds; and to put on the new self, created to be like God in true righteousness and holiness."* And then in Romans 12:2, we are told, *"Do not conform any longer to the pattern of this world, but be transformed by the renewing of your mind."*

The Greek word for mind in Romans 12 is *nous*. It is more than just your thoughts, but it is your mind (thoughts), your emotions (feelings) and your will (resulting actions), or in one word – your soul. If we can change the way we think and feel, then the way we act will also change.

Our beliefs without action will not change anything. It was when the disciples started testifying about Jesus in word and power that the world began to be turned upside down. The enemy knows that if the way we think and feel changes, then there is no stopping the advancement of the kingdom of God. So it is here that the first lines of battle are drawn. It is in our beliefs about who we are before God that the enemy first seeks to stop us. So he whispers the lies that we have heard all our lives, attempting to keep us in the bondage of deception that we are not worthy.

### Lovely

As we read through this book we must remember that what we are actually reading are the lyrics to a song. Here the two voices of the song sing out together in the midst of the battle fray. It reminds me of Broadway musicals and operas with many voices singing at once. Each sings their own words to convey the situation that they are now in. The believer calls out as she gets closer to the Lord, "I am dark," and He sings the truth to her even as these words come out of her mouth, "Oh, but you are lovely." She sings, "Dark like the tents of an angry war-like people," and He sings, "Lovely as the curtains that blow in the breezes of my spirit in My holy dwelling place."

As the battle rages, the Lord speaks to her about the truth of what He has done on her behalf. *"Come now, let us reason together,"* says the Lord. *"Though your sins are like scarlet, they shall be as white as snow; though they are red as crimson, they shall be like wool."*[8]

Here we see the believer is fully recognizing that her heart is black and that she is unable on her own merit to enter into the King's chamber, where she longs for Jesus to take her. It is only as she stands under the blood of Jesus, the perfect sacrifice, that she can be brought into the inner sanctums and be changed into His likeness. It is only by His blood that she is counted as worthy.

The enemy is relentless in the battle for her mind and beliefs. Yet the Holy Spirit is there whispering in her other ear the truth. "No, no – you are pure and beautiful! Lovely like the curtains in the temple." The curtains of Solomon's temple[9] were the very curtains that divided the Holy Place from the Holy of Holies.[10] They were blue, purple, crimson and white linen with cherubim woven into them. Each color in the curtains painted a beautiful picture of Jesus. Blue represented heaven, red His shed blood, purple His royalty and white His purity. Linen represented the righteous acts of the saints (See Revelation 19:8)

Both the proclamations of the believer and the Lord are true. But mercy triumphs over judgment. The Lord understands who we are and where we have been in our lives. He is good and kind and merciful while being Holy and just at the same time. The Lord sees the "yes" in her heart. Even the recognition of her dark heart brings Him much joy and shows her loveliness. She is not walking in pride or false humility, but in truth. And the truth sets us free. Now that she recognizes her own dark heart, she is free to receive the coal of fire from the altar that brings purity.[11]

## Spiritual Burnout

As she recognizes the lack of depth in her life she begins to look for a cause and make excuses. She says to the Lord, "I know I'm not perfect. I know that I'm not where I should be – but," she whines, "it's all their fault. Those other believers – they are just mean and spiteful – they told me to do it their way. They forced me into ministries I was never called to do. They were more interested in having a warm body in that place than they were about me and my life. All they care about is running their ministries and looking good, so now look at me – my life is a mess and it's all their fault!"

She has been spending all her time doing what her particular denomination, or those she considers more mature in God, have told her she must do to be a good Christian. She has lost sight of the whole reason for becoming a believer. She's burned-out and angry. It is very easy to "pass the buck" and blame others for our conditions. The maiden is not willing to taking responsibility for her present condition, but blaming the church. Isn't this what Adam and Eve did? They were caught and they found someone else to blame. If the enemy can get us to blame others, we will never have to face our own lack and in doing so we will never face the strength of God. *"For in our weakness He is strong."*[12] We have to stop being embarrassed before God by our sin, allowing the enemy to shame us and therefore keeping us from the throne of grace.

> *This is the message we have heard from Him and declare to you: God is light; in Him there is no darkness at all. If we claim to have fellowship with Him yet walk in the darkness, we lie and do*

*not live by the truth. But if we walk in the light, as He is in the light, we have fellowship with one another, and the blood of Jesus, his Son, purifies us from all sin. If we claim to be without sin, we deceive ourselves and the truth is not in us. If we confess our sins, He is faithful and just and will forgive us our sins and purify us from all unrighteousness. If we claim we have not sinned, we make Him out to be a liar and His word has no place in our lives.*[13]

*But He [Jesus] said to me, "My grace is sufficient for you, for My power is made perfect in weakness." Therefore I will boast all the more gladly about my weaknesses, so that Christ's power may rest on me. That is why, for Christ's sake, I delight in weaknesses, in insults, in hardships, in persecutions, in difficulties. For when I am weak, then I am strong.*[14]

So we find the believer realizing that her life thus far in the kingdom has been about works, not about love – about doing and not about being. And she is desperate to learn the art of waiting before the Lord. She is tired and weary. She has just been through a time of seeking man's approval versus God's. This is about ceasing from striving, ceasing from our own works and entering into the rest of the Lord. The believer is experiencing a spiritual crisis – burn-out. She has been doing all that she thought she was supposed to do, but she hasn't been experiencing life. She hasn't been experiencing joy, peace and rest. Recognizing that something has gone awry in her relationship with the Lord she begins to search for the pathway to bring true fulfillment. It's as if she is saying, "OK – I give up!

I'll stop striving. Just tell me where You are. Just tell me where to find rest for my soul" (Song 1:7).

## Rest for Our Souls

When we reach this place, often there is a sense of tiredness that comes over us, a need to find and enter into the rest of the Lord. Hebrews 4:9-11 says, *"There remains, then, a Sabbath-rest for the people of God; for anyone who enters God's rest also rests from his own work, just as God did from His. Let us, therefore, make every effort to enter that rest, so that no one will fall by following their example of disobedience."*

And Isaiah 40:30 says, *"They that wait upon the Lord shall renew their strength. They shall run and not grow weary, they shall walk and not faint."* When we wait we have the strength we need to do what the Lord is asking. We hear more clearly, so we are doing His work and not man's.

It is the cry from within the heart to know the Shepherd who David knew and wrote about in Psalm 23. David said, *"The Lord is my shepherd, I shall not be in want. He makes me lie down in green pastures, He leads me beside quiet waters, and He restores my soul. He guides me in paths of righteousness for His name's sake."*

The believer cries out in verse 1:7a, *"Where do You feed Your flock? Where do You rest Your sheep?"*

In his book *A Shepherd's Look at Psalm 23*, Philip Keller looks at what it is to be a shepherd and tend a flock. He observes, "In order for sheep to be made to lie down four requirements must be met. There must be a definite sense of freedom from fear, tension, aggravation and hunger."[15] Here the believer is crying out for the basic necessities of her life to be met so that she can enter into rest – to her promised land – to her destiny – to her calling. She is admitting her weakness, that she has, like a sheep, dumbly followed the advice of others, and she has lost her way.

The Lord answers back with a loud and joyous voice, *"Come to Me, all you who are weary and heavy laden and I will give you rest for your weary souls."*[16] How He runs to this precious lamb who cries, "I am lost, come find me!" He tells us He will leave the 99 to go after the one.[17] Once the one is found He will carry it back in His arms, not with chastisement – for that was placed on Him at the cross[18] – but with tender love and affection.

## Remove the Veil

Not only is the believer recognizing the need to rest and gaze. She is also recognizing that there has been a veil of separation between them. She says in verse 1:7b, *"For why should I [as I think of you] be as a veiled one straying beside the flocks of your companions?"* (Amplified Version)

This is one of those verses I struggled over. Many commentaries liken her to a prostitute following around the shepherds. And maybe this is what she does. Jumping from church to church, shepherd to shepherd, allowing men and women to meet her needs and becoming disillusioned when they didn't measure up to God and fill all her needs.

Indeed I do believe this is one aspect of this Scripture. The believer has just told the Lord that she wants to be fed by His very hand – not the hand of His servants. She is asking that she not look to others to get her needs met, wanting not to idolize other men and women of God, but to look only to the Lord for everything.

Another idea that we find in this statement is that her sin has become a veil of separation, and she is asking that all that separates her from the Lord would be removed. She has left her first love, chased other lovers. Now these things stand between them, and she wants them removed.

In the tabernacle of Moses the veil was placed between the Holy Place and the Holy of Holies. She wants to live in the truth that that veil has been rent in two, no longer separating us from coming before the Lord. There is no need to fear going into that intimate place, for the blood of the sacrificial lamb has been poured out on the mercy seat, so we can go boldly before His throne. Those who will go into the Holy of Holies are those who have allowed the Holy Spirit to kill the desires of their flesh. They have become so desperate for all of God that they will cry out like Esther, *"I will go, and if I die, I die"*[19] and there will be those who will add to that statement, "and what a way to go."

We were formed in the image of God, but our flesh conceals that image in *"jars of clay."*[20] Yet, Jesus tells us, the Kingdom of God is within us.[21] When we turn our lives over to the Lord He writes His law on our hearts. Our hearts are the very places in us that God wants to be enthroned. Yet there is a veil that separates us from the glory of God. That veil is our flesh: our selfish desires and self-interests. Our flesh consists of four parts – our mind, will, emotions and body. Before we come to know the Lord it is these four things that set the course for our decisions. But after we come to know Him we are called to bring the flesh into subjection to the Spirit of God within us.

## Dark but Lovely

Because of our sinful nature, that place where God wants to dwell is fully occupied with self. And self does not want God to rule as King, but to serve us as a slave, to be a servant. In order for this to change, our hearts must be circumcised. The circumcised (purified) heart is one in which the ruling love is utterly changed from self to God.

Circumcision was the sign of the covenant that God made with the Israelites. The cutting away of the foreskin in the natural created purity in intimacy. In order for us to have that purity we must allow God to cut away our flesh. To every person this will be different because every person has a different amount of flesh in their lives and different areas that need to be brought into subjection to the ruling love of God. I believe if we will cry out to God He will begin to purify our hearts and allow for a deeper intimacy, a deeper penetration of our souls, so that the things He desires to impregnate us with will be purely Him.

I believe this verse is also about removing her mask of "false-self" and being real before God and man. It is on our face that our emotions show. She is tired of hiding her feelings. Some can be learned by body language, but the place where we really expose ourselves is on our faces. She has been living out her life like a masquerade ball, looking perfect from the outside and hiding her feelings, masking who she really is. Being real before God and man can be a very scary thing. It will bring misunderstanding and vulnerability. Moses hid his face because of the glory of God reflected on it, for this glory caused fear.

Here the maiden has been betrothed to the Lord, she wants to remove the veil for two reasons: one, so that all can see she is married to the Lord and reflects His glory, so that all can see she has been in His presence; and two, so that all can see His glory, which will provoke them to jealousy and cause them to want what she has.

## Follow The Shepherds

The Lord now takes His turn to speak. I picture Him so much like a loving father and friend. He hasn't said much, as the believer has poured out her heart in verses 1:1-1:7. He just listened. I see Him smiling at her with great love and affection in His eyes. He calls her lovely, beautiful (Song 1:8). He is reaffirming His delight in her and encouraging her that she is asking the right questions. The Lord sees the heart even though the actions haven't followed. I have heard Mike Bickle say something like this: "The actions of the immature and the rebellious can be the same; it's the heart that's different." So when the Lord addresses us he doesn't merely address the actions – He addresses the real issue: the heart. The way He addresses her is tender and loving. Jesus is infinitely tender and loving in His personhood. He is so different than the religious image of God that the church has often taught.

As the Lord speaks He answers her question of how to find and grow in Him with three specific things that she can do. The poetic version says it this way: *"If you do not know, most beautiful of women, follow the tracks of the sheep and graze your young goats by the tents of the shepherds"* (Song 1:8). Again the Song is so full of symbolism. The word *"tracks"*[22] can be translated *"footsteps"*[23] or *"trail."*[24] The Lord is telling her that there are those who have gone before her and found the Shepherd of

Psalm 23. If she will find those people and get into relationship with them, they will help show her the way.

Secondly He said, "Graze your young goats...." This implies that she is leading others and nurturing others. The Lord wants her to think about someone besides herself. He is telling her to get back involved with believers and to find those both younger and older than she, learning from those who have been down the path and teaching others as she is going. Some may say, "But how can she teach if she is just learning it herself?" I have found that I learn more when I have to teach it to someone else. It takes it from just one learning style and helps utilize all of them, ingraining it deeper into our spirits. Being in fellowship with both older and younger believers helps to keep us humble and teachable.

And lastly the Lord tells her to feed those younger than her *"beside the tents of the shepherds."* In Scripture, shepherds are symbolic of spiritual leaders. In Jeremiah 3:15 the Lord declares, *"I will give you shepherds after My own heart, who will lead you with knowledge and understanding."* He tells her to get back involved with people and help lead others, and to do it beside the shepherds. In essence He is telling her not to be a "lone ranger" but to **submit to spiritual authority**. Not just to God in heaven, but the men and women that He has put into authority on earth. This will take a great deal of trust.

Now remember the believer has just been complaining to the Lord that the shepherds have taken advantage of her, and they don't know what to do with her. Yet the Lord tells her that it is in this very place she needs to be to grow and find healing. In this place He will enlarge her heart. The Lord wants her to get re-involved in the local community of believers. The Lord wants her back with people. He wants her to put aside her bitterness and anger and to search out those who can show her true food. It's about forgiveness. Young fervent believers tend to offend a lot of people because of their rough edges. Pastors and church leaders often don't handle them right, but God uses even bad leaders to produce godliness in us if we are willing to submit to them.

There are times that God puts us under the authority and leadership of ungodly shepherds. Now lest you go trying to blame your leaders as ungodly, remember only God can make that determination. Look at the story of King Saul and David. King Saul was a crazed madman who became jealous of David's fame and sought to murder David. For years he and his army chased after David throughout the land of Israel. It is in these years that the Lord forges David's heart to be set on one thing – seeking the beauty of the Lord.[25] David's heart could have been set on the throne of Israel or destroying the ungodly leadership of Saul, or even set in bitterness and anger. But David recognizes spiritual authority and that the Lord had placed Saul in this position, and the Lord must be the one to remove him.[26] Even when David had a chance to kill Saul and be set free to take his place on the throne that had already been promised him, David did not do it. He knew who it was who had anointed Saul King. It was the Lord, not man. In his book *A Tale of Three Kings*, Gene Edwards contends that you may never fully know whether the man in authority over you has the heart of Saul or the heart of David. It is only God who knows the deep things of the heart – and, Edwards contends,

*Dark but Lovely*

God will not tell.

We must realize that we all have hurts from the church. The church is run by and packed full of imperfect human beings – "dumb sheep," if you will – and sheep tend to bite each other. The fact is we are all walking around with sheep bites. Jesus, in fact, warned us to be ready for this, saying that we are not above our master, and if He was despised and rejected by men so would we. It was Jesus' own disciples who abandoned Him. It was the religious leaders that led Him to trial. But it was His love that held Him on the cross, and with that Love He cried out on behalf of all men, *"Father, forgive them, for they know not what they do."*[27]

After being in church leadership for a period of time I am beginning to see things a little differently than I once did. What I may have considered bad leadership when I was young in the Lord I now realize was more often than not me being a spoiled selfish two-year-old who wasn't getting my own way.

I will never forget the lesson the Lord taught me about this. I was involved with a great church. The pastor, in my opinion, because of his background, didn't know how to hear or follow the promptings of the Holy Spirit. My husband and I were leading a small group with another couple at the time. We had gotten together to discuss some of the issues in our group and pray about where we were to go next. In this context we were discussing some of the issues of the church that we were having personal problems with.

I, looking back, was one of those young fervent believers who thought I knew it all. I am unsure whether or not I had voiced my opinion that our pastor didn't know how to follow the promptings of the Spirit, but during our get-together there was a knock at our front door. Who should be standing there but our pastor? He had been on his way to get a cup of coffee and pray when he felt the Lord nudging him to "go to Terry's house." Note: it wasn't my husband's name nor our last name, but my name that the pastor heard. So feeling this strong prompting he was now on our doorstep wondering why the Lord would bring him there. Needless to say I was humbled that day. Falling on my face before the Lord, I repented for judging a man that I honestly knew nothing about. For, as you can see from the story, I was very wrong. This was a very valuable lesson for me, and one I pray I learned well.

## There Is Always A Remnant

We all have those moments when we think, in our arrogance and pain, that we are the only ones who really know how to follow the Lord. I know that is painful to hear, but let's be honest. It is a defense mechanism, and it is caused by feeling sorry for ourselves. This comes from myriad reasons, but the most prevalent is not knowing who we are to God.

Even the prophet Elijah experienced this. In 2 Kings, Elijah has just called down fire from heaven, killed the prophets of Baal, and shown Israel that God is who He says He is. Elijah is now running in fear because Jezebel has threatened his life. The Lord comes to him and says, *"What are you doing here?"* Elijah answers that he is running for his life, that he is the only one left in all of Israel who follows the Lord. The Lord responds, I believe, lovingly, *"I have reserved 7000 in Israel who have not bowed their knee to Baal."*[28]

Wherever you are, whatever is happening, there is always a remnant. There are always those hidden within every denomination and church who know how to find God. There are those in the body of Christ like Moses who know how to enter into the presence of the Lord, even in the midst of unfaithful, carnal people. The Lord wants His beloved back in fellowship with other believers. He wants her to find and follow those with hearts like Moses and Joshua, Moses' right hand man during the 40 years of wilderness.

Remember the story of the Israelites leaving Egypt and going to Canaan? Moses sent out twelve spies to survey the land that the Lord was giving them to possess. The spies came back with conflicting reports. Ten of those spies said, "The land is good, but the people are so big that we are like grasshoppers in their eyes." But two of the spies, Joshua and Caleb, disagreed. They said, "This is the land that God is giving us and He will fight for us. We need to trust God." The nation chose to trust the report of the ten over the confidence the two had in Jehovah, and they all spent 40 years going 'round and 'round the mountain of God.[29]

There were two spies who brought back the good report, but when it came time to enter into the Promised Land, although both were still alive, only one became their leader. That one was Joshua. Why? I believe it is because Joshua knew where to hang out during those 40 years. As we read through the tale of the desert journey, we find Joshua in one place continually. He is always at the "tent of meeting." He would not leave the tent of the Lord, even when Moses did. *"The Lord would speak to Moses face to face, as a man speaks with his friend. Then Moses* would return to the camp, but his young aide Joshua son of Nun did not leave the tent."[30]

It doesn't matter how perfect or imperfect our leaders are; what matters is where you choose to stand. Will you get fed by man, or by the very presence of God? If it is by the very presence of God, it matters very little what church you are in. For the Lord is far more interested in our character and our willingness to submit to the people He has put into authority than He is in us feeling good. Jesus said it this way, *"My food is to do the will of him who sent me and to finish His work."*[31]

There was a season at the church that I was attending that a lot of the reasons that I was drawn to the church were no longer an emphasis there. The things that were on my heart to grow in were different than what was on the leaders' hearts. Our church was wonderful and sharing Jesus with those who did not yet know Him. But for those of us who already knew the Lord and had a growing relationship with Him for several years, this was a difficult season. After a few years of this season had gone by people began asking me, "Why are you still here?" And my answer was always the same. "Within this body there is a group of people who have hearts that beat for intimacy as mine does. Early on God put me into relationship with these people and together we have gone for it, inviting others on the journey along the way." (More importantly – God had not released us.)

Not only had God given me friends who were walking into the deeper things of God with me, often leading me, but together we began to discover people from years past who had written of their journeys into the heart of God. With these encouragements as trail-guides, we began to explore new terrain together with people like Jeanne Guyon, St. Theresa of Avila, St. John of the Cross, and many others – some of whom were persecuted for their beliefs.

Wherever you are the Lord is. Just as David learned how to be a good king by being subject to a bad one, we too can learn to be a good leader by learning to be a good follower and by clinging to the Lord in humility.

## Selah

How much of Himself have you allowed God to show you? It is easy to see your darkness, but do you see His love for you?

Have you been blaming others for your spiritual state? Are you mad at the church or at leadership for what you perceive as a lack, and blaming them for where you are in the Lord? Are you guilty of grumbling against those the Lord has put into leadership? Are you using a lot of "if only" in your communication with Jesus?

Have you forgotten how to find rest and peace? What have you been chasing after? Have you been looking to men and women of God to nourish you instead of to the Lord?

## Further Reading

*Tale of Three Kings* by Gene Edwards

*The Three Battlegrounds* by Francis Frangipane

*Drawing Near* by John Bevere

*Secrets of the Most Holy Place* by Don Nori

*Under Cover* by John Bevere

## 4th Movement
# Rest

The music of the symphony takes on a soothing tone, bringing your heart to a place of comfort and rest. The images of the maiden and the King fill your mind as you think of Him holding her and comforting her while she has poured out her heart to Him. There is something deep within you that resonates with the maiden's life, and you find the desire to be in the presence of the King yourself. There is warmth in the music that speaks to you of being held safely in the arms of your Father.

The sound of the instruments turn majestic as the King's voice rolls out like thunder. It does not bring fear, as you would imagine, but rather a sense of security and safety. "And now, fair maiden, let us address the way you look." She looked at herself again, embarrassment beginning to show itself.

Wrapped in His arms she had nearly forgotten her appearance. "You see the dirt, you look on the outside. You see where you have let Me down. Do you think that when you come to Me with a heart of love and sincerity, recognizing that you are poor and broken, that I would be repulsed by you? That I could despise you?

"No, I see differently. I look on the inside. The dirt is easily washed away. And your dress – I have garments for you in My palace. I want you to come to Me as you are, for even your best garments are as filthy rags to Me. I am near to the brokenhearted. A bruised reed I will not break, a smoldering wick I will not put out. No. For I am not like others. My thoughts are not like those you have known before."

His words were like warm water bathing her. She felt as though she were being cleansed before His very eyes. He continued, "For I see what you cannot. You can only see yesterday and today. Your heart is such that you remember your failures more than your triumphs. But I see the victories that you do not, and I see what you will be. Would you like Me to share with you the maiden I see standing before Me?" He asks with a warm smile on His face. She nods vigorously, unable to speak or take her gaze from Him. She feels like a child about to receive an incredible surprise.

"I see a woman," He says. "Though young and immature, You send the hearts of those around you racing. I see the fire of love reflected in your face. Do not fear, for inside you have been planted the seeds of love. I will nurture that seed and we will bring about together the character of a queen. You will indeed look like a queen in the fullness of time. There is much we need to do to prepare you, much you will have to go through. For just as it is impossible to imagine a lump of coal becoming a diamond, you cannot see what you will become. But you will one day be a royal diadem in My hand." He held out to her the most beautiful gem she had ever seen. "One day you will be more impressive than this."

Oh how wonderful are the words of love from the King. The harsh words from the angry brothers had clung to the young girl like wallow on a pig. The words of love from the King washed her like a summer shower washes away the dust and the heat, leaving the earth refreshed and new. She sat beside Him clean, clothed in a golden dress. For, you see, in this enchanted kingdom, the effect of thoughts and words can be seen.

Now cleansed and refreshed she no longer felt ashamed in the presence of the King. Her heart even felt stronger. She felt that she could dare to believe all that He had spoken. She realized that the words of her brothers were lies. Here she could see so clearly. Here in this place she could even dare to believe in the King's love for her. As they lingered in each other's presence she began to recall all that the King had done for her. She remembered how she was a slave, constantly living in fear and hatred. Hiding as best she could from the eyes of all – especially the cruel Taskmaster – somehow he always found her, and nothing she did could ever please him. He kept charging her with offenses she had not committed, often blaming her for his mistakes. He would add on punishment and debt on a whim. He said he had not made her pay fully for her "mistakes." The Taskmaster said he was being merciful, yet he was always bringing them to her attention and reminding her how much she owed him. Somehow it felt that with each "gift of mercy," as he called them, another link was added to the chains on her ankles.

Then the King came. He came right into her world. He walked right up to the Taskmaster and claimed her. He paid for her. He paid far more than she was worth. He paid a price that could not be refused.

Suddenly like a lighting bolt from heaven it hit her. "He not only paid for me, but He took all the insults and abuse that the Taskmaster had put on me," she thought. "It is all so clear now. Why had I not seen it before? All that I have heard is true. That is why He had been away *for those three days. I had heard rumors that He had been beaten and even killed. I did not believe them, for then I saw Him walk back into His kingdom looking more glorious then He had before. But it is true! He took all that was for me – even death. But how could that be? If He had died, how could she be sitting here with Him? Oh, His Father truly must be more powerful then all the forces of the earth. For even death could not hold His Son."*

*Selah*

## *chapter four*
# FEASTING ON THE LORD

Song 1:12-1:14

As the last chapter ended we listened to the Lord telling the believer to forgive the church and those who had wounded her and to get back involved with His people. As He speaks to her about the fact that there is always a remnant of those who follow hard after Him, He leads her to dine with him at His table (Song 1:12). Later she calls it the "banqueting hall" (Song 2:4). The literal translation is *house of wine* or *house of intoxication*. If you will remember at the very beginning of the Song she had said, *"Your love is more delightful than wine"* (Song 1:2). She is now becoming drunk on His love as she sits within the presence of the King.

I picture a castle of old, all decorated and alight with torches and candles. The hall becomes filled with guests of the King; all are dressed in their finest. As you approach the castle from a distance you see the lights, and above it the flag of the King is unfurled. A beautiful ornate flag proclaims that the King is in residence and that there is joy and peace in the land.

As you enter the banquet hall itself you are overwhelmed by the opulence and beauty. We can get an idea of what the banquet could look like by reading what Solomon set on his table on a daily basis. (Remember that this whole song is using the natural king of Israel, Solomon, to show us a glimpse of our heavenly King.) We read in 1 Kings 4 of the abundance of the King's table:

*"Solomon's daily provisions were thirty cors of fine flour and sixty cors of meal, ten head of stall-fed cattle, twenty of pasture-fed cattle and a hundred sheep and goats, as well as deer, gazelles, roebucks and choice fowl."*[1]

If this was his daily provision, just think what a special celebration would have been like. This is nothing compared to what awaits us at the wedding supper of the Lamb.

At this banquet you are the guest of honor, not the servant. At this banquet you are to be served from the finest of the land sitting at the right hand of the King. For God raised us up with Christ and seated us with Him in the heavenly realms in Christ Jesus.[2] And you are eating of the best provisions the kingdom has to offer. Jesus said that *"the kingdom of heaven is not meat and drink, but righteousness, peace and joy...."*[3] At the banqueting table we are being filled with the fruits of the Spirit as we sit in the presence of the King.

But this is far more than a public feast – this is an intimate time for the believer, a time when she sits at the feet of the Lord contemplating all that He has done for her. Psalm 23 tells us that the Lord prepares a banqueting table for us and that the cup of blessing overflows. It is in these times of feasting on the provision of God for our lives that our hearts begin to overflow with love. The image these verses in Song of Solomon 1:12-14 paint is a beautiful picture of intimate fellowship between the Lord and the believer. Can't you just see them cuddled up together at a low table sitting on the floor in front of a fire eating, drinking and talking? It reminds me of several nights that my husband and I have waited on dinner until after the kids are in bed, opened some wine, gotten out cheese and crackers and fruit, and sat in front of a fire talking into the night, the perfume of our love wafting through the air; we laugh and listen and even at times just sit in silence, enraptured in the fragrance of the heart. This is what happens as we take time to sit at the banqueting table.

## The Fragrance of Myrrh

It is in this place of love and intimacy that the believer is contemplating the cost of the cross. It is going beyond head-knowledge; it is now becoming heart-knowledge and part of her life. Jesus told us when He was performing His earthly ministry that we must *"eat his flesh and drink his blood."*[4] In this same passage Jesus tells us that He is the bread of life that has come from heaven. When you eat you take food into your mouth, you chew it, you taste it, and you swallow it. The nutrients of the food get into your blood stream and are pumped throughout your body, giving life and energy to your being. As the believer is digesting the provision of the cross, the qualities of the bread of life begin to act on her being. She is feasting on the provision of the Lord, on His death and resurrection. She is chewing on it, digesting it and letting the truth get into her blood. As it does it flows throughout her whole body causing her to look and act like Jesus.

Remember the old adage "you are what you eat." What are your eyes "feasting on"? Your ears? What are you doing with your hands? All theses things feed your spirit. The question remains: Are you feeding your spirit life or death? Real food or junk food? Are you truly feeding your soul or killing the pain? Food has become the drug of choice for most Christians by which they kill their pain or fill their need. This is why fasting is a vital discipline for every believer. Jesus wants us to fill up on Him, the bread from heaven. For this will truly feed our every need.

As the believer feeds on the Lord, she begins to express how the Lord's provision has affected her life, what it has come to mean to her. Her first expression in Song 1:13 is that it is like a *"sachet of myrrh resting between her breast."*

Myrrh was not native to Israel; it was imported from Arabia and Africa and was very costly. Jesus was given myrrh at his birth, crucifixion and death. It was used for many different things: as an embalming spice, as a preservative to keep things from corrupting, putrefying and rotting; it was used in cosmetics because it takes away wrinkles and makes skin shiny and smooth; it was used in medicines, and it was used as a perfume. As the believer is feasting on the provision of the Lord, the effect of His life in her is to make her pure, without spot or wrinkle.[5]

The believer has entered into a time of intimacy with the Lord, His very words washing her clean, purifying her heart and revealing to her the cost of His love. It is in this place of fellowship that believers begin to truly understand the price love paid. It is a lifelong learning. The cross is the central point of our walk and relationship with the Lord and indeed the central point of all history. It is the place we all must come to find rest and provision, and this is the place we must continue to come back to all of our days. It is important to note that this time of contemplation is not merely an hour sitting in front of the elements, but it is a season of intimacy, of reflection and growing in spiritual understanding. This season can be different lengths of time and revisited often as the truths of Jesus' provision go deeper into our hearts.

One of the ways the Lord began to expound upon the sacrifice of the cross to me was through the study of Passover. I had been walking with the Lord for nearly 20 years when He began to have me look intently at these traditions. In this study came forth truths that gave me significantly greater understanding into the sacrifice that Jesus made on my behalf.

The Passover meal is replete with symbolism of the sacrificial lamb, Jesus, and the life that He gives us. How often we quickly take the bread and the wine during a church service but don't take the time to really consider what that sacrifice has done and continues to do for us. For most of us communion is at best a 15-minute thing we do – eating the cracker and drinking the wine. But to a Jew this is a four to five hour meal of remembrance in the celebration of the Passover, a time to contemplate the goodness and kindness of the Lord in all He has done for them. This time with the Lord is a time to linger and think on the mercy of God.

## Slavery to Friendship

From the very beginning of Scripture to the very end we see the history of God's relationship with man. God has always desired fellowship with us: to walk with us as He did with Adam and Eve in the cool of the evening.[6] Once our fellowship with God was broken by Adam and Eve in the garden, God began to implement a way for us to be back in His presence. He first made a covenant (a solemn promise) with Abraham. He then called a group of slaves, who had all but forgotten their God, out of the Land of Egypt to His holy mountain, giving an unknown people group His words, His laws and His heart. And then He gave us the Messiah.

The book of Exodus gives us the story of the slaves being brought out of Egypt. In brief, the Lord heard the cries of His people in captivity and delivered them from bondage by His very hand. The Lord led this group of former slaves by a pillar of cloud and fire through the sea onto dry ground, then to the mountain of God in the wilderness. When they reached this mountain the manifest (visible) presence of God came and settled like a cloud over the top of the mountain and Moses went into the cloud – into the very presence of God – and spoke with Him face to face.

While camping at the foot of the mountain the Lord told Moses to have the people prepare to meet with God:

*On the morning of the third day there was thunder and lightning, with a thick cloud over the mountain, and a very loud trumpet blast. Everyone in the camp trembled. Then Moses led the people out of the camp to meet with God, and they stood at the foot of the mountain. Mount Sinai was covered with smoke, because the Lord descended on it in fire. The smoke billowed up from it like smoke from a furnace, the whole mountain trembled violently, and the sound of the trumpet grew louder and louder. Then Moses spoke and the voice of God answered him.*[7]

The story goes on to tell us:

> *"The people saw the thunder and lightning and heard the trumpet and saw the mountain in smoke, they trembled with fear. They stayed at a distance and said to Moses, 'Speak to us yourself and we will listen. But do not have God speak to us or we will die.'* "8 *"Moses said to the people, 'Do not be afraid. God has come to test you, so that the fear of God will be with you to keep you from sinning.' The people remained at a distance, while Moses approached the thick darkness where God was.'* "9

The people so feared the presence of the Lord that they could not bear to hear His voice themselves. God's intention from the beginning was not to have a mediator, but to speak to them directly. He wanted to speak to them face to face as He did to Moses. God desired to have a personal friendship with the people at Mt. Sinai, but because of fear they walked away saying, "This is too much for us. Moses, you talk to Him for us." And so the priesthood was established.

*"But you are a chosen people, a royal priesthood, a holy nation, a people belonging to God, that you may declare the praises of Him who called you out of darkness into His wonderful light. Once you were not a people, but now you are the people of God; once you had not received mercy, but now you have received mercy."*10

I believe that it was always God's desire to have a priesthood of all believers, not just a chosen few.

God understood their fear and still understands ours today. He knows that we are but dust, yet He still desires intimate fellowship with us. In fact, we read of the direct fellowship the leaders of Israel had even after they told Moses to talk to God for them. It was as if God were giving them another chance by showing them that He is good. In Ex. 24:1 and 8-11 we read:

> *Moses then took the blood, sprinkled it on the people and said, "This is the blood of the covenant that the Lord has made with you in accordance with all these words."* (Sound familiar?) *Moses and Aaron, Nadab and Abihu, and the seventy elders of Israel went up [the mountain] and saw the God of Israel. Under His feet was something like a pavement made of sapphire, clear as the sky itself. But God did not raise His hand against these leaders of the Israelites; they saw God, and they ate and drank.*

I believe the Lord wanted, and still wants, for all of us to come meet with Him and eat and drink in His visible manifest presence where He can speak to us face to face like a man speaks to a friend.

Jesus said to his disciples, *"I no longer call you servants, because a servant does not know his master's business. Instead, I have called you friends, for everything that I learned from my Father I have made known to you."*[11]

> The Bible uses two consistent images in the representation of friendship. First, the knitting of souls – a companion of one's inmost thoughts and feeling, resulting in intense emotional attachment…. Characteristic expressions of this union of hearts are in affectionate embrace or kiss…. The second image the Bible uses to represent friendship is the face-to-face encounter, an interface…. This implies a

conversation of sharing confidences and consequently a meeting of minds, goals and directions.[12]

This is what God is looking for in you!

Is it scary to come into God's presence? Yes. Will it change you? You better believe it! In *The Chronicles of Narnia*, C.S. Lewis shares of the children's introduction to the lion Aslan, as they are being told about him Lucy asks, "A Lion, is he safe?" The beaver replies, "Safe, no! But he is good!"[13] Is God safe? At times yes, at times no, but He is always good.

## The Passover

In order for the Hebrew slaves to be allowed to leave Egypt, the Lord had to use a mighty hand against Egypt. We have read the accounts of God striking the Egyptians with 10 plagues. Each of the 10 plagues came directly against a god that the Egyptians worshiped. One by one the God of the universe came against the false gods of the world and showed His power. The last plague to hit the Egyptians was the death of the firstborn. Pharaoh's son, who was himself worshiped as a god, would die. At Mt. Sinai the Lord told His people that they were to have no other gods before Him. While in Egypt He showed them how much stronger He was than any other god. Here we see two significant revelations: God has the power of life and death, and Jesus, the firstborn son of God, died for our deliverance from the slavery of sin.

The Passover has been celebrated the same way since long before Jesus graced the earth. It is practiced today in the same ways it would have been in His day. The first Christians were

Jewish and knew the importance of what it was that Jesus had done. John the Baptist proclaimed, "Look, the Lamb of God who takes away the sins of the world."[14]

Passover as celebrated today is really the combination of three festivals: Passover, Unleavened Bread and First Fruits.

**Passover** - A one-day celebration that commemorates the deliverance of the Hebrews from Egypt and a time of looking forward to the coming of the Messiah.[15] For those who believe in Christ it is the day of His sacrifice and substitutionary death.[16] For both Christian and Jew it symbolizes Redemption.

**Unleavened Bread** - A seven-day feast that starts the day after Passover. This was to commemorate the bread of haste that the Israelites ate as they left Egypt and the purification of the Hebrews. Jesus was without sin (leaven), and therefore His body would never decay.[17] To the Christian it is the time that Jesus' body was in the grave. To both the Jew and Christian it symbolizes sanctification.

**First Fruits** - A one-day feast that starts on the second day of the Feast of Unleavened Bread. For the Jews this was the day to bring the beginning of the barley crop to the temple. The Lord would accept this offering of the first fruits as a guarantee for the rest of the harvest. Christ is the first fruits of those who will receive eternal life.[18] To the Christian this is the celebration of the Resurrection – Easter.

The Passover celebration is a long, involved party that lasts for several hours as the story of God's deliverance is retold. "The Lord's supper is actually a mini Passover seder (Hebrew word for order, it is the family ritual that is observed at Passover) fulfilled in Messiah, Yeshua, who said, *"Do this in remembrance of me.*"[19] The seder is filled with symbolism, but for space we want to look at three specific things: the bread, the wine and the Lamb.

## The Bread

The telling of the story is commemorated with unleavened bread that is pierced called matzo because the slaves had to leave in haste and didn't have time for their bread to rise. Even before the feast begins there is much preparation that goes into this joyous occasion.

In the Passover celebration there is a special piece of the bread called the *afikomen*. This is the only Greek word that appears in the *seder* and it means *I came*. The *afikomen* was one of three pieces of matzo that were stacked and put into a special wrapping. At a point in the celebration the middle piece is removed and broken in two. One piece would be eaten, the other piece hidden for the children to find. It serves as a reminder that the kingdom of heaven belongs to such as these. It was the piece that was broken and eaten that Jesus would have addressed the disciples with, telling them that the one who was dipping his hand in the bowl with Him was the one who would betray Him. Jewish believers who believed that Jesus was the Passover Lamb no longer participated in the sacrificial system; to celebrate Passover they incorporated the broken matzo to remember Jesus was the pierced unleavened bread, who was broken for us. In 70 AD the temple in Jerusalem was destroyed. Without the temple there could be no sacrifice,[20] and without a sacrifice there could be no Passover. It is believed that it was at this time non-believing

Jews took on the custom of the *afikomen* so that the Passover celebration could continue.

In Exodus 12:15 the commandment in observing the Feast of Unleavened Bread is that all leaven is to be removed from your house, and you are to eat no leaven for seven days. Since that time the Jews have practiced not only eating unleavened bread but also removing the leaven from the home. To this day the practice is to scald all spoons, wash all clothes and throw out all leaven. Exodus 12 gives a strong warning to any who would not remove the yeast from their bread and their homes, saying, *"They would be cut off from the rest of Israel."* Leaven in Scripture stands for sin. Sin will cut us off from the presence of God. Jesus tells us to beware of the yeast of religious people.[21]

In 1 Corinthians 5:6-8 Paul says,

> *Your boasting is not good. Don't you know that a little yeast works through the whole batch of dough? Get rid of the old yeast that you may be a new batch without yeast – as you really are. For Christ, our Passover Lamb, has been sacrificed. Therefore let us keep the festival, not with the old yeast, the yeast of malice and wickedness, but with bread without yeast, the bread of sincerity and truth.*

In the book of John we see Jesus himself clearing His father's house of yeast in preparation of the Passover and Unleavened feasts.

> *When it was almost time for the Jewish Passover, Jesus went up to Jerusalem. In the temple courts he found men selling cattle,*

*sheep and doves, and others sitting at tables exchanging money. So He made a whip out of cords, and drove all from the temple area, both sheep and cattle; He scattered the coins of the money-changers and overturned their tables. To those who sold doves He said, "Get these out of here! How dare you turn my Father's house into a market!"*

Matthew, Mark and Luke add that Jesus said, *"It is written My house shall be a house of prayer for all nations."*[22]

## The Lamb

Four days before the Passover the sacrificial lamb was to be chosen. A family would choose a lamb and take it into their house to inspect it and become familiar with it. In this way their attachment to the lamb would make the sacrifice more personal. As they would become attached to the lamb they would also renew their hopes for a Messiah.

After the four days of inspection and association, all the lambs were to be publicly sacrificed, signifying that all the people were responsible for the death of the innocent. Traditionally, the daily sacrifice was slaughtered at 3:00 pm, including the day of Passover. At that time the high priest stood at the pinnacle of the temple and blew the shofar announcing the atonement of sin.

The historian Ray Vander Lann explains to us the details of the specifications for the lambs that were to be sacrificed and similarities of how Jesus was crucified:

The lamb was the subject of strict ritual requirements. It was to be roasted on a cross-like spit, one branch penetrating the length and the other separating the front feet. Not a bone was to be broken. Each family was then to apply the blood to the doorframes of their house as a visible sign of faith. At that moment, the innocent lamb became the substitution for their sins, making it possible for the Lord's judgment to "pass over" their homes and the first born would live.

In the Roman custom of crucifixion the condemned were first flogged, the cross bar was tied to the prisoners shoulders and he was paraded through the streets to a public location.[23] Prisoners were crucified naked.[24] The cross was an upper case T and low to the ground. The condemned were nailed to the cross through the wrists and ankles.[25] Finally the sign identifying their crime was attached to the cross. The prisoner hung in excruciating pain and eventually died of asphyxiation and loss of blood.[26] Prisoners could remain conscious for days. Sometimes to shorten their pain their legs would be broken.

Vander Lann continues,

> Jesus, our Passover Lamb, was perfect. He was crucified according to the strict regulations – not a bone was broken.[27] As Jesus hung on the cross, He heard the blast of the shofar. He recognized that His hour had come. When the knife slit the throat of the Passover lamb, Jesus looked up to heaven and said, *"It is finished."*[28] At that moment the

Passover lamb and the Lamb of God died.

The curtain of separation in the temple was torn from top to bottom.[29]

## The Wine

During the Passover celebration participants partake of four cups of wine. Each cup different in its symbolism. The first cup is the "cup of blessing." It is a reminder of the Lord's promise, *"I will bring you out."*[30] The second cup is the "cup of deliverance," for the Lord's promise was, *"I will rescue you from bondage."*[31] From this cup 10 drops of wine are spilled, one for each plague against the Egyptians. The spilling of the wine is to remember with sadness the sorrow and suffering that our enemies went through. For the Lord does not wish any to perish but all to come to Him.[32]

The third cup of wine served is the "cup of salvation/joy," for the Lord's promise was, *"I will redeem you."*[33] At this time, traditionally the door to the house would be open in the hopes that Elijah, the prophet, would come in, drink a cup of wine and announce the arrival of the Messiah. And it was at this time that the Lord instituted the Lord's supper. For the spirit of Elijah had come in John the Baptist and announced the arrival of Jesus and the Savior was now making himself more plainly known. *"In the same way, after supper Jesus took the cup, saying, 'This cup is the new covenant in my blood.'"*[34] But when Jesus raised the glass and said this He added this to the traditional Passover, this is not in the seder; this was actually part of the marriage proposal.

Ray Vander Lann explains,

> During the times of Jesus when a young man was of marrying age, his family selected a bride and negotiated the "bride price." Once the price was agreed upon the man's father would pour a glass of wine and hand it to his son. His son would turn to the woman and lift the glass saying, "This cup is a new covenant in my blood, which I offer for you." In other words – "I love you and I give you my life. Will you marry me?" In essence as Christ added the covenant to the traditional blessing of the wine He was saying, "I love you, and the only picture I can think of that will describe the power of my love for you is the pure love of a husband for his wife."
>
> He is still saying, "I love you. I offer you my life. Will you be my bride?" In taking the cup we look to the Heavenly Father and say, "Yes, I will have your Son." And we look to the Son and say, "Yes, I will be your bride! I accept Your love and I give you my life in response."[35]

The fourth cup is the "cup of praise" because of the Lord's promise, *"I will take you as my own people."*[36] This is the cup that Jesus said He would not drink of again until we were with Him in heaven. After drinking this cup the Seder is concluded with a time of singing, praise and worship.

## Selah

Have you taken time to contemplate the provisions the cross

has made for you? Have you done so lately? The Lord stands at the door and knocks, will you let Him in deeper to your heart? What are you feeding on? What would it be like to eat and drink in the presence of the living God? What would it mean to you for God to bring eternity, by His manifest presence, into your life here on earth? How would this change your life? Do you desire this kind of encounter with the Lord?

What new understandings do you have of the sacrifice of Jesus? Are you willing to eat His flesh and drink His blood? Is that as startling to you as it was to the first disciples? Can you hear the Lord asking you to be His bride?

**Further Reading**

*The Tabernacle of Moses* by Kevin Conner

*The Feasts of the Lord* by
     Kevin Howard & Marvin Rosenthal

*The Feasts of Israel* by Kevin Conner

*Why the Cross?* by Ray Vander Lann, Focus on the
     Family Magazine, March 1997

*The Passover Journey: A Seder Companion* by
     Barbara Diamond Goldin

*His Body, His Blood* by Vander Lann,
     Focus on the Family Magazine, April 1999

## 5th Movement
# Romance

As the Maiden lingers over the thoughts of the Lord's payment for her, she finds that a perfume is coming from her heart, for in this enchanted place the thoughts of your heart become a fragrance for all to smell. To some they are the smell of life, to others the smell of death. Hers is the fragrance myrrh, the spice of burial that wafts from within. She turns to the King with tears of love streaming down her face.

"O, the fragrance of myrrh. It cleanses me, it purifies me, it takes away all the wrinkles and stains. Oh, how beautiful it is. It reminds me of the fragrant white henna blossoms You showed me that grow by the Spring of the Lamb. O, what a refuge, what an oasis is that spring."

"My darling," says the King, looking deeply into her eyes, "You are beautiful! Your eyes, they remind me of the dove. The dove can see only one thing at a time. I know your eyes are set on Me. I know that your heart is set on Me."

"O, my King, You are so handsome. You are really very charming, my love! This place," she says, looking around the inner room where they had wandered, "it is as if it were living and growing around us. I know that our life together will just keep getting stronger and stronger. Even the fragrance grows because nothing can come in here and destroy our love," proclaims the Maiden.

The King and the Maiden are in such unison, enraptured in each other's love. As they speak words of love they sing out in a single voice. "I am ordinary, but lovely. Like a bramble rose, like a lily, the fragrance and beauty of love flow from my heart. It is as a refreshing drink. With the eyes of a dove, love can be seen in the entire kingdom. It is like a beautiful mountain meadow carpeted with flowers."

"Yes, my love," adds the King, "You stand out pure and radiant in the midst of a crooked and dark world. I have walked the kingdom of slavery. I have seen the hardships there. I walked not in my royal robes, but as a commoner. So I know, from experience, what it is like there. And I see that you are different; you have found the entrance to the Kingdom of Love." "My King, You are the One who stands out. You are the One that is different from all the others. Even in the dress of a commoner You would stand out."

"This place, my love, is so refreshing. It is like coming upon an apple tree during a long journey," says the Maiden, looking around her. "It is so peaceful, so restful here, I can feel Your love over me like a majestic banner. Do you think all the kingdom can see it too? Your words of love have revived and refreshed me. I feel a strength that I have never felt before. The feel of Your arms embracing me; I have felt them before. They were always there, weren't they? I just couldn't always see them."

The Maiden goes to the balcony of the great hall that they are in and, leaning over the railing, raises her voice and calls out, "Is there any one who is listening? Is there any who can hear me? Do not awaken love until the King draws you to His side. Don't waste your love on the lesser lovers the world has to offer. Awaken the sleeping giant within only to the beckoning of the King.

"Love is a burning flame within your heart causing you to desire more and more. It is a precious thing. In the beginning it is fragile. But when you are ready, when the desire for the King rises up within you like a torrent, then the King will answer. Only He knows the timing. Don't rush it, but do yearn and desire it. Oh yes – unleash the passion within and desire it. For He will fulfill the desires of your heart."

As the Maiden goes back in, her heart is full of love and devotion.

"This great hall, this castle of love, is so glorious," she thinks. "I could stay here forever. I am never leaving here, never!"

She walks back over to the couch she has been sitting on with the Lord. Curling up beside Him, she lays her head on His shoulder. As warmth and comfort flow over her, she soon finds herself asleep, resting at last from the activity of life.

The curtain closes; act one comes to an end.

*Selah*

*chapter five*
# ROMANCE OF THE KING

Song 1:15-2:7

   The believer and the Lord are enjoying a time of intimacy as she contemplates the price paid for her. In my mental image they've left the busy gathering of the banquet hall and are now sitting in front of a fire enraptured in each other's arms, their thoughts, words, laughter, breath and heartbeats mingling together. What is our natural response at this time? It is to speak words of love from our hearts.

   The Lord really knows how to go straight to our hearts. Who doesn't love to hear words of affection? In the beginning of our journeys God is persistent in His revelation of His affection. This is the context in which maturity grows, in which love grows. Without this persistent revelation we lack faith and trust in God's love. The Lord tells her twice for emphasis how beautiful she is (Song 1:15). Rabbis say that when a phrase is repeated twice it is said once for the past and once for the present. The Lord is saying that He always **has** and always **will** find her beautiful. Oh, if we could only see from the Lord's perspective.

   As the believer is spending time with the Lord there is a recognition that things are changing. The two begin to talk about their dwelling place. Remember, Scripture says that we are the tabernacle of God.[1]  He dwells in our hearts.

The English language is so limited. The song here is sheer poetry. "Our bed is verdant, our house is cedar and fir" (Song 1:16-17). She could have just said, "Our bed is green." But how flat and comparatively undescripitive!

The word *verdant* means *green with leaves; fresh*. When I hear that word the color I see is the green of early spring. It is a yellow green, a new green. Have you ever noticed that the leaves change colors over the summer, not just in the fall? In spring they begin to bud a very light pale yellowish-green, and as the summer goes on and the leaves mature, they turn a dark forest green. Now can you see how descriptive she is being. It is not merely a growing love, but one that is young and beginning to spring forth in vitality and life. And yet, she goes on to say that it is stately and strong like the hardwoods of the forest. The cedar is a very strong, tall growing tree. Its root system is as deep as the tree is tall. It is a profitable tree used in building, and it has a strong fragrance that keeps pests away. The believer has been nourished, as we discussed earlier, and now is in a position of being able to rest in the Lord. She is not resting inside, in a sterile environment, but outside by the banks of the river of life, receiving all she needs from the hand of the Lord.

## Terms of Endearment

As the believer and the Lord share their hearts the words "I love you" come popping out like the cork from a champagne bottle. "You're beautiful" flows with emotion as champagne pours out into the goblets of their hearts. "You have dove's eyes." They compare each other to the lily and rose, dove and apple tree (Song 2:1).

In every intimate relationship we use "terms of endearment," nicknames that speak of love and acceptance. Growing up my father called me "Toots." I have no idea where the name came from or even what it means, but what it said to me was, "You are my daughter and I love you."

Names were very important in the Bible. The name of the person tells who they are. Elmer Towns writes in his book *My Father's Names*,

> Can you imagine two persons really getting to know and love each other without knowing each other's names? Somehow, our name becomes so intertwined with our personality that only those who really know our name can truly love and understand us...This is no less true of God.[2]

His names (of which there are 83 in Scripture) tell us of His personality.

God was continually changing people's names in Scripture. One example was the changing of Abram's name to Abraham. Abram means *exalted father* and Abraham means *father of a great multitude*. His new name spoke of the destiny that God had for Abraham. The Lord promises that He will give to us a name only for us that is from the very heart of God; these are terms of endearment that express to us the heart of love that God has for us, His beloved. It is a name that expresses the destiny and adventure that God has in store for each one of us. The book of Revelation says that we will receive a new name from God himself that is a secret between God and the individual.[3] To Israel, in Isaiah 62, He says her name will be *"My delight"* and *"married."*[4] And then again to the overcomers in Revelation 3 He says, *"I will write on him the name of my God and the name of the city of my God, the new Jerusalem, which is coming down out of heaven from my God; and I will also write on him my new name."*[5]

When a woman marries she traditionally takes on a new name, the name of her husband, telling all that she is married and has a new identity.

Unlike my pet name from my father, the names given from the Heavenly Father in the Song of Solomon have significant deep meaning. The Lord first tells her she has "dove's eyes." Doves are gentle creatures. They often sing in the morning as the sun is rising as if to herald the dawn of a new day. Doves are noted for their faithfulness and are unique in that they mate for life. Their most prominent feature is their eyes. The eyes of the dove can only see straight ahead and can only focus on one thing at a time. Can you hear what the Lord is saying to her? She is gentle and humble of heart. She can see the coming of the King, and she beautifully sings as He comes into her presence. She has eyes for only Him. She now has spiritual insight that is attractive to Him. She has the eyes of the Spirit.

The well-known lines of Song of Solomon are spoken here. *"You are a Lily of the valley. The rose of Sharon"* (Song 2:1). There is some debate among scholars as to who is speaking here, the maiden or the Lord. I think that it is actually both. Remember this is a song, a duet. Here the song of the lovers rises together as they speak forth the description of who they are to each other.

Can't you just hear the harmony as their voices rise and fall together? This is one place I wish that we could hear the song actually sung. The two voices swirling together, the couple at last has expressed their love for one another, and they sing together their refrains of love as they stand cheek-to-cheek, arm in arm. *"I am only a little rose or autumn crocus of the plain of Sharon, or a [humble] Lily of the valley [that grows in deep and difficult places]* (Amplified).

The rose referred to can either be the wild rose or bramble commonly found in the pasturelands of Sharon, or the rose bush, as we know it. The lily can either be a rose or a lily. They are often interchangeable in Hebrew thought.

> Neither the experts on Palestinian flora or the commentators agree about the identity of these flowers. [Different versions render them completely different.] Ultimately, however the botanical identity of these flowers may be less the point than their symbolic value in the Bible. The same two flowers are singled out about the restoration of Zion to her former glory.[6]

There is so much to this analogy of the lily. It is an image strewn throughout the scriptures. In the Song of Solomon it is mentioned eight times alone. If a lily, it would be the white Madonna Lily, which is very fragrant and holds water in its cup. It is a very tall and stately flower that is very fruitful. Here it speaks of us returning to our former glory, the glory of mankind before sin separated us from God.

## The Different Confessions

From the standpoint of the believer her confession here would be that of being the common bramble rose, not much to look at and full of sin. Her statement is one of humility. Yet there is a marked difference in the way she sees herself now compared to how she saw herself earlier when she said she was *"dark yet lovely."* Now she is seeing the fruit of that dark place, for it is in the darkness underground that seeds sprout forth life. Now she sees that she is beginning to look like Jesus. She still may be very common, yet she is lovely and fragrant, becoming one that can bear fruit. She is beginning to recognize the work of God in her life. Now as she learns more of who she is in God, as she comes to a deeper understanding of what it is Jesus has done for her and how He feels about her she realizes that He has indeed taken her to green pastures and here she "fits." Here she finds a home; she belongs.

As Jesus speaks forth the same words, I don't believe He is saying He is a common flower; rather I think He is saying He is a very exquisite one full of life and beauty. Yet we often miss the most beautiful and spectacular things of this world because we fail to see; we fail to even look, to "stop and smell the roses."

Isaiah 53:2 tells us, *"He had no beauty or majesty to attract us to him, nothing in his appearance that we should desire him."*

Even the most everyday things can become a thing of wonder when beheld with the eyes of love. At the same time the Lord is the most humble of all, and I think this is His statement of humility as well. In Paul's letter to the believers in Philippi he writes,

*Your attitude should be the same as that of Christ Jesus: Who, being in very nature God, did not consider equality with God something to be grasped but made Himself nothing, taking the very nature of a servant, being made in human likeness. And being found in appearance as a man, He humbled Himself.*[7]

The Lord then adds to the statement she has just made regarding herself. *"But you my love, you are a lily among thorns"* (Song 2:2). Thorns throughout scripture speak of the world and sin. Here the Lord tells her she is a beautiful, fragrant, pure flower in the midst of a crooked and perverse generation. Try to get the picture in your mind. Thorn bushes are brown, ugly, hard to get close to, and unattractive, yet, in the midst of this bleak picture rises a beautiful, white radiant flower. He is looking at her heart, a heart that says, "For you I will stand out against the world."

She stands out like a single star on a dark night. I love this. The Lord is singling her out. "You are different from the rest." She is a stark contrast to the world. A delicate, beautiful flower, that takes great care to cultivate, is living among thorns. And she is beginning to captivate the Lord's heart. He is beginning to take special note of her.

### Apple Tree

The believer likens the Lord to an apple tree. These names and these phrases seem so odd to us, but there is so much meaning in each and every word. Fruit trees are not the stateliest of trees, but unlike the noble cedar they provide nourishment and refreshment. Here we see the maiden telling the

Lord that she recognizes that it is not by the outward appearance but by the fruit that a person should be judged.

We see that, in the book of Genesis, fruit trees become a central figure in the story of mankind. Here we read the story of Adam and Eve in the garden. The Lord put two trees in the garden: the tree of knowledge of good and evil, and the tree of life. Adam and Eve were allowed to eat from any tree – even the tree of life – except one. They were not to eat from the tree of knowledge. Eating this fruit always will produce, shame, pain, suffering and ultimately death, which is eternal separation from God. When they tasted of the knowledge of good and evil the Lord said, "We must now remove them from the garden before they eat from the tree of life." I had always seen this as punishment and the anger of God, but I have come to believe it was not out of anger, but out of mercy, that God banned them from the garden. You see, if Adam and Eve had been allowed to stay in the garden after ingesting the knowledge of good and evil, they could have eaten of the tree of life; then mankind would forever be separated from God, living in evil for all eternity. Because God prevented them from eating of life after eating of knowledge, there is still a way back. That merciful way back to the tree of life is through the ultimate tree of death, the cross.

While John the Beloved is on the Island of Patmos, the angel of the Lord comes to him and gives him instruction for seven churches. In Rev. 2:1-7 we read the letter to the church of Ephesus. The Lord commends them for their good works and then speaks to them about the area they need to work on. Here we pick up in the letter:

*Yet I hold this against you: You have forsaken your first love. Remember the height from which you have fallen! Repent and do the things you did at first.... He who has an ear, let him hear what the Spirit says to the churches. To him who overcomes, I will give the right to* **eat from the tree of life***, which is in the paradise of God.*

According to Revelation 22, the tree of life is in the eternal city. If we overcome, we will be permitted to go to the city of God and feast with him on the fruit of life. What is it that we need to overcome? The loss of our first love! If we will repent and turn back with all our hearts to the lover of our soul, then the effects of eating from the tree of knowledge of good and evil are removed from our lives, and we can eat from the tree of life – and live as we were intended to live. *"Now this is eternal life: that they may know You, the only true God, and Jesus Christ, whom You have sent."*[8]

Fruit trees are generally found in orchards, not forests. But in the Song, the believer says in 2:3, *"Like an apple tree among the trees of the forest is my lover among the young men."* What a sight it would be to walk through the forest and find a tree that could nourish and refresh you. The believer is commenting that Jesus is different then all others because He gives life. Just as Adam and Eve were given a choice to eat from the trees in the garden, we too have a choice set before us: we can eat from the trees of the forest – the common trees of the world that provide the knowledge of good and evil – or we can eat from the tree of Life, which is Jesus. Because the maiden sees with doves' eyes she finds the small apple tree among the tall and stately trees of the forest; thus she finds nourishment and life.

She goes on to say in verse 2:3, *"I delight to sit in His shade."* This is a statement of protection and safety. It also denotes a secret place, a hiding place. We all sit under some sort of shade. There is something that hangs over all of our lives. It can be the shade of sin or the shade of righteousness found in God. There are trees more glamorous, larger trees that could offer complete shade, shade that would hide us completely from the trials and tribulations of life; or there is the shade of the seemingly less important fruit tree, shade that still exposes us and risks the possibility of getting burned again. She is choosing the food of life and partial exposure over hiding completely. She chooses the smaller shade of the fruit tree and delights in it.

In likening the Lord to an apple tree she is in essence stating she has found the tree of life. She is saying He looks totally different than the others, and His provision is totally different. She praises Him for His ability to fill her soul and to protect her.

### Lovesick

There is a cry in her heart for more. "Refresh me," she says, "give me more of you, for the mere thought of our lives entwined causes me to become weak and faint" (Song 2:5 paraphrased). There is an ache in her heart, there is a yearning that can't be filled by any other means. Love is the only thing that we cannot get enough of. When our stomachs are full, even the most luscious desserts lose their appeal. But the more in love you fall, the more you want. Love is something that the human spirit was created for and something we continually crave. She is recognizing this quality about the Lord and about love. She is saying, "I cannot go on without more of you. I am lovesick." The American Heritage Dictionary describes *lovesickness* as *stricken as with an illness by love; showing a lover's yearning.* Mike Bickle defines it as "being so much in love as not to be able to act normally."

David was a man after God's own heart. When he began his reign as king in Israel, he so desired the presence of the Living God that he moved the Holy of Holies from the Tabernacle of Moses to a tent on Mt. Zion in Jerusalem. The Ark was the throne of God and the place where His glory rested in the tabernacle and temples.

David loved the Lord so much and desired His presence so much that when he saw the Ark of the Lord's presence coming into the royal city he was overcome with joy and love. He could not act normally. David danced with all his might before the procession. David was lovesick! His wife said to Him later, *"How the King of Israel distinguished himself today."*[9] She did not understand his action or his desire, so she ridiculed and mocked.

Like David, the maiden has found in God something few others have – she has become lovesick. She is so overcome with the Lord that she can no longer act normally. She is giddy, weak and overcome with intense emotion. She asks to be *"strengthened with raisins and refreshed with apples"* (Song 2:5). She needs the concentrated resources of abiding in the vine (raisins) and the fresh word of God (apples) to go on in her journey.

## The Hand of Friendship

Let's go back to the stage setting. The maiden and the Lord have been dining together. They have retreated to a private place where they can be alone. They are speaking affectionately to one another using their intimate terms of endearment. We find them snuggled up together, the believer entwined in the Lord's arms.

Here we see the maiden in a spiritual embrace: *"His left arm is under her head, His right embraces her"* (Song 2:6). The very thing that she was crying out for in the last verse, to be sustained and to be strengthened, we see answered right away – she is enraptured in his arms. Her lovesick heart is being nursed in the arms of her creator. The hands of God represent His activities in our lives. His hands carry the marks of His love for us – the nail wounds from the cross.

The left hand of God under our head is a hand we are unable to see; it is out of our sight. This is symbolic of the activities of God in our lives that we cannot – or do not – see, those times of divine protection that we are unaware of, the hidden work of life in our hearts – like the growth of a seed underground.

In Isaiah 59:16 the Lord says, *"I have engraved you on the palm of my hand."* This engraving is literally carving into the palm and was part of the making of covenants. Covenants are sacred promises, and they were not entered into lightly. There was a very specific way by which a covenant was to be entered into in ancient times. There were two types of covenants: 1) Equal covenants, where both parties did each thing and had equal responsibility, and 2) Unequal covenants, where one party would do it all and the other party was just the beneficiary (i.e.,

Abraham and God; see Gen 15:1-17).

Richard Booker, in his book *The Miracle of the Scarlet Thread*,[10] shares the nine steps that were taken to enter into a covenant in the ancient Middle East and that are still used in some places today.

The first act of making of covenant was the exchanging of robes, representing the person. Next the two parties would exchange belts. Belts held the weapons and signified your strength. After belts were exchanged, the covenant was then cut. An animal was chosen and cut in half. It symbolized dying, giving up your rights, and beginning a new walk with your covenant partner.

The fourth step, which is the one we want to look at, was the intermingling of the blood of the two covenantal parties. In this step the right hands or forearms were cut and then clasped together, thereby intermingling the blood of each person. This symbolized the intermingling of lives, the putting off of the old nature and putting on the nature of our partner and becoming one. Jesus' hands were pierced, engraving forever our freedom on His hand. Once the blood had been intermingled the two parties became one, and next they would exchange names. The last name became part of the partner's name.

So that there was a permanent mark on the body, ash was rubbed into the cut so that it would leave a scar. This was a constant reminder to you, the covenant partner, and also aided in warning those who would come against you. If someone were to attack you, you simply held up your arm and showed your scar, thus saying, "I am not alone. You have to deal with my partner as well."

The next step was to celebrate. A memorial meal would be eaten. In place of eating the flesh of the animal and drinking its blood, bread and wine were eaten. When the meal had been eaten, the vows were said: "All I have is yours and all my liabilities are yours."

Lastly the memorial tree was planted. A tree was sprinkled with blood and planted symbolizing that now the two parties were friends. Once two parties entered into a covenant they were considered friends for life. In John 15 Jesus said that He now considers us His friends.

## The Arms of Love

As the believer is in the embrace of her friend, Jesus, she declares, His right arm embraces her (Song 2:6). In Jewish thought the right hand is the hand of power and of blessing. These would be the visible activities of God: those things He is actively doing that He is allowing us to participate in and to see.

The Lord uses His hands to mold us and make us:

> This is the word that came to Jeremiah from the LORD, "Go down to the potter's house, and there I will give you my message." So I went down to the potter's house, and I saw him working at the wheel. But the pot he was shaping from the clay was marred in his hands; so the potter formed it into another pot, shaping it as seemed best to him. Then the word of the LORD came to me: "O house of Israel, can I not do with you as this potter does?" declares the LORD. "Like clay in the hand of the potter, so are you in my hand, O house of Israel."[11]

Jeremiah watched as the potter used his hands to mold the clay. In this God showed the prophet how He has made us for His use.

I have had the chance to work on a potter's wheel. Those who are good at it can make it look so easy, but it really is difficult and takes much skill. When you begin working with clay, it has to be the right texture. If it is too hard it can't be moved, too wet and it won't hold a shape. When the clay is too hard, water is added. But it's not like a powder that instantly absorbs the water. The hands of the potter have to work the water in by kneading the clay. Once the clay is at its proper consistency it can then be put on the wheel. On the wheel more water is added, and the clay spins rapidly as it is pushed and pulled into shape. This is not a gentle process and takes strong relentless handling. This is such a beautiful picture of what the Lord does with us. When the Lord begins to embrace us He begins pouring the water of the Holy Spirit over us. He then takes His strong hands and works His words of life into our very being. As He does this we become softened by His love and moldable in His hands. This is just preparation for the seasons to come. For He will eventually put us on the wheel, spinning our lives out of our control, using circumstances to push and pull us out of the shape of the world into a vessel fit for His use.

## Awaken Love

Enfolded in the arms of the Creator a dawning begins to arise within the believer. It is the realization that this place of awakening love is not necessarily a safe one, and it should not be entered into unaware. The beloved and lover raise their voices together and proclaim: "Don't awaken this love before its time" (Song 2:7).

They first charge by the gazelles and the does of the field. Gazelles and does are gentle animals that startle easily. There is a caution to approach them tenderly so as not to scare them away. There is also the aspect that others cannot move us forward. We cannot be the Holy Spirit to others. John 6:44 says, *"No one can come to the Father unless the Father draws them."* The Father has to be the one to do the drawing to the next place. Only He knows the way you need to go and when. Everyone's road will be slightly different. As the Lord led the Israelites through the desert they followed His visible presence in the form of the pillar. When it moved they moved; when it stopped they stopped. It is the same with us. No one else can prepare the way for the Lord except the Lord himself. He prepares every heart and each heart from fullness to fullness. He is the one who enlarges the capacity of each heart, and He is the one who fills it.

The Lord is speaking to those around her. He says, "Don't bother her – she doesn't need to be running in activity right now." The believer needs to be resting and growing in the experiential knowledge of God's love for her. Lovesickness will take a certain amount of your energies, and you will require rest. But let us not forget that being lovesick is a
wonderful place to be, a place that the Lord doesn't want you to be disturbed from too soon. He loves you to be there because you experience some of His emotion for you – He is lovesick for you! She is experiencing a deep sense of rest and contentment. It is a time when she is being strengthened. "She is more pleas-

ing to Him in rest than she would be in all her external activity."[12]

## Selah

Where is your focus? Are you allowing life's circumstances to take your gaze off Him? Can you hear the Lord's words of tender affection for you? Do you believe them?

Are you aware of the growth the Lord has brought about in you? Are your roots as apparent as your fruit? Do you know that you are the temple of the Holy Spirit? What does the Holy Spirit's house look like on the inside? Are you striving or resting in the green pasture?

Will you dare to believe the words the Lord speaks over you, "You are beautiful"? What tree are you eating from? Are you settling for the lesser shade? Can you recognize the fruit of Jesus' life in yours? Can you find Him among the other more stately trees? What is hanging over your life?

Are you resting in the provision of the Lord? What does going to the banquet of the Lord look like? Are you immersing yourself in His Spirit to the point it intoxicates you? Are you approaching God as the lover of your soul who desires to be with you or as a mean, harsh taskmaster? What would it look like if you were lovesick? How would your walk look if you were touched this deeply by the Lord?

Have you allowed yourself to sit in His embrace, not rushing the moment? Have you felt the drawing of the Father? Have you responded to it? What things have you let keep you distracted and from resting in Him? What does "being still in God" look like?

## Further Reading

*Two Trees in the Garden* by Rick Joyner

*Bridal Intercession* by Gary Wiens

*The Miracle of the Scarlet Thread* by Richard Booker

*Under Cover* by John Bevere

## 6th Movement
# Signs of Spring

*Intermission is over. You find your seat again, eagerly awaiting the rise of the curtain. Once again the orchestra comes to attention and with unmatched precision the music begins.*

*There is a freshness in the music now. The sounds remind you of dawn arising. As the music sweeps over you, you imagine the sun beginning to peek over the snowcapped mountains, revealing alpine meadows bright with spring color.*

Your mental images focus as you once again see the Maiden. She is sleeping soundly, alone on her bed in the castle of the King. Suddenly she hears something. She is startled awake, unaware that she had fallen asleep. It is the King, her lover. She had not even realized that He had gone. Not sure if she is dreaming or awake, she sees Him on the mountaintops leaping over them as if they were hurdles for a runner. She sees Him skipping over the hills as though they were stones in the pathway.

He calls to her…"My beautiful one – arise! It is beautiful out here. Come see the flowers, come hear the birds, come skip with me over the hills. See, it's easy; it brings lightness and joy to the heart. I am capable of overcoming anything that stands between us. Anything that has scared or hurt you I can jump over, I can skip over it. They are as nothing to me."The Maiden sits up and rubs her eyes. "I must be dreaming. Where am I? Oh yes – the palace of the King." Her memory begins to flood over her as she remembers the banquet of wine, the *time of intimacy and romance. These thoughts bring a comfort to her heart and she settles back into her bed relishing the memories of His touch. "He truly does love me! Where is He now?"*

*Getting up, she looks around the room for Him, then seeing His figure outside she says to herself, "Oh, there He is. He is standing behind that wall we built together. That wall does really work well to keep others out. It is also a great shield from the eyesore that the kingdom of slavery is. I really do not like to look at that place. I don't know why the King doesn't do something about it. If He has the power to raise His Son from the dead, I don't see why He won't use it to get rid of that place. It even smells bad." She turns away from the city in the valley below, slightly wincing as she does. Thinking of that place brings back such wounds, such scars. She pushes all thought away, unwilling to even test the healing powers of the King in her life.*

*She hears His voice again. "Darling, My beautiful one! "With these words her heart races. He is looking for her. She listens more, hiding coyly within as He speaks. "Wake up, arise! Come on, it's time to go. I want you to come outside with Me. It is beautiful out here. You have to come out and see it. The sun is shining, the birds are singing, the winter is over. There's warmth in the air again. Even the spring rains have passed. Come out and smell the flowers. You can even see the buds on the vines; it is going to be a wonderful harvest. Come out and look upon all the kingdoms. Come on, My darling, My beautiful one, come with Me."*

*Still not having a response from her the King continues...."O, My dove, I know you are still frightened. I know that you find it hard to* look at the kingdoms of slavery and hatred. I know that you are hiding in our secret place. But please come out and let Me see you; let's talk. Didn't I just show you My ability to handle all that could possibly separate us? Do not fear the other kingdoms. For I am with you always. Come out, My love, I want to hear that sweet voice. I want to see your lovely face."

It is amazing to the Maiden that the King could know her heart so well, that He has the power to even speak to her in her dreams. She feels as if she were naked. Still hiding behind the curtain she speaks in barely a whisper: "I cannot go out there." Shame starts to creep over her. She pulls the curtain closer around her like a blanket. But it holds little comfort.

Her thoughts become troubled. "I cannot, not until that wicked Taskmaster is caught. He still sends his little servants around; they buzz in my ear like flies, telling me that I can't trust you. They encourage me to live the way I want. They tell me that being comfortable is important, that it is something that I should seek. They spoil everything."

Her heart starts to ache as fear creeps over her, her body trembling at the thought of leaving this place. Her thoughts begin to race, "Those servants of the Taskmaster spoil the beauty of all the King has just described. I know that the King likes to be around all that is gentle and lovely, that He surrounds Himself with the beautiful and pure." The King is my lover, and I am His. Why should I go out into that dark, dreadful place?" She thinks, "That could not have been the King; that was just one of those pesky messengers of the kingdom of hatred. He *would never ask me to leave here. Oh, they are so clever, making their voices to sound as His."*

*Convincing herself that this is a messenger of the enemy she yells out the window, "****NO!*** *Whoever you are, you just go by yourself. You are just trying to trick me. I am not one of those Noble of the kingdom who can walk around in the kingdoms of anger and slavery and not be overtaken. No, not until the King has perfected me and made me a Noble woman will I venture out there. This is our place together. This is the only place the King would ask me to be. So you just go, be triumphant on the mountaintops if you can. But you will not drag me down with you. I've been there before; it is a place of pain and hurt. I will stay in this place of love. I will never leave, Never!*

*Selah*

*chapter six*
# THE CALL

Song 2:8-2:17

The curtain had fallen; the lights had dimmed on the stage. Now as the lights come on again, a new scene emerges. The music fills you with images. You can see the maiden asleep in her room, but she is no longer entwined in the arms of the Beloved; she is alone. She suddenly wakes as she hears sounds outside her window. You can hear the excitement in her voice: *"Look! Listen!"* (Song 2:8)

The maiden has been in a time of rest and sleep. She was tired, overworked and underfed, and she needed this time of rest. This has been a time to tend her soul and be refreshed. This is something that the Lord not only allows, but also insists upon. Often we think of sleep from the spiritual perspective as a bad thing. But in verse 2:7, the Lord commanded the church to not disturb her. We are made to need rest.

The Lord knows we like to "do," and given the chance we will "do" rather than "be." So He creates times for us to find the rest we need. In Genesis, at the creation of the world, we are told on the seventh day God rested from all His work.[1] Later when the Ten Commandments are given the Israelites are told to consecrate the seventh day unto the Lord – not to work, but to rest. He also commands them to give the land rest every seven years. In Matthew 11:28 Jesus told the multitudes to come to Him, all who were weary, and He would give them rest. And that is exactly what He has done for this weary, burned-out believer.

## Overcoming Obstacles

The last revelation that the believer had of Jesus was that of the Lamb of God on the cross who took away the sin of the world. Here, in the Song, the believer describes the Lord in "superman" terms – able to leap mountains in a single bound. The Lord comes to the believer and shows Himself as the resurrected Lord.

Mountains and hills stand for the trial and tribulations of life, the obstacles that separate us from the Lord. We use mountains and hills to describe difficult and impossible circumstances. Even in our own vernacular we say, "Let's not make a mountain out of a molehill." We name our problems and trials as impassible mountains, or we state that we are "climbing uphill." But then Jesus shows up – nothing is too big for Him, nothing is in His way. David says, "The mountains melt like wax before the Lord."[2] It reminds me of the old song: "Ain't no mountain high enough, ain't no valley low enough, ain't no river wide enough to keep me from gettin' to you…"

The maiden has so completely entered this time of rest and fallen so soundly asleep that the Lord left and she didn't even notice. He was out working on the mountains that separate them. How long she is asleep we are not told. Our times of rest in the Lord will vary. I believe that those times can be shortened if we fully embrace the rest we need, not looking for what we can do next. Often the body of Christ remains weary and wounded because we fail to embrace the Sabbath rest. Instead we cease one activity only to search for another to fill our time, thus providing another distraction from dealing with the pain in our hearts. When the time is right the Lord will come and awaken us to "do": don't rush it.

## Come Out, Come Out

This is one of those places where I think the music turns robust, changing courses in an instant. Its tumultuous sounds awaken us from our slumber. Here the lover of her soul has just come to her, leaping effortless over the difficulties of life. Then in verse 1:9, she sees him standing behind "their" wall. She sees Him not coming inside to her, but rather peering at her through the lattice. He is not looking at her through a fully open window, but rather one that is shuttered to keep things out.

She had asked earlier that anything that is between them be removed, yet we find a wall that she says is "theirs," a wall that she thinks they have built together. This would be easy to do since God was the one that said, let her stay there undisturbed for a while. Walls are built for several reasons: to provide protection and safety, or support for a roof. She has been inside protected. And in fact the Lord probably did help her build it, but it was to be a rest stop along the way, not a permanent address.

We all, throughout our lives, have built walls around our hearts, walls of self-protection. Indeed if we don't know Jesus we need to protect ourselves, but once we come to know him

He calls us to remove the barriers. But we tend to build our walls so thick and so strong we even keep Him out. We fear being known deeply. We are afraid that if God were to really see what is inside of us, He will reject us. So we keep Him outside looking in.

I believe that there is also an innate knowing in us that if God were to come inside these areas of our hearts, things would never really be the same. Things would have to change, and most of us don't like that kind of really deep change.

You see, we are the temple of God. Solomon, in his prayer of dedication of the temple declares, *"Will God in very deed dwell with men on the earth? Behold, heaven and the heaven of heavens cannot contain thee; how much less this house which I have built!"*[3]

And therein lies the problem: how can God dwell within the walls we have built in our hearts? God, in His mercy, stays outside of our walls of self-protection. He will not, indeed cannot, come inside those barriers. For Him to do so would reduce Him to our mere image of who He is, and He would not be true to the reality of the complexity of the Godhead – and for this reason He cannot come within our puny confines. He just can't fit. When God comes in something has to change. Either He must change to conform to our images of Him, or our images of Him must become reality and conform to who He really is.

Please note that I am not talking about salvation; Scripture is clear that when we come into a saving knowledge of Jesus Christ He takes up residency within. I am talking about sanctification. I am talking about ownership, about control. Is God living within our hearts as a guest does, sleeping where we tell them to, eating what we prepare and not touching anything?

Or is He coming into our hearts living as the owner of the house, rearranging the furniture whenever and wherever He wants, throwing away things He doesn't like, and making it a place that suits His desires and tastes? There is a vast difference.

## Walls of Separation

So here is the Lord looking within her heart and calling to her. The words He speaks are not ones of rebuke that we normally accredit to the Lord, but rather of words of love. He understands the hardships and trials of life. He even understood that she needed a time of rest and recuperation, and He made provision for it. But there comes a time when the resting is no longer healthy, and it is time to get involved in life again. It seems to be our human nature to want to stay at the last place where we met with God, pulling away from our pursuit of Him. This was Peter's reaction to seeing Jesus in His transcendent glory on the Mount of Transfiguration.

*"Then Peter answered and said to Jesus, 'Lord, it is good for us to be here; if You wish, let us make here three tabernacles: one for You, one for Moses, and one for Elijah.'* "[4]

Isn't this what we all want to do? We say, "Hey, Lord, that was so great, let's build a permanent monument to that revival you just did, and we will just live in it. No need to go anywhere else, this is great right here." Oh, but God is so much bigger than that!

So the Lord in His love and mercy is calling her out of her comfort zone. He speaks with such words of love and admiration. He calls her his *"beautiful one, My beloved!"* In His great mercy He calls us out and brings down the walls as gently as He can. Mike Bickle says, "The Holy Spirit will always take us the quickest and easiest way possible." But that doesn't mean that it is always quick or easy. The speed and ease will be affected depending on how we respond. The first step is for Him to bring our attention to the walls and how they limit our relationship with Him and others.

## Unity of Heart

In John 17 the Lord is praying in the garden before His death. Here He prays for the unity of the believers, that they would be one as He and the Father are one, that our walls of separation would be removed. I think through the years we have tended to limit the meaning of unity, to mean one church denomination getting along with other denominations. This is true from a corporate standpoint. But I believe there is a personal one as well. There is also the unity of family, like the intimacy that the Father and Son shared. We come to know the Father as Jesus did, and we come to know Jesus as our heavenly Bridegroom. Another area that we have often ignored is the unity of our hearts within ourselves, which brings us to a place of health and wholeness.

The Lord gave me a picture while praying one morning as I was going through an intense time of emotional healing. It was a bleak picture – black and white, without any color at all. I saw what looked like a city that had been under siege: half-walls and partial buildings, debris on the ground and no plants growing. I saw myself at various ages and stages of life hiding behind walls of varying heights. From time to time I would

## The Call

pop up and look over the wall and wave at another part of me, only to find fear overcoming me, and I would duck back behind my various walls again.

As I watched this scene, Jesus spoke to me of recovering those lost parts of me. Life had caused me to seclude parts of who I am behind walls of self-protection. But in reality these walls could offer little protection and there was no real comfort in them. The Lord was calling me out from behind these walls wanting to bring them down, thereby unifying my heart, making me whole again.

The Lord has placed within each of us a unique combination of gifts and talents and personality. I believe it is His desire that we come into unity with His Spirit and who He says that we are and to walk in the fullness of that. The Lord never intended for us to hide the various parts of who He created us to be. But sadly, many of us don't know who we are because of the times that we have been mocked, laughed at, scorned or beaten because we dared to let a part of who we are venture out.

### The Winter

The Lord is not calling her out to the same old–same old. He is calling her out of the winter season into the warmth of spring, a new season. The winter seasons are cold, bleak months when you stay inside and try to keep warm. One year I was in the midst of teaching Bible study and doing ministry in our church. I also had two children and a small home business at the time. Over a period of a few weeks I began to hear the Lord speak to my heart about giving up my business and cutting down on ministry. In fact I felt him say that I was going into a winter season.

    Living in the mid-west, I know about long dark winter months. Often winters here are not all that beautiful. We don't get much snow, but we do get a lot of gray, cold days where the temperature hovers at 33 degrees and it rains, creating a cold that chills you to the bone. The bleakness and damp cold zap your strength and energy. Needless to say, with this picture of winter in mind, I was not too excited about going into a winter season. As I contemplated this time I began to have pictures of the fun of winter. Playing in the snow, cozying next to a fire having hot chocolate and generally enjoying myself. I began to get a sense of anticipation for this time. I backed out of the things I was doing (which was very difficult emotionally) and prepared for the winter. Little did I know that the things that were coming in my life would require me to be rested and free from commitment.

### Spring

    Winter does not last forever, and as spring begins to emerge the spirit begins to lift. Sometimes, though, the calendar says that spring is upon us – but the earth does not look that way. The trees are still bare, the cold winds still howl and the dark clouds still hang overhead. This is when you need faith in the calendar and that the earth will do what it has done since its creation. It will indeed rotate on its axis toward the sun, the earth will once again warm and the flowers and birds will once again appear.

    The Lord is encouraging the believer that this is indeed happening on a spiritual level. The heart is indeed warming, and the time of seclusion and hibernation is coming to an end. C.S. Lewis gives us such a wonderful illustration of this in his book, *The Lion, the Witch and the Wardrobe*. In this enchanted book, four children find themselves walking through a wardrobe into the wintry land of Narnia. The wicked White Witch has seized the kingdom of Narnia; she has put everything under a spell of winter, eternal winter where it is never Christmas. She keeps it always cold, damp and gloomy, and the joys of the winter season are never enjoyed.

When Aslan, the great lion, arrives back in Narnia, the first thing that happens, even before the snow melts, is that joy returns. Father Christmas brings in the celebration with gifts for all. Then rather quickly spring appears, the snow stops, the sun comes out, flowers begin to bloom and the birds begin to sing. The King has returned to His kingdom. There is nothing more to fear. Once the witch has been defeated, the great lion travels through the land setting the captives free. He goes to all who have been turned into stone by the White Witch, and by His very breath gives them life again.

This is such a vivid picture of what is happening here in the Song. The Lord speaks to the believer about the signs of spring that she has been unable to see for herself. Flowers are bursting forth onto the gray and dreary landscape of her soul, the outward sign of fruit being prepared on the plant. Beautiful fragrances are beginning to waft on the warm breezes of this season of life. The Lord is encouraging her that there is life within. The birds have returned, and they have come with a song of love floating on the gentle breezes. It is not time to stay inside, but to come out and hear the song of love.

### The Cleft of the Rock

The Lord ends this beautiful interlude with a repeat of His call, *"Arise, My beloved, My dove in the cleft of the rock, and come with me"* (Song 2:14). Here He again refers to her as a dove, one of singular devotion with eyes only for Him. Here she is, caught in this place of self-centeredness, yet the Lord doesn't speak to her harshly – rather He reminds her of whose she is. The Lord is kind and wants only the best for her; He will never call her out totally unprotected. In fact, what the Lord is calling her to is a place much more secure and much more vast than any little hut she could build on her own. In calling her out of her walls of self-protection, He calls her into the depths of His heart. He calls her to the *"cleft of the rock."*

There is a tremendous amount of symbolism here. The cleft of the rock refers to the Lord. He is our rock, strong and mighty.

> In the ancient world where explosives and powerful drills were unknown, rock – abundant and varied in size and shape – was a ready image of impervious solidity. A rock provides a solid foundation, protection and security, a safe refuge and a fortress. It almost always is associated with God.[5]

David said, *"The Lord is my rock, my fortress and my deliverer; my God is my rock, in whom I take refuge."*[6]

The Lord is calling her out of her self-built walls of protection to the place of true protection – the Rock, the Fortress, Jesus. The Lord is letting her know that where He is, is the safest place to be.

She is not just called to come to the rock; she is called to come to the cleft of the rock. Webster's defines "cleft" as *a space or opening caused by splitting*. In this definition we can find a clear link between the split rock and Jesus. While Jesus hung on the cross, one of the solders took a spear and pierced His side.[7] A cleft was made in His side. And it is this side that we are to run into and abide, to hide and find refuge. *"For our life is hidden in Christ."*[8]

Running into the rent side of Jesus is the place of protection, but the pathway into that is through the very path that Jesus walked, death to self. Jesus told his followers that unless a grain of wheat falls into the ground and dies it will remain a single seed, but in dying it produces many seeds.[9] It was in dying that Jesus was able to produce a bride.

The Lord gave us an illustration of how this would happen when he created man and woman. Mankind was made in the image of God. God made Adam and said, *"It is not good for man to be alone,"*[10] so He caused him to fall asleep and from Adam's side produced woman. In order to form a suitable helpmate, the Lord created two from one, taking the one that was the exact representation of the Godhead and dividing it in two. When Adam saw Eve for the first time he was so overcome that he declared, *"This is bone of my bone, flesh of my flesh."* And the command was given that they should cleave to one another and be one flesh.[11] As the two came together in marriage there would once again be a complete representation of God.

Just as in the first Adam so in the last – Jesus[12] – just as God created the counterpart of Adam by causing him to fall asleep and taking woman from His side, so too Jesus tasted death and from his wounded side was brought forth the bride. Jesus willingly fell to the ground so that we could be His. Therefore when we go into the cleft of the rock – Jesus' torn body – we become one with Him, becoming the true representation of Christ, the true representation of His bride on the earth.

## Treasures of the Deep

To come to the cleft of the rock is an invitation to come into the depths of Jesus and to hide in Him. The cleft of the rock is not only a place of safety, but it is a place of receiving the deep things of God. It is within the depths of rock that gold and precious gems are found. The Lord tells us in Isaiah 45:3, *"I will give you the treasures of darkness, riches stored in secret places, so that you may know that I am the Lord, the God of Israel, who summons you by name."*

He wants us to have the treasures of His kingdom. But it takes searching; it takes going on a treasure hunt.

> *If you accept my words and store up my commands within you, turning your ear to wisdom and applying your heart to understanding, and if you call out for insight and cry aloud for understanding and if you look for it as for silver and search for it as for hidden treasure, then you will understand the fear of the Lord and find the knowledge of God.*[13]

The knowledge and understanding of the Lord are compared to riches and hidden treasure. God says it is His glory to conceal these things and our glory to search them out.[14]

## The Call

In 2000 while visiting my sister in Georgia, we went to a small town in the mountains for some sightseeing. While there we went to visit a gold mine. I had an inclination from the Lord that this was more than just a sight-seeing trip, that He had something to show me. As we walked through the mine hearing explanations of drilling and mining techniques, we found ourselves standing some 300 feet underground. Here our tour guide had us stop and look up. There was light streaming in from an opening in the rock high above. As we looked up the man began to tell us that in the place where we were now standing the most concentrated vein of gold on the east coast was found. Here so many veins of gold ran together that it was several feet wide and several hundred feet long. The concentration of the gold was so great that this single vein that was dug out resulted in an opening 300 feet underground. It became known as the "glory hole."

Gold is symbolic of divine character. Just as in the depths of the mountain in Georgia was found a rich deposit, so in the depths of the cleft of the rock, our Savior, is found the richest vein of gold. It is here in the cleft of His side that divine character will be mined. But it is not without diligent work and removal of much debris. It takes digging in the word and digging out our flesh to uncover the glory that resides within.

> *We have this treasure in jars of clay to show that this all-surpassing power is from God and not from us. We are hard pressed on every side, but not crushed; perplexed, but not in despair; persecuted, but not abandoned; struck down, but not destroyed. We always carry around in our body the death of Jesus, so that the life*

*of Jesus may also be revealed in our body. For we who are alive are always being given over to death for Jesus' sake, so that his life may be revealed in our mortal body.*[15]

It is in the hard pressing, the crushing and the persecution that the vein of gold, the glory of God within us is revealed. This is the pathway to the cleft.

## Show Me Your Face

The Lord is wooing the believer, gently calling her out of her into Him. It is in this place of going deep within the life of God that the Lord says to us, *"Show me your face, let me hear your voice. For your face is lovely and your voice is sweet"* (Song 2:14b). For it is in this place that we recognize how unworthy we are to be in the glory of God, so we want to hide our faces and silence our voices. For what words are adequate here? However, it is precisely in this place that the Lord says, "Now let Me see the beauty of My Son radiating from your face. Now, let Me hear the voice that sounds like My Son; it is like music to my ears." It is in this place, as we lay ourselves on the mercy seat, that the Father and the Son and the Holy Spirit see us through "rose-colored glasses," the blood of Jesus. Does this mean that their view is distorted? No, it means that they see us as we were created to be, not half an expression of God, lacking and incomplete. Rather, they see us like Adam was first created, being the full expression of the Godhead.

In the midst of these loving words from the Lord the maiden suddenly breaks in, *"Catch for me the foxes that are spoiling the vineyards"* (Song 2:15). Or in non-poetic words, "Lord, there is so much that is hidden within that seems to be killing the depths of my heart. Will you show me what those things are?"

David said, *"Search me, O God, and know my heart; try me, and know my thoughts. And see if [there be any] wicked way in me, and lead me in the way everlasting."*[16]

It is in this place of being called out that the inner fears and views of ourselves begin to rise to the surface.

She uses foxes because they are extremely crafty and cunning animals that come out mainly at night. They are diggers. They will dig into chicken coops and dig at the roots of a plant. The fox is adept at hunting and concealing themselves from their predators. They learn their terrain very well, making it extremely difficult to catch one on its own ground. They can out maneuver a pack of dogs, and they know how to conceal their trails by walking through streams and backtracking, and by mixing their scent with those of other animals.

Just as these creatures are hard to catch, so are the hidden dark sins of our hearts. Foxes represent our thoughts that keep us from abiding in Christ, that keep us from holding fast to God: things like fear, selfishness, unbelief, envy, strife, anger, jealousy, unforgiveness and gossip. The list could go on and on. Foxes represent all those things that sneak into our thoughts and cause our hearts to harden and rob us of joy, peace and love. Some of these things have been a part of who we are for so long they have become concealed within our hearts, causing us to bury deep in old habits and mindsets.

Here the maiden speaks up at last in response to the Lover's bidding that He enjoys hearing from her. She speaks of the damage theses crafty creatures have done to her root system and her ability to abide in the vine. She is crying out to the Lord to catch the little crafty sins that are ruining her fellowship with the lover of her soul. It's as if she takes a deep breath and speaks. "I don't trust it." She proclaims, "I've been out there and there are too many dangers. There are too many of those sly foxes out there trying to turn me from you. I am not strong enough to face them. No, I cannot come out until you catch all those foxes in my heart that have ruined what you have planted." And here she refuses to trust in the work of the cross and the work of the winter season.

## View from the Other Side

Again the question can be asked, "Who is asking for the foxes to be caught? (2:15)" I see both voices coming together to sing these words. They are the same words – the same melody but different connotations.

Let's now look from Jesus' perspective. We see Him asking the maiden to at least come look out the window and see what is happening to the vineyards. His perspective takes on the corporate element. The Lord is always concerned with the individual believer, but each believer has a corporate position, for it is all who call on His name who will make up the bride.

Remember she spent a lot of time in those "vineyards," working for the church, working in the fields. Those vineyards were the very things that caused her to draw her attention away from the Lord. It's as if the Lord is saying to her, "Now that we have things in their proper order – your relationship with Me is first – it's time to get back into the game. Look at My people. The enemy has gotten in and is destroying the place of abiding, in both your personal vineyard and in the corporate vineyard. Because you will not come out of your little incubator the enemy is stealing, killing and destroying those I love. Will you get up and help Me? You asked that we run together, I am asking that you put your hand to this job. This is not about working for My approval; this is about working with Me."

"No"

As the thoughts of leaving her comfort zone begin to sink in, fear begins to race in upon her. The father of lies masterfully turns things around, and instead of recognizing this call to come out as the voice of the Lord, she believes it to be the enemy and fear takes hold. Her fear allows a place within her that the enemy can manipulate, causing the believer to deny the call. The believer seems to have forgotten here that the Lord called her *"a lily compared to the thorns,"* that it is out in the world that she looks different, for in the next breath she denies that she is able to conquer on the heights as He is and sends Him away without her. She says, *"Until the day breaks, until the shadows flee, go..."* (Song 2:17). She is telling him that until all darkness is gone from her life she cannot go with Him.

I can hear the selfish whine in her voice, "But Jesus, You are mine. I am your lily. We don't need others. Let's just stay here where it's warm and comfortable." And then seeing the look on His face she adds in an attempt at manipulation, "Fine. Be that way. Just go, but You will have to go without me." Oh, then comes the self-pity: "I'm just not good enough. There are still too many sins in my life. I won't be any good to you out there. No, I can't make a difference."

Now, we don't usually say things this bluntly, but it is the underlying motive of the heart. Oh, how many of us have refused to move forward in our relationship with the Lord because we feel we have to get it all in order first, because we fear being hurt again. We forget the words of Isaiah: *"All our righteous deeds are as filthy rags before him."*[17] For indeed it is only by the blood of the Lamb that we can approach His throne of grace and find help in our time of need. But in order to take hold of that help we cannot come in our own righteousness, but rather with the blood of the perfect sacrifice covering us. Then the help comes to fight the battles and catch the foxes that spoil our ability to abide in the vine.

She refuses to obey because of fear that is due to immaturity, not necessarily rebellion. When you are struggling, even when you end up in compromise as she does in verse 2:17, the Lord does not want you to give up. Stumbling is not the same as failing. You are only a failure if you quit. *"The righteous fall seven times and rise again."*[18] When you discover your sinfulness and your fear, run **to** him, not **from** Him. Run into the safest place there is, the Cleft of the Rock – Jesus!

## Selah

Have you resisted the season of rest? When God has brought you into rest have you picked up other things? What does the conquering God look like? Can you see the Lord overcoming the obstacles in your own life?

Are you hiding behind a wall? Is this your season to come out? What frightens you? Are you hesitating to look outside? Do you hear the Lord saying, "Come out! It is safe"?

Do you realize that your voice lifted to Him is sweet to Him? Do you withhold your voice? Are you willing to go into the cleft of the rock, to hide yourself in Jesus? What does that mean to you? How do you do that?

Are there things that the Lord is trying to draw your attention to? What is spoiling your vineyard? What does abiding mean? What things need to be taken hold of? Are you judging yourself rightly or taking on the lies of the accuser?

Are you finding excuses for staying in your comfort zone? What are they? What will it take to get you to respond in confidence and faith? Do you trust what God is calling you to do?

## Further Reading

*Divine Romance* by Gene Edwards

*God Chasers* by Tommy Tenney

*The Sacred Romance* by Brent Curtis and John Eldredge

*Hinds Feet on High Places* by Hannah Hurnard

*Ruthless Trust* by Brennan Manning

*God's Favorite House* by Tommy Tenney

## 7th Movement
# Turning

*With some doubt in her heart that she just did the right thing, the Maiden closes the window and pushes away lingering doubt that could have been the King's voice. She will control her will and emotions. She will be strong and not leave this place; she will not yield to the beckoning of that voice. She knows that the King's enemy, the Taskmaster, can often change his voice and sound very close to the King; the Taskmaster can disguise himself as a beautiful messenger of His.*

*"No, I will not fall for it!" she tells herself.*

*With these thoughts she resolutely goes into the palace to look for the King. She goes to the places He always meets her – in the garden, the courtyard, the secret chamber. She calls for Him. But He does not answer. She does all that she knows to bring His presence to her. But it does no good.*

*Desperation begins to rise within her, like a mother searching for her lost child. All night long she searches for her beloved King – even going to places that He has told her about in the palace but she has never ventured to go, but to no avail. She cannot find Him anywhere. Slowly reality begins to dawn, and she wonders, "Maybe that was the King. Maybe it truly is safe outside. Whoever it was did speak to me in ways that only the King does. He told me things that only He could know. Oh, was I wrong? Could that truly have been the voice of my Beloved?"*

*His voice did seem to stir my heart. The servants of the Taskmaster send my blood cold, but that voice – it warmed me to the very core. Oh, I was wrong, that was my Beloved! I cannot stay here anymore. The beauty of this place has vanished; without the lover of my soul this place is just an empty shell. It is so cold and lonely here.*
*I must find Him!*
***I will go!***
*I will venture out into the dark.*
*I will go anywhere to find Him."*

Hastily she grabs her cloak and begins to run into the dark night. Panic grips her heart as she realizes she sent the King away. But where should she look? Where would He be? As she runs she looks up and sees the walls of the city. "That seems safe at this time of night. I will go there," she tells herself. Frantically she searches the beautiful places of the city. She goes to the palaces of the Nobles, and the homes of the well-to-do, the places that it would seem most likely to find Him. But He is nowhere to be found.

Despair begins to nag at her heart. As she walks the streets some of the Noblemen, the leaders of the city, find her. She has seen them before. In fact, she thinks that they had been the ones who told her angry brothers how to treat her and where she should work. Fear begins to creep in on her. With all her heart she wants to run from them, but she does not. Instead, in great humility, she walks up to them and asks in a shaky voice, "Have you seen the King? Have you seen the One my heart loves?"

"Oh, yes," they answer, as they begin to puff out their chests. "Oh, yes, we have seen Him. It was a glorious time. He brought so many gifts for us. He touched us in ways that we will always remember," they respond, as if they were the only ones who had really ever seen Him, and puff out their chests all the more. She thinks they resemble a school of blowfish more than the chosen ones. She can barely contain the giggle rising in her as she looks upon these leaders.

They continue in their pontificating. "In fact, we have built a monument to that visit." They are speaking more amongst themselves than to her. "Have you seen it? It really is spectacular – only the best will do for our King. We spent more on that monument than any other in the city. It truly is the nicest around. We had to make it the nicest, because the visit He paid us was far superior to the ones He paid to the others in the city (actually in all the world). Once you've been to our monument you won't want to be anywhere else. We have everything that He gave us. It's all in its original package. Oh, we use it from time to time, but we do not want to tarnish the awesome gifts He brought us, so we set them under glass and look at them. We even hold events at which time we take them out and show them to all who come in."

"Let's see, how long ago was it that He came?" asks one to another. "Oh that visit, let's see, it must be 20 years now...."

"Yes, yes..." says the Maiden, having a hard time getting in a word. "But have you seen Him lately? I know He has visited you in the past, but has He been with you today? Have you seen Him today?" Caught a little off guard, the head Nobleman clears his throat. "Well, no, no. I don't think today. Now let me think....We have heard rumors that He has been seen in the slums in the company of the undesirables. Some say He likes the slums, that He actually enjoys being around the poor and broken of this city. We don't believe it to be true. Why would He ever go there when He can be in the beauty of our monument? It's just preposterous, to think that the King would even think about going into those dirty sections."

"Are you sure that He wouldn't go there?" asks the Maiden, suddenly remembering some of the stories that He had told her, and remembering where He had found her. Oh, but that seemed so long ago, like a nightmare of her childhood.

Another statesman continues, "Are we sure? Well, no. We can't be 100% sure. We won't go into that place ourselves. You can go there if you want. But we warn you – it is very dirty and smelly there. You will be considered unclean should you venture there."

The Maiden looks down the road where they are pointing. She can vaguely remember the slums. She was once a slave there, but she had not dared to go back in many years. What would her old friends say? How would she explain her new look, her new actions? Oh, this would be harder then she thought! Taking a deep breath she braces herself and thinks, "If I could just face those of His kingdom who had hurt me so badly, as I just did, then surely I could face those who do not know the King at all."

Turning to the Nobles she says, "Thank you for your kindness," and turns in the direction they are pointing. Mustering all the strength she has left she begins to walk down the alley to the slums. As she turns the corner the sights and smells come back to her like a ton of bricks, assaulting all her senses. She had forgotten what a God-forsaken place this was. The smells of refuse are so strong that she thinks she might be sick. Covering her nose she continues to walk into the dark places.

Suddenly the Maiden looks up. There standing in the road is the King Himself. Startled for a moment she stands there, and then, as she realizes this is truly the Lord, she runs into His arms and clings to Him as if her whole life depends on it. For indeed it does! "Thank you for coming out," the King says to her. "I know you were scared, but you bravely faced the watchmen." The Maiden looks puzzled. "How…?" "I've been with you all along," replies the King. "I will never leave you or forsake you. But sometimes I must hide from you so that you will obey Me and learn to trust Me."

"My King!" she says, holding Him tightly. "Lover of my soul, let me take You to my household. Let me take You to those who raised me. They do not know You as You have revealed Yourself to me. Let me take You to them so that You can take away their anger, so they can love You as I do. I will tell them of Your love. If there is anyone who is listening, if there is anyone who can hear me, I will tell them…."

"Oh, My dove," replies the King, smiling into her eyes. "Remember that not all will be ready to hear what you have to say. Not all are in the place of knowing their desperation."

"Yes, I know. But I have to try. I have to speak to them about the abundant life that You have. I will be cautious, and I will tell them *'not to awaken this love until the King draws you to His side. It is a precious thing. In the beginning it is fragile.'* I will tell them, *'When you are ready, when the desire for the King rises up within you like a torrent, then the King will answer. But He alone knows the timing. Don't rush it; yearn and desire it, for He will fulfill your desire.'*

*That is what I will tell them.
If I don't, how will they know?
If I don't share the realities of Your kingdom,
which are more real than anything here,
how will they desire more?"*

"Lead the way!" the King replies, still smiling with much love.

*Selah*

*chapter seven*
# DIVINE DISCIPLINE

Song 3:1-3:5

It is truly remarkable how much this book reflects our hearts and lives. How many times must the Lord speak before we hear? She has refused the call of the Lord telling Him, *"Until the day breaks and the shadows flee, turn my lover and be like a gazelle on the rugged hills"* (Song 2:17). He has done as she bid and gone about His business, withdrawing His manifest presence from her.

Here she is experiencing the chastisement of a loving father who promises to pry her fingers off the things that hold her in bondage. The Father loves her too much to allow the growing maiden to come up short of being the glorious bride of the Lord Jesus Christ. Hebrews 12 gives us a vivid picture of the love the Lord has for us – the love of a good father for His legitimate children. *"My son, do not make light of the Lord's discipline, and do not lose heart when He rebukes you, because the Lord disciplines those He loves, and punishes everyone He accepts as a son."*[1]

There is no wrath or anger, but tender discipline so that she will share His values as a mature bride. If she knew her full inheritance to reign with Him as a heavenly bride in heavenly places, then she would understand the necessity and value of this loving discipline. You see, the Lord loves each of us so much He will do what He must to get us to move out of our place of comfort, into the destiny He has for each of us.

## On My Bed I Looked

The Lord has called her to arise out of her bed, her place of complacency, and come with Him. She has refused on the grounds that she is still too sinful and, in reality, too afraid of venturing out into ministry again. She has told Him, "I can't go until the shadows flee" (Song 2:17a). Shadows are the areas of sin and compromise in our lives. That is all she can see right now. She is relying on her own strength and ability and not on the Lord's. Oh, how we allow the thoughts and pain of failures to rob us of the abundant life in Jesus. God always calls us from glory to glory, not from defeat to defeat. However, all she can see is her failures. She is forgetting to look at herself the way the Lord does.

As she refuses to obey the Lord, she goes back to where she had been with Him before – just like Peter, who, after denying the Lord, feels such despair that he goes back to the only thing he knew how to do, going back to his old way of life by going fishing.[2] The maiden doesn't go fishing, but she tells us, *"All night long on my bed I searched..."* (Song 3:1). Beds represent our places of comfort and inactivity. How active can our search truly be if the only place we are looking is in the place that we are comfortable and where we have found Him before? We must come out of our place of comfort. We must arouse ourselves from the sleep of the soul and press into the places we haven't been before to pursue the Lord.

As she searches she finds the Lord is no longer there, in her bed or in her chamber. You see the Lord will not, indeed cannot, stay within a box. He detests being restrained. So, as she goes back to her bed, He goes on about His Father's business. Indeed, this is what she said she wanted in verse 2:17. She told Him to go about His business without her. And He listened.

It is important to understand that God will never leave us, but He will remove the sense of His presence, the feeling of His nearness. Just as a good teacher will not interfere when we take a test, but remains silent, so does our heavenly Father remain silent at times like these. The Father will treat us as He did His son Jesus. When Jesus hung on the cross He felt the withdrawal of the manifest presence of the Father. His Father looked away. We can hear it in Jesus' cry, *"My God, My God why have you forsaken me?"*[3] Jesus had to endure this trial without the interference of His heavenly Father.

Jeanne Guyon speaks frequently about these experiences in her many writings. She teaches that God really wants nothing more than to give you all of who He is and it is for that reason that He frequently conceals Himself. "He flees, He hides, that He might draw the believer after Him."[4] You see it's not out of anger or disgust but because of His abundant goodness and faithfulness to us. The Lord loves us too much to let us stay the way we are. He already sees in her a beautiful mature bride and He will do what He must to bring her forth. He has already prophesied over His church: *"You shall love the Lord your God with all your heart."*[5] And He will fulfill His word.

## Discipline

There is always a wonderful aspect to the discipline of God.

Discipline is different than punishment. Discipline is training, like an athlete who disciplines his body to run a race. It is the coach who helps to implement the discipline. It's not because the runner is bad; it's because he is in training. It can hurt greatly, yet the outcome is far greater than the pain.

God's discipline isn't a discipline of earthly fathers who rage out of control in anger and frustration, but that of a perfect Father who patiently calls us forward into the very things that will fill our lives and hearts with meaning. This discipline of God's withdrawn presence is drawing her out to do the very thing she feared and thought herself incapable of doing. Yet the Lord knew that all she needed was a little motivation and she would be on her way. The motivation the Lord uses is the felt absence of His manifest presence. This is one of the ways the Lord brings discipline to our lives. James tells us: *"Consider it pure joy, my brothers, whenever you face various trials, knowing that the testing of your faith produces endurance. And let endurance have its perfect result, so that you may be perfect and complete, lacking in nothing."*[6]

The discipline of God's withdrawn manifest presence causes the believer to do the very thing God had called her to do in the first place – to get up off her bed, go out of her comfort zone and begin to walk in the ways of God.

## I Will Go

Finally she cannot take it any longer. She is more desperate for His presence than she is to be comfortable. She obeys the challenge to arise. At last she gets up and leaves her comfort zone in search of the Lord. How long it takes to get to the point of frustration that causes you to respond can differ for every believer. Some may never reach this place; instead they hide the fear behind good things, safe things, but they never answer the call. Here the believer has reached the place where it is better to face her fears head on and have the presence of the Lord than to be without Him. She proclaims, *"I will get up now and go about the city"* (Song 3:2).

When the Lord called her out, we are not told where He wanted her to go, just that He wanted her to be with Him. Often the Lord doesn't tell us. Abraham was told to go to a place that he did not know, yet his willingness to do so was credited to him as faith.[7] The Lord loves mystery and surprise. And he loves obedience that comes with faith. He loves the faith of Abraham that says, "I have no idea where You are leading me, but if You are there, I will go."

There are several places we can speculate that she was called to go, based on the verses we have already studied. In verse 1:8 the Lord tells her that in order to find Him she needs to go the tents of the shepherds, to get back in fellowship with His people. In verse 2:3 he speaks to her of the vineyards and their blossoming vines. This could be the corporate church or our personal lives to which we must tend.[8] In 2:17 she tells the Lord to go back to the mountains. Mountains are both the obstacles in our lives and the place of God's abiding. But interestingly, she doesn't go to any of those places. Instead she goes to the city.

The city differed from a village in that it had a wall. It was not unusual to find the city walls to be 20 to 30 feet thick. The wall had one or more gates that were closed during the night.

The gates were strengthened with iron or bronze bars and bolts and had rooms overhead. From the top of the wall or from a tower by the gate, a watchman was on the lookout for approaching danger. Cities represent security, safety and permanence. So the city seems like a safe choice. She wants to stay behind some sort of wall of protection. As we can see she is just taking a baby step, still staying in some place of protection.

## The Watchman

As she goes on her way in search of the Lord we are told she comes to the watchmen, or the noblemen of the city, as I called them in the allegory. There were several different types of watchmen. There were watchmen who were hired to watch a garden, the fields, or the flocks, to keep away wild animals and robbers. And there were watchmen in the cities. It was their job to stand in the tower on the walls or at the gates of the city and patrol the streets. They were required to call out the hours of the night. Also, they were charged to watch and announce the arrival of visitors of importance coming into the city. In the spiritual realm there are five offices given that are to function as the "watchmen" of the Church: They are the prophets, evangelists, pastors, apostles and teachers.[9]

Here in the Song, I believe the watchmen that the young maiden encounters are the church leaders. But she didn't set out to find them. She accidentally ran into them. I believe a reason for her not going to the tents of the shepherds was pride and unforgiveness in her heart. Remember, she has blamed them for her lack of spiritual depth. So she says, "I'm not going back to those that hurt me. They have already demonstrated to me that God isn't there." How often in our hurt do we become prideful and begin to belittle those who have hurt us. Can't you just hear her saying prior to this point, "Oh, they are so sinful; they can't possibly know anything real about the Lord. Look at how they treated me. Would anyone who truly knows Him treat another as they did? God came to me and comforted me, didn't He?"

The Lord is so loving. I can just see Him watching her, knowing what she really needs to do. So in His love He says, "If you won't go to the shepherds, I will bring them to you." As they come in contact, and out of her desperation to find the Lord, she reaches out to them and humbles herself. She asks them if they know where the Lord can be found. This takes great humility. God wants her to see the truth that there is something of God within these people, even if they are not perfect. And so, she humbles herself; she goes back to the very ones who kept her so busy that she didn't care for herself and asks them, "Have you seen Him?" In essence she is admitting that she has lost God; she is admitting her own weakness; she is admitting that she doesn't know it all.

## Found Love

Now an interesting thing happens. The church leaders, the watchmen, don't show her where the Lord is. From the account given us they say nothing (Song 3:3-4). Whether she doesn't give them the chance or they just don't know is uncertain, but either way the direction to the Lord isn't given through the watchmen. She must pass them by before she finds the Lord.

There is a strategy here. It isn't to show the maiden that they don't have God, but I believe it is to ensure that she doesn't trust in man again to fill her need. If they had been able to give her what she was requesting, then once again her relationship with the Lord would have been dependent on men. She would have eventually found herself in the same position in which she was when this whole book started – doing instead of being, and in doing, finding herself depending on others. We cannot find the depths of the Lord through another person. They can point us in the right direction, but ultimately it has to be about us and God individually. The Lord continues to elude her until she forgives, humbles herself and looks beyond the boundaries of what she has known before, until she steps out in faith and trust in Him.

## Clinging to the Lord

As the believer humbles herself and admits that she still has a lot to learn, the Lord suddenly appears to her. The Word says, *"God opposes the proud but gives grace to the humble."*[10] What more grace could there be than to know the presence of the Lord again?

When the Lord's presence floods back in, the believer grabs hold of Him as if her life depends on Him. There is a desperation in her words, *"I held to Him and would not let Him go"* (Song 3:4). There comes a time that your love for Jesus so compels you that when you finally are caught by the Lord, you cling to Him with all your strength, like a drowning person who is thrown a life preserver or lovers who have been apart.

In Genesis 32:24-31 we are given an account of Jacob's night of finding God, which ends in him clinging to God with all his strength. Jacob was coming home after being on the run from his brother Esau, from whom he had stolen the inheritance and blessing of the firstborn. Now returning as a rich man with two wives, things were obviously different for him. The question was, were they different for Esau? Did Esau still hold a grudge? Was Esau still intent on murdering him? As they approached Jacob's homeland, he sent his family on ahead of him, and in the night a man came and wrestled with him until the break of day.

The Bible says that Jacob was *"prevailing."*[11] To *prevail* means *to win control over something.*[12] I have often wondered what this wrestling may have been about, what was going on. Was Jacob fearful about going home? Was the Lord trying to get Jacob to see things differently? Or was Jacob up to his old tricks? Jacob's name means *trickster*. He was known for manipulating circumstances to his advantage. He was shrewd. I imagine that he was using every last trick in the book to get his own way in this wrestling match with this man. Did he know it was God? Some things we will never know. Nonetheless he was holding nothing back and not bending to the man before him. Jacob was not giving up control; he was not giving into God.

Jacob was a stubborn man, used to getting things his own way and doing whatever it took to get ahead. Now a man comes to Jacob as he is alone for the night, as Jacob is probably trying to figure out how to manipulate his brother into not killing him. Maybe he thought this man was one of his brother's servants. Now he is using every trick he knows and winning. As they wrestle the man says, "Let go of me." And Jacob replied, "Not until you bless me." Seeing that Jacob was "prevailing," the man touches Jacob's hip and puts it out of joint. The Lord then changes his name from Jacob to Israel, for *"as a prince you have power with God and man and have prevailed."*[13] The name Israel itself means *"God prevails."* The man literally injures Jacob's hip. Jacob is now in extreme pain and still will not let go until he gets what he wants from this man. As a result he gets a new name, and he gets a new way of walking.

## Wrestling with God

When we step out we will begin to wrestle with our inner man, we will begin to wrestle with the Lord. We begin to wage war within our hearts and minds about the decisions we have made, because in the natural they don't always make sense. But the good news is God always wins. To the heart that says "yes," God will overcome and overpower every fear and worry and argument that sets itself up against Him.

*For though we live in the world, we do not wage war as the world does. The weapons we fight with are not the weapons of the world. On the contrary, they have divine power to demolish strongholds. We demolish arguments and every pretension that sets itself up against the knowledge of God, and we take captive every thought to make it obedient to Christ.*[14]

Often we wrestle with God in the same way. Thinking we know better than He, we presume upon Him for things to go our own way. Fortunately mercy triumphs over judgment, and God cripples us instead of destroying us. Now I must clarify here that I do not believe that this crippling is physical. I do not believe it is sickness, disease or anything else in our body. I believe it is an utter changing of the way we walk through life. Suddenly the things we wanted to do, we have no desire for anymore. Suddenly there is a hunger in us to go after all there is in God, regardless of what others think. Suddenly we become radical and ravenous. Suddenly we see ourselves for who we really are in light of who he is. It is in these encounters with the Lord that everything in our lives seems to change. The Lord visibly embraced Jacob, His hand visibly touched him, and in so doing the Lord permanently changed Jacob's very character and nature. Jacob became lovesick.

When the Lord comes into our lives and allows us to prevail upon Him, it does not change God, **but it changes us**. This is what wrestling with God or contending with Him in prayer is all about. These encounters with the Lord touch our lives so deeply that our spiritual walks will never be the same. We will "limp" through life constantly lovesick, constantly unable to act in a normal way, unable to walk like others do. Jacob saw God face to face and could no longer walk normally; Isaiah saw God and declared, *"Woe is me, I am ruined."*[15] The Scriptures are full of believers who wrestle with God and come away never to walk the same way again. Moses, Joshua, Gideon, Mary, Daniel, Esther, Paul, Peter, and countless others whose names are written in the book of life somehow wrestled through fear and doubt and the natural ways of man to come to know God in a way few others had, and they would walk through their lives different from others. They would walk with a "limp." When we encounter God in deeper degrees we too become ruined for anything less than all of God. When God "kisses" the human heart, when we encounter Him more deeply, there is no turning back.

## Let Me Take You

The believer is clinging to the Lord, unwilling to let Him go. She says, *"I would not let Him go until I had brought Him to my mother's house, the room of the one who conceived me"* (Song 3:4). Mother's house is representative of the Church, the one that birthed her into the second birth. As her love and understanding of the heart of God grow, her desire to show forth who God is and what He has done in her life comes bursting out, and she has an overwhelming desire to take this new-found level of the presence of God back to the very ones who have hurt her, back to the body of believers.

Have you ever known someone who has gone through an incredibly hard time? They are struggling with their faith, with core issues of who God is, who they are and how to walk according to His plan. They come to the end of that time, and they are so on fire for the Lord that they begin to walk and function in the Church in ways they had not before. It seems that this trying time has solidified their faith. They have grown in understanding of who they are and who God is. They begin to show the Church aspects of the Lord that it had not seen before. This has happened many times in my life. God created me to be a person who wears her passion on her sleeve. But until I came to the place of understanding that we have a passionate God and that He wants us to be passionate about Him, my passions were poured out on myself in very worldly ways. Eventually God took me to the end of my rope, and I experienced the consequences of that lifestyle. But as I clung to the

Lord and learned from His discipline, He began to show me that passion does have a place in the church. Now I have the privilege of bringing that good news to the people of God. This is exactly what is happening to the maiden in the song. She has grown in her understanding of God, and she wants to share it with all.

## Do Not Arouse or Awaken

As the maiden comes back to the church and begins walking in intimacy again, there is a decree sent out – I believe by the Holy Spirit – not to arouse or awaken love until it desires (Song 3:5). It is an admonishment to the believer that love cannot be stirred by mere words and to be careful how she approaches the church, for the Lord doesn't want her to scare off those who are much younger or those who are not ready to know the Lord as she does. She is reminded of what the Lord said in John: *"No one can come to the Father unless the Father draws him."*[16] It takes God to love God, and it takes the Holy Spirit to draw them. Don't try to push them, and don't expect God to be working on the same areas in others' lives that He is working on in yours.

I remember several years ago as my heart was awakening to the passion of God, I tried to share what God was sharing with me with people who weren't ready yet. We were in a couples' small group. In trying to decide what to study next, I suggested the Song of Solomon. There wasn't a whole lot of interest, but they humored me. We had a new couple in the group the first night of the study. In introducing the topic of Song of Solomon, I played a tape from the conference I attended (which I shared about in the book's prelude). The speaker was a man named Allan Vincent. The message was a powerful teaching called "The Intimacy of Covenant." The message so startled this couple that they never came back to the study. They admitted that the subject was just too "out there" for them.

Another time I wanted my husband Steve to hear and understand what God was doing in my heart. We were on a weekend away and I had brought along Mike Bickle's teaching on the Song of Solomon – all 16 hours. After 20 minutes into it Steve looked at me and not too kindly asked, "Can we turn this guy off?" Steve was not there yet. But unlike the other couple, Steve could not run from me. Instead he watched over time as my life was being changed. Now ten years later Steve has listened to those teachings five or six times.

As your life begins to change and the fire of intimacy begins to burn, listen to the admonishment of the Holy Spirit, "Do not arouse or awaken love until it so desires."

### Selah

Are you having a hard time feeling the manifest presence of the Lord? Do you feel like you have lost your way? Has the Lord given you instruction in something that you have failed to obey? If so, what? Are you not sure, ask Him. Are you searching for Him in the right places? Is God showing you the hindrances to your finding Him? Are you harboring fear, strife, selfish ambition, anger, resentment, unforgiveness, offense? What things do you need to get beyond?

Are you willing to pass by the things that you have known before? What is it you need to pass by? Will you take up your cross? Can you see the joy on the other side of the cross? Have you found Him before and let go too soon? Have you held out for the blessing? How do you hold on? How do you press in to go further?

Are you trying in your own strength to push others further than they are ready to go? Are you allowing your life to be the thing that spurs them on?

## Further Reading

*Spiritual Torrents* by Jeanne Guyon

*Experiencing the Depths of Jesus Christ* by Jeanne Guyon

*God Chasers* by Tommy Tenney

## 8th Movement
# Who is This?

*The music has changed once again. It seems calm, almost surreal, bringing with it images within of the maiden and the King together in their secret place. The King holds the Maiden tenderly. He speaks to her in tones of love, so rich the sounds seem to go to her very heart. He speaks in low tones, almost whispering. These are words for her ears only.*

"May I show you something?" He asks, pointing into the air. "Look, what do you see?"

As the Maiden looks, slowly appearing in a swirl of mist, something begins unfolding before her like a movie screen. For in the kingdom of love the thoughts of the King become visible to those who have doves' eyes. Enraptured in the arms of the Beloved, eternity becomes reality, and what isn't yet is seen as if it is.

Looking at the screen-like image, she answers, "It looks like someone coming out of the desert." Continuing she adds, "It reminds me of the caravans that I have watched coming on the horizon bringing the abundance of other lands. I can see the dust rise around them; it must be a large caravan to cause such a stir. I always loved watching those caravans with their beautiful coverings and exotic trappings. Oh, it must be a grand and successful merchant or the caravan of a very special person," she concludes with joy.

As she watches the scene before her, she begins to smell their fragrance as well, for visions from the King can touch every sense our natural bodies have. "What is that I smell?" she asks more to herself, searching her memory for the identity of the scent in the air. "Oh, I know, its fragrance is of incense and spices. I think I smell myrrh, and frankincense, and cassia.

In a moment a question comes to mind. "Who is it?" she asks, turning her attention again to the King. "What special person are you showing me? And where are they coming from?" It suddenly occurs to her that the place that they were coming from may be very important.

The King looks at the Maiden intently. "You have grown in your observation skills. And your questions are good. For it is just as important to know where they are coming from as to know who they are. First let us address the 'where.' They are coming up from the scorched barren desert. And they bring with them the treasures that are found only in the desert places." The Maiden looks at the King, puzzled. "The treasures found there? I didn't think there was anything out there."

"Very few do," answers the King, "but for those who are willing, there is a treasure worth dying for." A vague shadowy look comes over the King's face as He says this. Shaking it off, He adds, "Not many are willing. But if they were, oh, if they were...!"

As you listen to the symphony your mind begins to wander to one of the last statements you heard the King make. "There is a treasure in the desert." This, you think, is something to ponder.      - Selah

*chapter eight*
# THE DESERT SEASON

Song 3:6

As the maiden and the King connect, they are once again having a chamber experience. While together, the Lord shows her a vision of the future. In verses 3:6-11 she describes the vision to us. It reminds me of Peter, in the Book of Acts, when he is sitting on the rooftop in prayer and sees what he describes as a sheet lowered before him with a parade of unclean animals.[1] As the believer watches the scene unfold before her she asks, *"Who is this coming up from the desert like a column of smoke, perfumed with the crushed spices of the merchants?"* (Song 3:6)

Earlier I shared how I believe that the kisses of God are meant to encounter every one of our five senses. Here three of her senses are being used: hearing, sight and smell. As she watches the scene before her eyes, she can smell the fragrance that accompanies this parade through the desert. She tells us that what she is smelling are "the crushed spices."

Fragrances are very important. God loves them. Look at the earth. Everything has a scent: the flowers, plants, animals, even the ground. If you read through the books of Exodus and Leviticus you will see that the temple was filled with many different fragrances. There was the fragrance of the burning sacrifice, the holy incense, and the holy perfume called the holy anointing oil. These things were so precious to God that He commanded them to be made by a skilled perfumer and set apart as holy. God guarded it fiercely, telling any who would to try to make these for themselves that they would be cut off from the rest of the people if they did so.[2] Why? Because it points to something far greater; it points to Jesus, and it points to the process of sanctification in our own lives.

In order to smell the fragrance of a spice, it needs to be released. This can occur in a few different ways. One way is as the container holding the spice is opened or broken, as one would do with perfume. Another way is that the substance itself is heated, like incense. And yet another is when the substance is crushed, like cooking spices. Just as there is something that must happen to the spices to release their fragrance, so there is something that we must go through to release the fragrance of God in our lives. We must be broken, put on the heat or crushed. Paul says this is something to be thankful for because *"[God] always leads us in triumphal procession in Christ and through us spreads everywhere the fragrance of the knowledge of him. For we are to God the aroma of Christ among those who are being saved and those who are perishing. To the one we are the smell of death; to the other, the fragrance of life."*[3]

One of the major ways the fragrance of God is released is as we go through the desert season, a season that Jesus himself experienced, first in his 40 days in the wilderness fasting and then in his beating, crucifixion and burial. Jesus was crushed, so to be like Him we also must be crushed. While speaking to the multitudes about the kingdom of God, Jesus said, *"The stone the builders rejected has become the capstone. Everyone who falls on that stone will be broken to pieces, but he on whom it falls will be crushed."*[4] The maiden had asked to be drawn after Him, but she was unaware of the sovereign times of crushing. She was unaware that this is a place we all must pass through. But again we must stress what Paul said, *"Thanks be to God,"* for He is the one leading us.

When I read this phrase in verse 3:6 it always makes me think of the story of Joseph. As a young boy, Joseph angered his brothers by always sharing his dreams and visions with them. Although the dreams were from the Lord, they put Joseph in such a high position over his brothers that they burned with jealousy. In their anger they plotted to kill Joseph, but as they were considering how to do so, a caravan of merchants came by, and they sold him into slavery instead.

From here conditions went from bad to worse. As a slave Joseph was falsely accused and imprisoned. Joseph went through the crushing and crucible process, a process he had to endure in order to fulfill his destiny and calling, to see the very dreams and visions that God had given him come to pass and have a life that smelled of God. Just as the temples of old were filled with fragrance, so must we, the living temples, be filled with the fragrances that please God. Like Joseph and the maiden, there is brokenness and a crushing that we must experience in order for our lives to become the dwelling place of the Lord.

## Breaking Open the Jars

In Matthew 26 we are told the story of Jesus on a night shortly before his death:

*While Jesus was in Bethany in the home of a man known as Simon the Leper, a woman came to Him with an alabaster jar of very expensive perfume, which she poured on His head as He was reclining at the table. When the disciples saw this, they were indignant. "Why this waste?" they asked. "This perfume could have been sold at a high price and the money given to the poor."*

*Aware of this, Jesus said to them, "Why are you bothering this woman? She has done a beautiful thing to Me. The poor you will always have with you, but you will not always have me. When she poured this perfume on My body, she did it to prepare Me for burial. I tell you the truth, wherever this gospel is preached throughout the world, what she has done will also be told, in memory of her."*[7]

Here this woman took what has been estimated to be the equivalent of one year's salary and poured it on Jesus. She poured out everything she had in extravagant worship and devotion and love. The fragrance of that act of love wafted through the house. To some this smell was offensive, but to Jesus it was pleasing.

Think on this for a moment. Jesus said she had prepared Him for His burial. At His crucifixion it is quite conceivable that the fragrance still clung to Him. I can picture how as Jesus stood on trial, beaten and bruised, a few wisps of hair would pass by His nostrils, and the aroma of the love of this woman would once again steady and uplift His heart. Later, while hanging on the cross He could look out at the face of Mary and be touched again as the fragrance still clung to His hair and His body, rising as a memorial to Him that He was not completely rejected by all.

Three days after his death, Mary went to the tomb with some other women to prepare His body properly, only to find He was gone. But as she stood there, angels appeared, and the Lord Jesus himself stood before her. Mary clung to Jesus just as the maiden in the Song had done because she had once again found the lover of her soul. Jesus then said to Mary, *"Do not hold on to Me, for I have not yet returned to the Father."*[8] This is amazing. After His resurrection, before returning to His father, Jesus made one stop. He came again to the garden in which the empty tomb stood and there met with the one who had already anointed His body for burial by her extravagant love and devotion – the woman who poured out everything she had upon the man Christ Jesus.

Jesus is the same yesterday, today and forever. Just as He stopped to minister to Mary in her time of grief because she had poured out everything she had on Him, so will He stop and be with us when we empty out our jars of clay, our hearts, on Him. When we willingly waste our lives and smash our jars, the glory of God will be revealed.

## The Desert

As the believer describes the vision placed before her eyes, she notes that the caravan not only is fragrant but that it is coming out of the desert. This is a very important piece of the vision that she is noting. What is this desert? The desert is a dry arid region with little water and therefore little vegetation. Deserts in some translations are called *"wilderness."* "The wilderness designates a land burned by the summer heat, generally wasted, rocky and sandy with minimal rainfall, in which only nomadic settlements were found."[9]

Metaphorically, deserts are those long dry arid times when we don't feel the presence of the Lord and life is hard. It is times like the season the maiden just went through. Biblically, it has negative implications as a site of danger, death, rebellion, punishment, temptation and a dwelling place of evil spirits. But there are also positive times when God gave guidance and help, miracles and revelation. You see, when we enter into these long, arid times when we don't feel His presence, it causes us to become dry and hungry. The need rises up for us to search for the water of life, which is not readily available. This causes us to dig.

Throughout the scriptures we see journeys through the deserts. All the stories of the wilderness times have amazing pieces of instruction for us. But let us concentrate on two. The most well-known stories of the desert are the Israelites' journey out of Egypt to the Promised Land and Jesus' 40 days in the wilderness facing the temptations of the devil.

At 40 years of age Moses killed a man and was driven by the pharaoh into the desert. There he made a new way of life as a shepherd. Then after 40 years he had a divine encounter with God, in which the Lord calls him to go back to Egypt to set the captives free. After doing as the Lord has asked, Moses brings this motley group of slaves to the mountain of God in the desert region in which he has spent the last 40 years of his life, only to find that because of the Israelites' unbelief, he would spend the last 40 years of his life wandering around the desert

## The Desert Season

rather than entering the Promised Land.

When Jesus went into the desert it was just after being baptized, when the audible voice of the Lord told him that He was God's "beloved Son in whom [He is] well pleased." From this place of knowing and being assured of the pleasure of God, the New International version says Jesus was *"led."*[10] The King James version says He was *"driven"* into the desert by the Spirit of the Lord for 40 days. The Greek word for driven means *to eject, to bring forth, cast out, drive out, expel*. This is a violent word. It wasn't a gentle leading, but a force that could not be controlled. The Holy Spirit expelled, ejected, thrust Jesus into the desert. At the end of 40 days the devil came to Jesus and tempted him. In those temptations we see He was offered earthly power in religious, economic and political arenas, in exchange for His soul. But Jesus did not fall for it. He knew why He was on the earth in bodily form and what He had to do. Jesus came out of the desert a "seasoned," "spiced" man who had overcome.

If these two men, Moses and Jesus our Savior, needed a season in the desert, how much more do we? But what does that look like for us? And what does this season do?

### Our View of the Desert

Many of us we have a repulsion of going into this place; the very sound of it makes us cringe. I am no different. A few years ago my husband and I were on a romantic weekend getaway in Oregon. We had been there once before and decided to take a trip to the coast, just a short one-hour drive. Coming in from the east at a straight shot you have your choice of following the coastal highway north or south. We had taken the northern route the year before and thoroughly enjoyed it. This year, having a sense of adventure, we decided to go south to explore the amazing wonder of the Oregon coast. Turning southward from our point of intersection we immediately hit the Oregon Dunes, 35 miles of sand dunes that disrupt the rocky northwest coast of the United States.

Within minutes of turning south the tourist billboards began: "Dune buggy rides." Upon seeing the signs our hearts stopped in unison, but for completely different reasons. Steve's stopped from the rush of testosterone and the need for a very male activity, mine from the dread of participating in this very male activity.

Seeing the look in Steve's eyes I encouraged him to go and enjoy – without me. But because this was a romantic get-away he appealed to togetherness and told me how much more fun it would be if we were to share the experience. In a moment of weakness I agreed.

Now, I have a great sense of adventure and was raised spending my summers backpacking in the mountains of Wyoming and camping throughout the United States. But by age 35 I had learned that there is a difference between what most men and women would consider fun. This was not high on my list.

After getting geared up in helmet and goggles, we began our adventure. Steve offered to let me drive; I passed – this was to be his moment. So we set out into the open terrain of the beautiful Oregon sand dunes.

As we crested the top entrance dune, we were met with a

## The Desert Season

spectacular view of these amazing dunes, some of which reach as high as 70 feet, ending in the surf of the Pacific Ocean. I began thinking that this might not be such a bad ride after all. It was truly beautiful!

We began our descent slowly, abiding by the speed limit. Then once out of the start gate the ride really began. Dune buggy rides, for those who have never experienced them, are far from smooth. The constant wind coming off the ocean continually changes the terrain, causing many shifting, unsteady hills. Sunny days are harder to maneuver on the dunes because the sun plays tricks on the sand. What looks like a shadow can turn out to be a deep puddle or pond in the middle of the vast ocean of sand. And what looks to be small ripple in the sand can turn out to be a 10-foot drop.

Being the passenger in one of these crafts is an experience of being out of control. You may see things coming, but you can do nothing about them. We bumped along at upwards of 35 miles an hour. To most of us who are used to speeding along at almost twice that on roads it doesn't sound fast, but when the car you are in consists of a few frail bars and no top or bottom, sitting mere inches off the dunes, your perspective of speed quickly changes.

As we toured around in our buggy I sat in silence. It was not out of anger, but out of the fact that the engine was so loud that you had to scream to be heard and if you did dare to open your mouth it would be quickly filled with sand.

Steve took great joy in speeding along and turning suddenly left, always left, creating a beautiful arching spray of sand which, inevitably, landed on my lap. About a half an hour into the ride (one of the longest half-hours of my life) Steve was careening along toward one of these "little" ripples in the sand that neither of us could see. As he revved the engine and we crested the ripple we began to hang in mid-air, and we realized that this was no mere ripple. Rather it was a six-foot drop. Flying through the air my body tensed, bracing for impact. As the buggy landed nose first in the sand every bone in my body jarred. The small bruise that had begun on my tailbone from the jostling screamed in pain and my muscles ached all down my back. As we settled into the sand Steve looked at me to see if I was all right and could barely stop from laughing as he saw my goggles down around my neck and my whole body buried in sand.

Upon seeing the look on my face, Steve suggested that we had been out here long enough. After returning to the starting point I proceeded to empty the dunes from my contacts, hair, mouth, pockets and underclothing. Steve continued to thank me for the rest of the day. I just smiled, thankful that the ordeal was over, and reminded him he owed me one!

For many Christians the desert or wilderness becomes synonymous with the teeth gritting, sand eating, painful time of unknown sudden drops, with God doing his "male" thing and enjoying the fact that He's in control and we're not. But the reality of the desert is far, far different.

## The Desert Fathers

Although it is true that God is in control and that there can be some pain and teeth gritting, there are those, like the early monks, who feel differently about the desert. The first monks were men who chose to literally leave society behind and go into the deserts. They became known as "The Desert Fathers." To them, the "world, was regarded as a shipwreck from which each single individual man had to swim for his life."[11]

Thomas Merton writes,

> [The desert fathers] sought a God whom they alone could find, not one who was given in a set, stereotyped form by someone else...There was nothing to which they had to 'conform' except the secret, hidden, inscrutable will of God...[a desert father] could not dare attachment to his ego, or the dangerous ecstasy of self-will. He could not retain the slightest identification with his superficial, transient, self-centered self. He had to lose himself in the inner, hidden reality of a self that was transcendent, mysterious, half-known and lost in Christ...the old superficial self had to be purged away, permitting the gradual emergence of the true, secret self in which the believer and Christ were one spirit.[12]

For the desert fathers this happened in the literal desert.

These fathers of the monks sought to find themselves in God in the only way they knew how, withdrawing from society and living in the actual desert. For some today, their calling may be to live the life that the desert fathers lived – that of a monk or nun – but most of us will find God another way, perhaps an even more difficult way. We have to go through emotional and spiritual deserts. The purpose of the desert season is to kick out our crutches from underneath us. It is to rid us of all that we hold onto that isn't God himself. It is where the soul is brought into health and fitness.

## The Purpose of the Desert

The reality of the desert season is harsh. It is a barren place, and it is a hard place. The purpose of the desert is to provide a place where the flesh can die, for it dies more easily in this barren place. The Israelites were brought out of slavery and needed to spend time in the desert to learn to walk in a new way; they had to learn how to walk as free men and women before they could go into the Promised Land. When they had the opportunity to enter the Promised Land, they shrunk back from the inhabitants there. They were too afraid to face their fears. Jesus, too, had to face His enemy head on in the desert.

We all need the desert because it is there that our aspirations for personal power and prestige are challenged. Our egos are cut to size and we begin to see who God is compared to us. It is here that the ways of the world in our lives are challenged and here that we must die to self. For in so doing, we will come out the other side a new creature, a new person in Christ.

As we come to Jesus He leads us out of captivity. Then we must go through the process of learning to walk in faith and the ways of freedom and health. In the desert we too must strain against the chains from our past that have bound us and face the giants that loom before us in order to become who we are made to be. The Lord is calling us to be brave enough to leave behind the old and known and to flow with the Spirit to the new, to be what He created us to be and make His joy complete in us. It is here that we face the giants within, the enemies of our souls that can stop us from fulfilling our destiny.

As I have stated earlier, the Holy Spirit will take you the quickest and easiest way possible. The length and ease depend on you, and it is not always quick or easy. I believe that there are times when we will find ourselves in the desert without warning. And there are other times when we will have a choice, like the desert fathers, to go into the desert as if "swimming from a shipwreck." It is here we are called to put ourselves to death. Like Abraham we are called to place our promises and dreams on the altar, for we can have no promise or dream but Jesus himself.

## The Grave

The desert season is about death to self. Madam Guyon speaks much in her writings on the death process. She writes of how we get to the place where there has been so much of our soul that has died that what God goes after next is the very core – or what we think to be the very core – of who we are. Then, within us, rises up the very God-given instinct of self-preservation. There comes a time when we cannot kill ourselves; only God can do it.

It is here in the desert that we learn submission. Hebrews 5:8 says, *"Although He [Jesus] was the Son, He learned obedience from the things He suffered...."* The surrounding verses talk about being a priest unto God. The desert is the place we learn how to minister unto the Lord; it becomes about Him and not about us. I have heard it said, "To learn obedience means to fully come into what you are created to be. An acorn is complete, but it is perfected when it becomes a tree. It must go through death to be perfected." This is not about failure, for Jesus never failed. It's about being perfected in Him.

In the same vein, Hannah Hurnard eloquently depicts this

in her book, *Hinds Feet on High Places*. In the chapter titled "Grave on the Mountains," the heroine of the story, Much Afraid, and her companions Sorrow and Suffering are following the path of the shepherd to the high places. Again and again the path has turned in directions that don't seem to be leading up to the places of the kingdom of love.

> [Once again] the path led forward to the edge of a yawning chasm, then stopped dead. This grave-like gorge yawned before them in each direction as far as they could see, completely cutting off further progress. It was so filled with cloud and mist they could not see how deep it was, nor could they see across to the other side, but it spread before them like a gaping grave, waiting to swallow them up.[13]

The story goes on as the three do the only thing they know to do – jump into the chasm. There at their feet is an altar in the mist. Behind it, shrouded, is a priest. He says nothing, just watches. Much Afraid kneels at this altar and begins to try with all her might to pull out the self-love that is within her heart. She cries out to God – imploring Him to help do what she cannot do. At this point the priest steps forward to help.

Much Afraid looks at Him and says, "I am a very great coward. I am afraid that the pain may cause me to try and resist you. Will you bind me to the altar in some way so that I cannot move? I would not like to be found struggling while the will of the Lord is done."[4]

The priest does so, and then with a steely hand he reaches into her heart and removes self-love; every root comes out.

With that she passes out. Later she awakens to find herself being carried in the arms of her beloved Shepherd.

What a beautiful picture of that place in the desert where all of self is removed and we are perfumed with Jesus.

## Treasure Hunt

One very important thing that we must remember – the desert is a place to pass through, not to take up residency. As the maiden is watching this prophetic picture of destiny before her, she is not seeing the desert season, but rather the result of that season. She is watching the emergence of a person from the barren places. She proclaims, *"Who is this coming out of the desert?"* (Song 3:6) Maybe the person is at such a distance that she cannot see who it is, or perhaps the person is so changed she does not recognize them.

There is a promise that we can look like Jesus. The desert is the place this transformation happens. But there is a condition. Are you willing to drink the cup?[15] Are you willing to face the experiences that Jesus did, to the degree that God knows you can handle? Or, as Paul writes, *"to know the fellowship of His sufferings and the power of His resurrection"*?[16]

Oh, how often we ask for the things that we truly have no idea what we are asking about. I constantly cry out, "Make me more like You" and then cringe when I'm asked to go into the desert place. I am amazed that the Lord loves me enough to put up with my whining and complaining and to take me through the desert, to help me leave behind the worthless and grab hold of the eternal.

As I was in prayer one night the Lord spoke to me very

clearly, "I am driving you into the desert." Needless to say I was less than thrilled at this statement. In fact I cried for the remainder of the prayer watch, which was around four hours, as the words of the Lord echoed through my spirit. As I contemplated what this would mean, I began to see that there were some exciting things in the desert. It was here that Moses met with God at the burning bush, and here he would meet with Him again on the mountain of fire and smoke. It was here that Moses would speak to God "face to face." The Lord began to speak to me that the journey into the desert was to be a treasure hunt.

In the desert, treasure is buried in the tomb of mummies. Treasure hunters often died in search of treasure because when they disturbed the dead there were toxins released into the air. And just like treasure hunters of old, in searching for the treasure that He had placed within me, I had to face the tomb.

I found my personal tomb, and when I began to disturb what was put to rest there, I died. I was trapped, ensnared in the tomb of my ancestors, succumbing to generational curses and decisions of my past. Everything had to die there; my heart was bound and cold. Yet He was faithful, when all had died, to call me out. Like Lazarus, the Lord makes sure we are good and dead before He calls us to come forth.[17] He called me out of the mindsets that caused death; He called me out of such things as self-hatred and offense.

The Hebrew word for *offense* means *scandal, stumbling block, snare, shame and humiliation.* A snare is the trap of the enemy to catch us in offense. This term *snare* means *a noose, a network for hunting and violent death; to slaughter.* We are called to love the

Lord with all we are. When we operate from an offense or curse, our mind is ensnared by the enemy, effectively decapitating and slaughtering us. This keeps us from fully being able to observe the first commandment. And so our hearts become hard.

It is out of the desert the voice calls, *"Prepare the way of the Lord."*[18] The Lord spoke to me and said, "Why would you think that I would lead you into the desert and not give you a voice? For the voice comes out of the dry and barren places. Here you dig for water that is not seen by the natural eye. Here you get perspective that fertile places lose. Here you have lost the echo of other voices and are finding your voice, the voice I have given you."

Like Peter the Lord says to us, *"Satan has asked to sift you like wheat* (the you here is plural), *but I have prayed for you, and when you turn back again strengthen your brothers."*[19] The Lord speaks this to us all and says,

> *You are not disqualified. In fact now, in this desert place, you are becoming qualified, for it is not you, but Me in you. When you have come through this time I will use you, like Moses, to deliver My people from bondage. Don't conjure what that will look like, for it will look different than you expect, yet I will use you to bring them out of despair. And because you have gone into the desert you can lead them to my holy mountain, where some will wander for many years. But like Moses, because you have spent time in the wilderness, you will know your way around it: you know the pitfalls and you know where the water is and you will be a help and a guide to those in the dry and barren places.*

> *As you reach into these dry and barren places to help others, you will again be as Moses standing humbly before your God, able to commune with Me within the cloud.*

> Heb 12:1-2 says (in my own words),
> *Therefore, let us throw off everything that hinders us and the sin that so easily entangles us, and let us run with perseverance the race marked out for us, not for someone else. Fix our eyes on Jesus, the One who spoke into existence and gives us our very breath that we may be like Him, who, being able to recognize with eternal perspective what the purpose of the cross was. Therefore He could bear with tolerance the pain and agony of this horrible death and consider the guilt and disgrace of this death a joke. He looked down at it as a means to an end, not an end in itself. He then heard his Father say, "You are My Son, today I have become your all and all. Ask of me and I will make the nations your inheritance.[20] Sit at My right hand, the place of honor and power and authority, until I make your enemies a footstool for your feet."[21] Look to Him who bore with tolerance mankind so that you will not grow weary and lose heart.*

This is how we are to look at the death of ourselves, to see it as a means to Jesus not an end, to bear with tolerance all that God brings to buffet us, knowing that it is bringing about eternal perspective. For unless a seed falls to the ground and dies it cannot bear fruit.[22]

During my desert experience, while having a quiet time one morning, the following poem came bursting out of me.:

The Desert Season

## Desert Treasure

*Deeper, deeper still, we dig;*
*plunging, lifting, heaving unbearable loads.*
*Rocks, rubble, dust,*
*Sands of time, windswept over treasures unknown,*
*hardened to stone, entombing the heart.*
*Shifting sands reveal hints of what lies beneath.*
*Once a lively pulsating heart,*
*now forgotten, forsaken, buried alive.*
*Winds howl – uncovering gemstones here and there.*
*Blistering, biting winds circle back in unrelenting repetition.*
*Treasures disappear from view, buried in the shores of the dead*
*all but forgotten.*

*Provisions for the afterlife?*
*What are we doing here?*
*Are we grave robbing or is sleeping beauty waking?*
*What mysteries lie in the still darkness of my inner sanctums?*
*Are the dead better left undisturbed?*

*Like Juliet reviving in the tomb of her ancestors,*
*bone of her bone, flesh no longer there.*
*Is there life within this tomb?*
*Does His heart still beat for me?*

*"Lazarus, come forth!"*
*The voice of my Beloved booms from beyond the grave.*
*The voice of sweetness itself.*
*The voice that shatters mountains.*

## UNQUENCHABLE FIRE

*Can that voice calm the storm within?*
*Or does it just shake to the core of existence?*

*Longing, illusive, unrelenting violence opening heaven – or hell?*
*Will His voice open the tomb I am?*
*When did I retreat to the sepulchre within?*
*Why?*
*Hadn't I come out once – twice – a thousand times before?*
*When will this grave truly be forsaken?*
*When will life completely consume the death within?*

*Pain, fear, emotions beyond words.*
*Can a body endure and not be shattered?*
*Should it?*
*Can I look back? Can I look deeper?*
*Will this looking cause implosion?*

*Oh, loving hands of the miner – dig gently,*
*dig deeply – dig unrelentingly!*
*With all my cries – don't stop – press on – dig!*
*Within the dust and debris there must be a vein of gold.*

*The never ending search for the pure and holy amidst the vein and vile.*
*Smelting, refining, intensifying heat.*
*The unbearable to bring forth beauty – a pure reflectionof you.*
*A vessel of honor – You promised.*

*You spoke:*

*"Refined to purest gold.*
*Set with a rainbow of gems.*
*A treasure that I gave all for.*
*A treasure lying buried, but not forgotten.*
*A treasure worth dying for!"*
Me?
Oh Dig! My Lord,
*dig deeply and may this grave be shattered and empty forever.*
*Look! My beloved stands behind the gravestone,*
*His voice breaking the deafening silence, speaking to me,*
*"Arise, My beloved, and come with Me.*
*Leave the grave behind, embrace the longing within.*
*For that is your treasure.*
*That is the treasure I fight for,*
*I die for, and I live for!"*

*"Lover, Come Forth!"*

## Selah

Have you been through the desert yet? How will you respond to this drawing? Can you hear Him calling you there? Can you see that this is a treasure hunt, and you are the treasure? Will you go with Him into the tomb of your ancestors? Will you wait for Him to call you out? Do you trust in His resurrection power? Can you see that this death is unto life? Can you see the treasure that you will gain?

Is there joy in your heart to embrace the cross? Have you found those around you who will walk through this with you? Are you listening to the Holy Spirit as He battles on your behalf? Do you trust the Lord to take you through this season? Do you trust Him to call you out? In the midst of this do you hear Him say, "Beloved, you are My favorite"?

**Further Reading**

*The Journey Begins* by Rick Joyner

*Journey of Desire* by John Eldredge

*Wisdom of the Desert* by Thomas Merton

*The Way of the Heart* by Henri Nouwen

*Hinds Feet on High Places* by Hannah Hurnard

Bridal Carriage, Funeral Pyre

## 9th Movement
# Picture of Destiny

*After some time of pondering the "treasures of the desert" your mind is drawn back to the music; its sounds are regal and triumphant. Horns seem to be heralding the coming of royalty. There is a jubilation in the music that speaks of the coming of a concurring army. You allow your mind to pick up the vision from where it had stopped. The images of the vision the Maiden is seeing dropped before her like a movie screen returns. The processional from the desert is coming into closer view.*

You hear the King ask, "Can you see more clearly now?"

"Yes," the Maiden replies, "it looks as if they are coming closer to us. There are great men, soldiers, surrounding something in the center of the caravan. It looks as if they are carrying something on their shoulders. "What is that? A royal carriage?" There is a sense of excitement in the Maiden's voice.

"You are seeing correctly," replies the King. "Those men are 60 of the bravest men in My kingdom. They are knights who have all experienced battle. They have their swords by their sides; they are not frightened by the terrors of night, nor by the dangers of the desert."

The Maiden continues to look in awe at the scene before her eyes. "Whose carriage is it?" she asks in great wonder.

"It is Mine.
I made it from the choicest wood, silver and gold. The inside is more beautiful than the outside. It is the carriage of My presence. I had your closest friends decorate it for you."

"For me?" the Maiden says in shock.

"Yes, for you. Listen to what the warriors are saying. They are calling to you." The King turns her attention back to His thoughts.

She watches as the processional begins to move out of the desert towards the gates of the city. As they do she hears the proclamation go forth, "Lift up your heads, O you gates; Be lifted up, you ancient doors, that the King of glory may come in."

As she watches them walk through the gates into the city streets she can hear the captains of the guard proclaim, "Come out, O daughter. Come out, entire kingdom. Come see the King wearing His wedding crown. His wedding day is approaching. This is the day His heart will rejoice. "The entourage continues to chant their refrain as they walk through the city streets, calling all to come and look. The Maiden looks at the King, not sure what all this is about. "I'm not sure I understand." The King explains: "Many proclaim they love me. Many say they will follow Me anywhere, but they won't leave the comfort of the city. Fear overwhelms them and they will not leave their places of seeming protection. What they don't know, what I am showing you right now, is that I do not ask them to go through the wildernes of death alone. I don't even ask them to do it in their own strength. For those who will go where I go, for those who are willing

## Bridal Carriage, Funeral Pyre

*to follow Me anywhere, to look for Me anywhere, like you did today, I have a carriage for them. I will take them through the wilderness. They need only to trust Me enough to climb in. So look again, My dove. This carriage is for you. If you will just climb in and trust Me, it will carry you through and you will be prepared as My bride. On that day My captains will proclaim that My joy is complete and you, My bride, have made yourself ready."*

*Selah*

*chapter nine*
# BRIDAL CARRIAGE, FUNERAL PYRE

Song 3:7-11

As you listen to the music the tempo becomes somber yet royal. What is it the composer is trying to say? As the music begins to sink into your soul the vision becomes a little more in focus as the smoke clears slightly, and you see a royal carriage surrounded by armed guards. What a picture!

What a sight this picture must be to the maiden! She sees a procession carrying a litter, and it is surrounded by the army's most valiant leaders in their finery (Song 3:7-11). Then Solomon becomes visible behind the procession, dressed in all his finery. Is he dressed as priest or king? Does she really understand what she is being shown? Does she really understand what she must first go through to be transported in the carriage? Is this a funeral pyre or a wedding carriage?

The answer is both. For this is not unto death, but life.

The picture is reminiscent of Shakespeare's *Romeo and Juliet*. The young couple from feuding families, desperate to be together, fake the death of Juliet. She drinks the potion of a friar and goes into such a deep sleep that it is believed that all life has left her. The family takes her body and dresses her as a bride. Flowers in hand, she is laid in the tomb of her ancestors. The plan is that her beloved Romeo will come to her in this place of death, and there the two will find new life together.

We all are familiar with the star-crossed lovers. And in many ways Shakespeare had it right. But the Lord created the stars. He does not get confused or tricked by them. Can you see the correlation here? We are at enmity with God. We are told that there is no intimacy possible with Him because of who we are. And in this there is truth, for the only way to break that enmity is to die to our carnal flesh and live hidden in Him.

We are told of the time during Jesus' life when His dear friend Lazarus became deathly ill, and his sisters sent word to Jesus.[1] Yet Jesus' response was to wait. Apparently by the time Jesus got the message Lazarus had already died, yet Jesus still chose to wait.[2] Not until Lazarus was fully dead and decaying did Jesus go to him. Jewish thought was that the spirit lingered around the body for three days. Jesus arrived on the fourth day, when his spirit was believed to have been departed. Jesus gave the family time to embalm his body, wrap it, and lay him in the tomb of his ancestors.

I imagine the funeral procession: myrrh and frankincense so thick that it is a cloud of smoke wafting around; women weeping and wailing as they follow behind. But Jesus was not mourning; He was not sad for Lazarus. Oh yes, he wept, but He knew what was about to come. I believe He wept at the sorrow in the hearts around Him, and perhaps He wept at the lack of faith He saw in His own friends. In our finite minds we often miss the life that comes from death. And misunderstanding can delay God's coming. Often anger and grief overcome our ability to trust.

Lazarus' sisters, two of His closest friends, missed the purpose, on the front end of Lazarus' death, of what Jesus was doing. Both Mary and Martha said the same thing to Jesus: *"If You had been here he would not have died."*[3] Those closest to Him didn't see what this was all about, but Jesus could see the life that comes from death. He had told his disciples earlier, *"This is not unto death. No, it is for the glory of God, so that God's Son may be glorified through it."*[4] But they still misunderstood. *"So then He told them plainly, 'Lazarus is dead, and **for your sake I am glad** I was not there, so that you may believe.'* "[5] Amazing! Jesus was glad that Lazarus had died. Why? So He could show forth the unsurpassed glory of God: so that all could see resurrection power.

## Fully Dead

After four days Jesus goes to His friends. Upon coming to the tomb Jesus tells them to remove the gravestone. Martha protests, *"But Lord, by this time he [is decaying and] throws off an offensive odor, for he has been dead four days!"*[6] The King James Version says, *"But Lord, he stinketh."* Oh, how we must come to understand the delays of God.

We must understand that the Lord won't come and kiss us awake when we are "mostly dead," in the immortal words of the movie *Princess Bride*. Oh no, He waits until we see decay, until there is no possible signs of life left and we ourselves smell the stench and even say to the Lord, "Oh, don't remove the stone now, the stench is too bad."[7] This is the place where we repulse even ourselves and everyone around us. But this is the place of bridal preparation. It is at times like these the Lord says, "Now is the time I can do something, and all will know it is Me and that you have nothing to do with it." Could it be that Paul saw this very picture when he wrote to the Corinthians,

> *Thanks be to God, who always leads us in triumphal procession in Christ and through us spreads everywhere the fragrance of the knowledge of him. For we are to God the aroma of Christ among those who are being saved and those who are perishing. To the one we are the smell of death; to the other, the fragrance of life....*[8]

In Christ our triumphal procession is the march to the death of ourselves, and simultaneously it is the bridal procession. The Lord is showing her the altar of her death. But this is not a death unto death, but unto life in the lover's arms, a place where the believer can say with Paul, *"For to me, to live is Christ and to die is gain."*[9]

John Piper says it this way:

> If you want to glorify Christ in your dying, you must experience death as gain, which means Christ must be your prize, your treasure, your joy. He must be a satisfaction so deep that when death takes away everything you love – but gives you more of Christ – you count it gain. When you are satisfied with Christ in dying, He is glorified in your dying.... So Paul's point is that life and death, for a Christian, are acts of worship – they exalt Christ and magnify Him and reveal and express His greatness – when they come from an inner expression of treasuring Christ as gain.[10]

## Bridal Carriage, Funeral Pyre

As the believer yields, laying herself on the altar, being willing to let the Lord carry this chariot into the grave, she experiences great gain. There she becomes a new creature. There her name is changed. There she is no longer the maiden – but the bride. The hope that sustains us is knowing that there will come a voice from beyond the grave that says, "My beloved, arise! Come forth!"

What the believer is being shown here is the procession of the sacrifice, the procession of a funeral and the procession of a wedding – all together. For it is in the death to our flesh that the Lord can come close. It is in being shrouded in the smoke and incense that we can enter the Holy of Holies. And what is the Holy of Holies for us? Intimacy. The smoke? Our prayers and our sacrifice.

### Escorted By the Noblest

As the believer watches the vision before her eyes she says, *"Look, it is Solomon's carriage, escorted by the noblest of Israel"* (Song 3:7). In this place of death the King doesn't go to the bride; the bride comes to the King. He sends His carriage to bring her to Him and to bring her safely through the wilderness. However, the Lord doesn't send us out alone; He says that He will never leave us or forsake us.[11] He sends with us our own company of warriors. In Hannah Hurnard's allegory, *Hinds Feet on High Places,* the companions of little Much Afraid are Sorrow and Suffering. Sorrow and Suffering will be part of our company as well. For Jesus told us that we must drink His cup and pick up our crosses and follow Him. Jesus told us that we will experience the things He did, but we will not go through them alone.  He will send His comforter to us, the Holy Spirit.

I believe that the Holy Spirit will come to us in several ways. He will come directly, speaking to our hearts and showing us the things we need to do to be prepared. He will give us the strength from His very hand to endure what we must, trusting that His grace is sufficient for us.  And His power is made perfect in our weakness.[12]

Another way the Holy Spirit will come is indirectly, through His servants and other followers of the Lord, the others who have traveled the path before us.  Remember in verse 1:8, the Lord told her the way to find Him was by following the tracks of the sheep.  Those tracks lead through the desert, but it is a well-worn path that will lead to the mountain of God. The Lord will send the counselor, and He will send his friends who know His ways first-hand.  They can lead her through the dark night of the soul.

The writer of Hebrews says, *"The Lord is my helper; I will not be afraid. What can man do to me?"*[13]  The Lord sends with us people who know that *"our struggle is not against flesh and blood, but against the rulers, against the authorities, against the powers of this dark world and against the spiritual forces of evil in the heavenly realms."*[14]

They continually remind us to look beyond the natural, and they come along side us and as Aaron did with Moses when they fought the Amalekites; they hold up our arms in worship and prayer so the enemy can be routed.[15]  Yet those He sends to help us do not come empty-handed; they come with the sword.  The sword of the Lord stands for the Word of God and the Spirit of God. These companions speak words of life into areas of our lives that seem dead. They act as surgeons, wielding with precision the knife to go in and cut out that which is not God, circumcising our hearts, thereby removing the flesh. They bring truth into our lives. The sword of the Spirit acts as both a defensive weapon in protecting us and an offensive weapon in purifying us. God, in His faithfulness, will surround us with men and women of God who will yield the sword of the Spirit in our lives.

And let us not forget that the Lord will sometimes even use unbelievers. He will use people who do not know Him to both bless and discipline us. He will often use them to help provide the circumstances by which we are purified or brought to death to self, as He did with the nation of Israel.

## The Heavenly Bridegroom

As the prophetic vision comes to a close, it goes beyond just what the Lord is doing for her, and she now sees the heavenly Bridegroom adorned for His wedding. She says in verse 3:11, *"Look at King Solomon wearing the crown, the crown with which his mother crowned Him on the day of His wedding, the day His heart rejoiced."* God is happy; He is rejoicing! Isaiah says, *"As a bridegroom rejoices over his bride, so will your God rejoice over you."*[16] Why is the Bridegroom rejoicing? Because *"the bride has been made ready"*[17] and He is being crowned for His wedding day.

A few years ago I was privileged to hear Rabbi Frankle of Rock of Israel, a Messianic itinerant minister, share on the ancient Jewish wedding. This sent me on a journey of investigation. Through his teaching and Jewish books on the history of weddings, the Lord began to expound to me this beautiful picture the believer is painting in the song.

## The Ancient Jewish Wedding

The primary view of marriage in the Jewish mind is that it is the "creation of new life." Second Corinthians 5:17 says, *"Therefore, if anyone is in Christ, he is a new creation; the old has gone, the new has come!"*

The wedding is viewed as a spiritual Yom Kippur (Day of Atonement), a day of repentance and forgiveness. The Midrash, which is the running commentary on the Old Testament, considers marriage the work of heaven, and it states five times that marriages are made in heaven. The rabbis believe that the whole of the Torah (the Old Testament) is the marriage contract between God and Israel.

Marriages were arranged by the matchmaker. The matchmaker was usually a servant of the father or a friend of the groom, and it was his job to speak of the groom to the young woman and win her hand for the groom. This has been the job of the Holy Spirit from the beginning of time, to prepare a people to spend eternity ruling and reigning with the Godhead.

In Hosea God says, *"I will betroth you to Me forever; I will betroth you in righteousness and justice, in love and compassion. I will betroth you in faithfulness, and you will acknowledge the Lord."*[18]

In Malachi 3:1, the Lord is speaking to the nation of Israel and says, *"See, I will send my messenger, who will prepare the way before Me."*

In the New Testament, we see the first fulfillment of that

promise in the person of John the Baptist. Mark begins his account of the life of Jesus by saying,

> *The beginning of the gospel about Jesus Christ, the Son of God. It is written in Isaiah the prophet: "I will send my messenger ahead of You, who will prepare Your way—a voice of one calling in the desert, "Prepare the way for the Lord, make straight paths for Him." And so John came, baptizing....*

And then in the book of John, John the Baptist said of himself, *"I am not the Christ but am sent ahead of him. The bride belongs to the Bridegroom. The friend who attends the Bridegroom waits and listens for him, and is full of joy when he hears the Bridegroom's voice. That joy is mine, and it is now complete."*[19]

John the Baptist declares himself the friend of the bridegroom, the matchmaker whose job it is to prepare the bride for the Bridegroom. In the Holy Spirit coming at Pentecost we see a broader fulfillment, for the Holy Spirit leads us in the ways of the Lord and raises up a generation of fiery men and women who know the sound of the Bridegroom's voice.

## The Bride Price

Once the girl was chosen by the matchmaker, the negotiations would begin. The father of the young woman, or another residing male, would require payment be made to the girl; this is called the *mohar*. The bride's father in return gave a dowry. This could have included household goods, but it had to include 100 pieces of silver. The groom then would match the 100 silver pieces. Often the coins were made into decoration for the veil. If anything happened to the groom or he divorced the woman, those 200 pieces of silver and the *mohar* would belong to the bride to care for her needs. We are told in 1 Corinthians that *"you are not your own; you were bought at a price."*[20] Jesus paid the price with His life. We can even see that it was paid for by the religious leaders to the sum of thirty silver pieces paid to Judas.

## The Ketubah

The *ketubah* is the wedding contract itself. Traditionally it was not a contract between bride and groom but a document signed by two witnesses who testify that the groom "acquired" the bride in the prescribed way. The document itself states what the groom will do for the bride as her husband. It is an unequal covenant like the one God made with Abraham in Genesis 17. It was not a mutual agreement; the bride only had to accept the proposal of marriage. The contract itself became her property, a continual reminder of the promises made to her. The Midrash (Jewish commentary) states that all of the Torah is the *ketubah* and it was given to Israel at Mt. Sinai. As the New Testament unfolds and we see the promise of the Messiah fulfilled and Jesus adding more promises to it, it becomes part of the *ketubah* as well.

## Betrothal

There were two very distinct ceremonies in the Jewish wedding: the betrothal and the nuptials. Today they are performed on the same day, but until the 11th century, they were performed about a year apart. Today the two ceremonies are separated by the presence of two cups of wine: the cup of joy and the cup of sorrow, because life is filled with both.

The betrothal ceremony was the one in which the legalities were taken care of designating the bride and groom for each other. Prior to the betrothal ceremony, there would be "the veiling of the bride" by the groom so that he knew whom he was marrying. This came about because Jacob was tricked into marrying Leah when he thought that he was marrying Rachel.[21] Once veiled, the bride would then be considered set apart, and the veil became a statement of betrothal as well as a symbol of modesty.

## The Kinyan

The *kinyan* then took place. The *kinyan* was the formal, physical acquisition of the bride; without the groom's giving and the bride's acceptance there was no marriage.

When the negotiations were complete, the father of the groom would pour a cup of wine and recite the blessing over it, and he then would hand it to his son. The son would then raise the glass and say, "This is a new covenant in my blood, which I offer for you." He would then leave the cup on the table, and if then young lady accepted his proposal, she would at some point in the night lift the cup and drink. Then the two witnesses would sign the marriage contract, declaring that the bride had been acquired in the correct manner.

Next the formal betrothal ceremony would take place, at which time the marriage contract would be handed to the bride as the bride and groom stood under the chuppah (bridal canopy) together. Once the contract was signed and given to the bride, the blessing was said, and the second cup of wine was drunk and the ring was given. The betrothal was now complete.

What a vivid picture we have here of what Jesus did. *"The Lord Jesus, on the night He was betrayed...took the cup saying, 'This cup is the new covenant in my blood, do this in remembrance of Me.'"*22

Here Jesus set before His followers the proposal of eternal life. He was about to pay the price to acquire the bride. All that was required of them was to say, "Yes, we believe. Yes, we love you," and to remain faithful until His return. When we drink the cup of the Lord's supper we are proclaiming our acceptance of Jesus as our eternal Bridegroom until His coming for us at the end of the age.

## Time of Preparation

During the year between the betrothal and the nuptial ceremonies, preparations were made for the nuptials and the couple's life together.

The bride would prepare a white dress to symbolize her purity. Revelation 19:7-8 says, *"The bride has made herself ready. Fine linen, bright and clean, was given to her to wear."* Along with the white dress and veil discussed earlier, something blue was to be worn to represent their faithfulness to the word of God and to the vows they were to make. During this time of preparation if you were from a wealthy family, clothing was prepared to provide for the guests who were to attend the wedding as well. Jesus spoke of this in his parable about the wedding at the end of the age in Matthew 22:11.

During this time of separation the groom would go back to his home and prepare a house for his bride. Only the groom's father could say when the house was ready and when he could go get his bride.

In John 14:1-3, Jesus said, *"In my Father's house are many rooms; if it were not so, I would have told you. I am going there to prepare a place for you. And if I go and prepare a place for you, I will come back and take you to be with Me that you also may be where I am."* In Matthew 24:36, Jesus, speaking of his return, said, *"No one knows the day or hour, not the angels in heaven, nor the Son, but only the Father."*

When all is prepared the heavenly Father will look at Jesus and say, "Son, go get Your bride."

## Cleansing

Another thing that the couple would do in preparation for their wedding was to take a ceremonial bath in a *mikvah*. A *mikvah* is any body of "living water" (which is running water as opposed to stagnant). The bride and groom would separately go into a pool of running water and immerse their whole bodies. Jesus was baptized in a river, by John, the friend of the Bridegroom, thus fulfilling His requirement of cleansing. And the bride is washed both in physical baptism and continually in the water of the Word of God.[23]

## Fasting

As the day of the wedding approached, the couple would fast. The fast is a time for prayers and repentance. The fast is broken under the chuppa with the first cup of wine. Later the couple will eat a meal together.

Jesus spent 40 days fasting in the wilderness immediately following His baptism.[24] In Matthew 9:14 we are told the story of John the Baptist's followers coming to Jesus to ask about Jesus' disciples and their seeming lack of fasting. They came to Him and asked, *"How is it that we and the Pharisees fast, but your disciples don't?"*

Jesus answered them, *"How can the [friends] of the Bridegroom mourn while He is with them? The time will come when the Bridegroom is taken from them; then they will fast."*

Jesus said, in essence, that His disciples didn't fast because He had not gone away to prepare the home for the bride yet, and that they would indeed fast while He was away. It is in fasting for our heavenly Bridegroom that we go through repentance and cleansing, thus preparing us for His return.

## Escorting the Bride

Once all was prepared and the father said that the house was suitable to bring the bride home to the groom, he would come for the bride accompanied by friends. They always came at night and they would search for the light in the window. During this time of separation, the bride was to keep a light burning in her window every night.

Jesus said,

> *Therefore keep watch, because you do not know on what day your Lord will come.... At that time the kingdom of heaven will be like ten virgins who took their lamps and went out to meet the bridegroom. Five of them were foolish and five were wise. The foolish*

## Bridal Carriage, Funeral Pyre

*ones took their lamps but did not take any oil with them. The wise, however, took oil in jars along with their lamps. The bridegroom was a long time in coming, and they all became drowsy and fell asleep. At midnight the cry rang out: "Here's the bridegroom! Come out to meet him!"*[25]

The groom's entourage would enter her city or street blowing shofars (rams horns) and shouting, calling all to come to the wedding feast. In 1 Thessalonians 4:16 we are told, *"For the Lord Himself will come down from heaven, with a loud command, with the voice of the archangel and with the trumpet call of God."*

More than one groom could come on the same night, so it was important that the bride knew the groom's voice. Jesus said, *"He calls His own sheep by name and leads them out. When He has brought out all His own, He goes on ahead of them, and His sheep follow Him because they know His voice. But they will never follow a stranger; in fact, they will run away from him because they do not recognize a stranger's voice."*[26]

Upon hearing the call of her bridegroom, the bride would come out of her home covered with a veil. She would sit upon a litter, or carriage, and was moved through the street in the wedding procession from her father's house to the nuptial ceremony.

This is what I believe the maiden in Song of Solomon 3:6-11 is describing. She sees the wedding carriage and sees it coming out of the dark night parading through the streets of the city. The believer is shown from the Lord a vision of the second coming of the Lord when the bride of Christ has been prepared and is being taken to seal, for all eternity, her marriage to the

King of Kings.

## The Nuptials

The Hebrew word *nissuin* (nuptials) literally means *to carry or lift* and refers to the day when the bride was carried through the streets to her new home. This ceremony was also known as chuppah and was a symbolic act of intimacy.

As the ceremony started, the bride was to walk under the chuppah and circle the groom three to seven times, based on Jeremiah 31:22, which says, *"The Lord will create a new thing on earth – a woman will surround a man."* The rabbi then welcomes the couple by saying, "Blessed is he who comes in the name of the Lord." With the bride and groom covered with a single *tallit* (prayer shawl), seven blessings were recited. "[T]he blessings mention the beginning of time when life was whole and the end of days when that wholeness is restored…the day that offers a taste of paradise as bride and groom."[27]

A cup of wine would then be blessed and the bride and groom would eat bread and drink the wine together, breaking their fast under the wedding canopy. Jesus said to His disciples as they partook of the Passover with Him on the night before He died, *"Do this in remembrance of Me."* It was the last cup of wine in the Seder that the Lord said He would not drink of again until *"the day when I drink it with you in My Fathers Kingdom."*[28] The fourth cup of wine in the Seder is the "cup of praise" because of the Lord's promise, "I will take You as My own people."

At some point during the nuptial ceremony part of the bride's veil is temporarily removed and placed on the groom's shoulders with the statement, "The government will be upon my shoulders."[29] The pronouncement of bride and groom would be made, and a glass they drank from was stepped on and broken, representing the cutting of the covenant, and that marriage is a transforming experience that changes individuals. With this the crowd shouts, "Mazel tov!" or "Congratulations!"

No tears are allowed at a Jewish wedding. If a mother wants to cry she must leave the room.

The book of Revelation tells us, *"He will wipe every tear from their eyes.*[30] *There will be no more death or mourning or crying or pain, for the old order of things has passed away."*[31]

## The Party

The bride and groom would preside over a feast as the "king and queen" for the evening. They would then retire into the wedding chamber for seven days. During this time the friends and family would continue to party. The bride would remain veiled to the public and in the tent for those seven days.

Colossians 3:3-4 says, *"Your life is now hidden with Christ in God. When Christ...appears, then you also will appear with Him in glory."* At the end of this week of seclusion, the couple would then come out and share in as much as another week of festivities.

When Jesus walked the earth, He fulfilled all the law and the prophets. He followed all the rules and regulations set before Him. God, in His infinite wisdom, gave the Jewish people an order to their wedding ceremony that points to the Messiah coming as our heavenly Bridegroom. How all the details of

Christ's return will look may be unclear, but one thing is certain – all who call on His name will appear as a glorious bride without spot or wrinkle. And this will be the day that His heart will rejoice.

## Selah

Are you willing to climb on this carriage? Can you see that this carriage is for you? Can you trust that the process, even though difficult, is out of love? Is there an understanding within you that all that God is doing in you is because He loves you? Will you willingly submit to the things that God brings that will purify and cleanse you? Do you know the voice of the Bridegroom? Do you have oil in your lamp? Can you see yourself as the bride of Christ?

## Further Reading

*The New Jewish Wedding* by Anita Diamant

*Divine Romance* by Gene Edwards

*Bridal Intercession* by Gary Wiens

*Destined for the Throne* by Paul Billheimer

*Dangerous Duty of Delight* by John Piper

## 10th Movement
## I Will Go!

*The Maiden stares in wonder at the scene of the carriage before her, silently trying to comprehend all that it means and all the King had told her. "For me?" she whispers under her breath.*

*The King turns His attention to the Maiden again, as the screen before them rolled up and faded away.* "Do you know how beautiful you are to Me, My darling? Your eyes are singly on Me. Your dedication is showing in your outward service to Me. You have the ability to take the words that I have spoken to you and make them part of your very being. I see your willingness to wear the cloak of humility.

You are beginning to think like Me and to think like My Father. It brings peace and truth to those to whom you speak. You are now able to start training others in the ways of My kingdom. Your thoughts, oh they are beautiful. Did you know that you have learned to take your thoughts captive, that your thoughts are pleasing in My sight? You have become strong in your worship of Me. You are a woman after My own heart. You even have the ability to fight off the pesky lies from the Taskmaster. You, My darling, are beautiful!"

*The words of the King rush into the Maiden like an artesian well, filling her with love and joy and confidence. She bursts out, unable to contain herself any longer.* "I know that I have not reached perfection. I know that I have nothing to offer you and I know I have not yet done anything for you, but **I WILL GO!** Yes, I will get in the carriage, I will go through the wilderness of death. I will even go to the mountains and hills, the ones I saw in my dream, and even though they make my heart fear, I will go wherever you ask," she says breathlessly.

"Oh, you are beautiful!" announces the King. "Do you know how much joy it gives Me to see your heart say YES to Me? To see you beginning to trust Me? Come, let Me take you to the mountain tops. I wanted to take you there with Me when I called to you from the window. Come with Me now. I want to show you some very personal things. I want to show you what my Father sees. For at the top of the mountains the air is different, the view is clearer. From the mountain peaks you can view eternity. Here you will learn truth, how to put on your armor, and you will learn My ability to conquer the enemy through you. But, I must warn you, there are dangers on the journey to the top. The Taskmaster doesn't want you to go there. He doesn't want you to grow and learn more of Me. You see, the more intimately you know Me, the less chance he has to capture you again."

Looking intently into the Maiden's eyes, the King speaks again: "Oh my bride, **You have ravished my heart! When you look at me I am overwhelmed.** Your beauty is rare. Your love for Me is so unusual even for those who are in My kingdom. There are few who love Me so much that they would willingly travel through the wilderness of death. But you have said you will, you have said YES! You have captured my heart. Your love delights Me more than all the riches of this Kingdom. Your heart of love spreads a perfume that is better than all the spices the merchants carry. Your voice is pure sweetness to Me. Your words feed My spirit."

A look of fierceness comes onto the King's face as He adds, "You have been made for only Me, and I will not share you with another." His face softens again as He continues to speak to her of His love. "Your presence, my bride, brings Me pleasure and tranquility. The fountain of your love is for only Me to drink from. For in your heart flows the purest of love. Growing within your heart are many virtues. I see your obedience unto the wilderness of death; there is holiness growing, there is honor for My Father, uprightness, forgiveness, faith, purity, authority, worship, praise and thanksgiving; there is truth with mercy, and there is intimacy with Me. The fountain of your love flows like the River of Life from My Father's throne."

"Oh, my King," bursts in the bride,"I know that for me to mature there is more work to be done in my heart. Just as the gardens need the winter and the summer for the produce to be sweet, I need different seasons in my life. I no longer fear the winter. I am no longer afraid of the harsh times in life. I do not look forward to them, but You know what my life needs to produce fruit pleasing to You. Do what You must. Send whatever You will, for I trust You! I want my life to mature in its pleasure for You, so I yield to the training conditions that You deem necessary. For I will always love You!"

"My bride." says the King, as He pulls her closer to Himself. "What joy it gives Me to hear you say these things. I long to bring you into maturity. You fill My heart with joy. Just your willingness to get in My carriage has already produced wonderful things in you. You can now be used to tell others of My Kingdom. You bring Me much delight. You are a crown of beauty to Me. No longer will you be called Maiden. For today you have been betrothed to Me. And just as I *rejoice over you, My bride so My Father rejoices over you. There is much you need to do to prepare for our wedding. I must leave now. But I will leave My servant with you; He will guide you in all you need to do. Though I tarry, remember that one day is as a thousand to My Father, and a thousand is as a day. Don't forget – I will come for you."*

With that, the King kisses her hand and leaves her. How long they were together the bride does not know. She only knows that she is enraptured with the King. He had called her "My bride." He had told her they would one day be together as husband and wife. "Oh, to be the wife of the King!" she sighs as she climbs into bed and drifts off to sleep.

*The curtain falls. There is a warmth in your heart as the lights in the auditorium come on. Even though it is now intermission, few begin to stir. A whispered murmur starts to be heard; there is a sense in the audience that if they were to raise their voices even to a normal conversational tone, something would be disturbed.*

*Selah*

*chapter ten*
# ANSWERING THE CALL

Song 4:1–5:1

The Believer has just walked through one of many desert seasons. She has experienced the Lord's divine discipline and gained understanding in some of His ways. The Lord is revealing the significance of and need for these seasons in our lives. These are times of divine training, and they can look different for everyone. The Lord knows what it is that is holding us back. He withdraws the feelings of His nearness to make us so hungry and thirsty that if we don't come out we feel as if we will die. He knows that we do not always have what it takes to follow Him, so He says, "In your weakness I will be strong." The result of this "desert" experience is that the believer has come to the point of desperation, of recognizing that she would rather have the manifest presence of the Lord, feel His warmth and nearness, than stay in the place of comfort. She comes out of the desert season loosed from the chains that have bound her and free from any crutches that have held her up. All she has left is the Lord to lean upon.

As the believer responds to the call, even though late, the voice of God comes flooding in again with the sweet songs of praise for who the believer is, not what she has done. He says, **"How beautiful you are, my darling! Oh, how beautiful!"**

(Song 4:1) Obedience is beautiful to the Lord. But the believer's obedience isn't religious obedience following do's and don'ts, but the obedience of love. It is an obedience of the heart that says, "I must have more of Him!" The Father is looking at the heart, not at the actions. We must recognize that the believer has not yet done anything to advance the kingdom. She hasn't won any souls to the Lord; she hasn't won some great spiritual battle that has advanced the kingdom on the earth. All she has done is come out of her place of comfort – and she has done so reluctantly. But even a reluctant obedience is pleasing, for God is looking for the "yes" in our hearts.

Here we see the loving Father heart of our God. It is like the proud parents who are watching their toddler learn to walk. The baby stands by himself, and all around applaud. Then the child is encouraged to take one step, then two. When the baby falls, the parents rush in and lovingly pick him back up and put him on his feet, smiling and encouraging the child. The parents continue this process until the child is running around so much that they cannot catch him. As the child is learning to walk, there is joy in the heart of the parent, not anger because he keeps falling.

Scripture tells us that God is a good Father and that He does all things well. The believer has taken a huge step by walking out of her comfort zone, and Abba God lavishes on her great words of encouragement as she takes one step and then two, until she is running with joy down the highway of holiness. Like any loving Father He disciplines, but then He loves and encourages. The true definition for *discipline* is *training which corrects, molds and perfects*.[1]

## The Garden of Our Hearts

As the Lord speaks, He gives her words of encouragement. He speaks things that strengthen her resolve. He tells her what He sees in her, extolling the inner qualities of her heart. There is nothing that energizes and moves the human heart in courage more than being told how wonderful we are, who we are and how another feels about us. It is not ego; rather it is truth, and the truth sets us free from the confines of life and of the lies of the enemy, and we begin to move in power and authority. The Papa tells the believer in the Song in verses 4:1-5 of the maturity that He sees growing in her and what she is capable of doing. He gives her a list of all the things He sees coming to life within her, things growing in the rich soil of her heart.

Jesus told many parables when He walked the earth. One He told was about the kingdom of God being as a seed.[2] A farmer (the Lord) went out to sow seed (the kingdom of God). That seed fell in four places. The first place it fell was a path; here the birds of the air came and snatched the seed away. Jesus said this represented the person who didn't understand the kingdom, and the evil one came and took it from him. The second place the seed fell was in the rocky soil. Here the seed had been given to those who had no depth, and even though it was received it eventually died. The third place the seed of the Kingdom was sown was in the thorns. Here the believer was too concerned about the cares of life, and he lost the life of the kingdom of heaven. Lastly the seed was sown among good soil. Good soil is soil that is free of stone and root and has been tilled – overturned and loosened – making it receptive to the seed of the kingdom of God. This means that the enemy could not snatch it away, that there was depth for the seeds to grow and an understanding of who God is and in His provision, resulting in an abundant harvest.

What was the issue with the believer? As with all of us, all of the above. She didn't understand the ways of God, she didn't have depth and she was filled with the cares of this world. In verse 2:2 of the Song the Lord told her she was a "lily among thorns." He was commenting that she was growing in a place that had the potential to choke the life out of her. And, as we have seen, it nearly did, for out of her fear, out of looking at herself and not trusting in the provisions of the cross, she refused His call. But God in His mercy came and revealed that it was in the walking out of her comfort zone that the things that held her in bondage would be broken. Now after going through a season of discipline, a season of training, the soil of her heart has been prepared, and she is not only open and receptive to the Kingdom of God, but it is starting to grow within her and she didn't even know it.

The Lord comes to her and speaks words that fill her with the courage she needs to take the next step, telling her of the hidden qualities within that He sees growing. There are seven attributes the Lord highlights. Seven is the number that represents perfection. He is telling her that she is indeed becoming the pure spotless bride and is clothing herself in white robes.[3] Those attributes of perfection are: 1) singleness of vision, 2) consecration and dedication, 3) the ability to take in the meat of the word, 4) a soft and pliable will, 5) a gentle and quiet spirit, 6) the strength of a warrior, and 7) a sacrificial life. She is not perfect yet, but the Papa encourages her that she is indeed walking in the right direction.

## I Will Go!

We are made to respond to praise, to words of love and affection. We are made in the very image of God, and God himself responds to our praise. We are told that He will inhabit our praises. He will live in the praises of His people. God knows that the way to motivate our hearts is to speak to who we are made to be. So as the Lord is telling the believer how He sees her, the maiden cannot hold back any longer; she interrupts the Lord and proclaims, *"Until the day breaks and the shadows flee, I will go to the mountain of Myrrh and the hill of incense"* (Song 4:6).

According to most transcripts, the phrase in verse 4:6, "I will go…" is still spoken by the Lord. Once again, I see it as a place in the duet where the two voices sing together. The Lord is responding, "I will go to the mountains that you told Me to go to." But I see the believer so overwhelmed with the thoughts and praise of the Lord that she bursts into His song of love and proclaims, "I AM RUINED! I can't take any more. Whatever it is you want of me, wherever it is you want me to go, I will go! I am Yours! Do with me whatever You wish. I'll die to myself; I'll even face the thing I've feared the most because You have overwhelmed me."

I am reminded of a scene in the children's Christmas movie *Rudolph the Red-Nosed Reindeer*. The time comes for little Rudolph to join the other reindeer at flying lessons. None of these little guys have ever done this before. As they start the lessons, a young doe looks into Rudolph's eyes and says, "I think you're cute." His heart races, and with the proclamation on his lips, "She thinks I'm cute! She thinks I'm cute!" he takes off soaring through the sky, amazing all around him.

In the Song, the believer hears the Lord say, "I think you are lovely!" And with that phrase resounding through her heart, she knows she can go anywhere, she can do anything. She says to the Lord, *"Until the day breaks and the shadows flee,* **I will go to** *the mountain of myrrh and the hill of incense."* In her own way, she repeats the scene with Rudolph. "He thinks I am beautiful! He thinks I am beautiful! Look at me! I can fly over all the obstacles that once held me earth-bound."

### The Mountain of God

Oh, how the Lord loves this response from the believer. I can see the smile on His face. He knows she really has no idea what she is saying. He knows that she is saying this in the heat of passion, but He doesn't care. He knows this is her true heart's desire and that the "yes" is genuine. Even though she does not fully understand what she is saying, He says, "I will take that 'yes'!"

The Lord never lowers His standards nor surrenders His purposes for His chosen ones. He bides His time and waits until developing maturity prepares us for the fuller response demanded. With her "yes" He begins to share with her in verse 4:8 about the adventure that awaits her – the places she'll go and the things she will see. The Lord is calling her to heavenly elevations. He is asking her to come to high lookouts from which she can view the world.

I can hear the excitement rising in the heart of the Lord as

## Answering the Call

He is telling her about all the wonderful things they will do together. The Lord says, "OK, this is where we are going; I want you to come with Me to the mountain peaks. But to do so you must leave the lush fertile comfortable life, like Moses, and take a journey through the wilderness, where nothing seems to grow, where it looks like death all around, and come to the mountain of God. Continue on your journey up the mountain. And there, at the top, you will meet with Me and see Me as I am."

In Exodus 24 is told one of the most amazing stories. The leaders of Israel have just committed to do all that the Lord commands and follow with all their hearts.

Then in verses 9-11 it reads, *"Moses and Aaron, Nadab and Abihu, and seventy elders of Israel went up [the mountain] and saw the God of Israel. Under His feet was something like a pavement made of sapphire, clear as the sky itself. But God did not raise his hand against the leaders of the Israelites;* **they saw God and they ate and drank."**

Wow! How would you like that? This, I believe, is not just for the leaders of Israel, but any believer who will journey up the mountain of God. This is what we are beckoned to; this is what awaits us.

There are three peaks from which the Lord wants to give the Believer heavenly perspective: Amana, Senir and Hermon. These are mountains on the northern side around Israel. *Amana* means *confirmation or truth. Senir* means *a flexible armor known as a coat of mail.* Hermon means *devoted* and denotes destruction and Jesus' ability to destroy the works of the enemy. It is a snow-covered peak from which the Jordan River is fed, and it is the most likely location of Jesus' transfiguration.

As the believer willingly leaves the comfort zone below, she is beginning to live a life of total commitment. Jesus' affirming words give her the strength to embrace the cross. As the Lord calls her to the higher places He warns that there is danger along the way. The enemy hides there setting traps. I have heard it said this way: "New levels, new devils." She will encounter more warfare because she is becoming a threat to the enemy. Satan's biggest threat is a Christian who is totally sold out. As she ascends the mountain of the Lord she will gain the ability to take her place in God's purposes as a lover of God and also as a warrior in full partnership with Him and His purposes.

As she goes with the Lord to the tops of these mountains she will see the truth of her being seated with Christ in heavenly places and the enemy being made a footstool. She will eat and drink with God. For it is as she goes up these mountains and faces her fears she will be knighted with confirmed truth (Amana), given a coat of mail for protection under her armor (Senir) and learn to use the divine weapons capable of pulling down strongholds (Hermon).

For us the mountain of God is not a natural place, but a spiritual place. To climb higher up the mountain is a metaphor for growing closer to God and becoming holy and righteous.

David wrote in Psalm 24:3, *"Who can ascend the hill of the Lord? Who can stand in His holy place? He who has clean hands and a pure heart, who does not lift up his soul to an idol or swear by what is false."*[4]

As we yield to the discipline of the Lord, as our hearts are purified and we are in the place that God is on the throne of our hearts, then we have journeyed up the mountain of the Lord.

## The Ravished Heart of God

Here we reach the climax of this song, the turning point in their relationship. As the believer responds to the Lord and says she will go to the mountains, the Lord tells her where they are going. As if He cannot contain Himself any longer, He breaks in with what I believe to be some of **the most astounding words in the scriptures**. He blurts out His deepest heart's emotions, *"You have stolen my heart!"* (Song 4:9) The King James reads, *"You have ravished me!"* To me this is the single most amazing and life-changing sentence in this whole song. And perhaps, it even sums up the whole of creation, the whole of Jesus' willingness to go to the cross. It shows us the joy that He willingly died for. It reveals His heart in four short words: *"You have ravished me!"*

The word *ravish* means *to capture by force, by violence*. Here the Lord speaks an almost unthinkable phrase to the human heart and mind; the very impact of these words is mind blowing:

**We mere mortal man, dust and ash, can violently capture the heart of God. We can move the very heart of God. We, you and I, His creation, can make His heart beat faster!**

In Matthew 11:12, Jesus says, *"From the days of John the Baptist, the kingdom of heaven has suffered violence and the violent take it by force."*[5] To take the kingdom by force means to seek the kingdom of God with the most ardent zeal and intense exertion – in other words, going for it with everything you have. John the Baptist, in John 3:29-30, proclaims himself to be the friend of the Bridegroom, and his joy is complete because he hears the voice of the Bridegroom on the earth. Jesus says it is from this day forward that there is a violence in the kingdom. John's life gives us an example of one who sought the kingdom violently. He was to be a priest in the synagogue. He was to be of the upper echelon of Hebrew society. But he gave it all away for the glory of God. John gave it all away so that he could have the joy of knowing the voice of the Bridegroom. As John reveals that Jesus is the Bridegroom that all the earth has been waiting for, for all eternity, the ravished heart of God is exposed, creating a violence in the heavenlies for the advancement of the kingdom. Jesus made known that His heart can be ravished by mankind. He let his love for us be known. He made known the way to take, own, and influence the Kingdom of Heaven. How is this done? By us merely looking into the eyes of Jesus and saying, "Yes." This is the violence that advances the Kingdom. Love captures God's heart by force. Amazing!

Oh, the magnitude of these words cannot be overstated, and yet I find my words inadequate here. *Father God, I pray that these words would sink into our hearts and our souls. Oh Father, let us know the love of your Son that is so overcome with His bride that He literally moves heaven and earth to bring us into full union with Him. Lord, I ask that you would convince our hearts of the height and depth and width and length of your love, this love that surpasses all understanding.*[6] *This love that allows the God of all creation to be moved by the love of humankind.*

Oh, can we understand this? The Lord is not captured by

force as she works and strives to do things for Him. Verse 4:9 says that His heart is ravished by *"one glance of her eye."* To *glance* means *to take a quick look at something.*[7] The Lord is captured by force as she simply looks to Him. As she just quickly looks in His direction He is undone. We come to this place of abandonment and obedience and say, "Yes," and the Lord is undone. Amazing!

Oh how the Lord lavishes His love on us. He doesn't stop at saying the most astounding thing of all time. No, He goes on and adds to it. He says, *"Your love is better than anything that I created. There is nothing in all of creation that fills Me with joy like your heart aflame for Me. This is why you were created. This is why I redeemed you. And it is good!"* (*Song* 4:10-11 paraphrased)

## A Garden of Delights

As if these words are not enough, the Lord goes on to tell her in verses 4:12-15 that her life is a pleasure to Him, literally a paradise. He speaks in terms of a hidden garden to which He alone holds the key. He begins to share with her the joys of what He has found in that garden paradise. He sees that she has kept herself pure for Him. He tells her that she is a *"spring enclosed, a sealed fountain"* (Song 4:12). It is not a cistern that is stagnant; rather it is a spring that has had a cover put on it to keep out the dirt, dust and impurities.

The Lord, throughout the Scriptures, is described as a good farmer. He knows how to care for his livestock and His harvests. Here the believer is described as a garden, as a place that is tenderly cared for and cultivated. Wild plants that are not tended are not as productive as plants that are cared for by a gardener. One of the most important ways to care for a plant and help it to yield an abundant crop is by employing the process of pruning. "Pruning embodies a paradox of life – that growth and productivity require deprivation and stress. If left unattended a vine or fruit tree will produce lush foliage, but little fruit. Pruning is associated with life rather than death."[8] We also must allow the pruning process to take place.

In his book *Secrets of the Vine*, Dr. Bruce Wilkinson teaches on the process that a vine must go through in order to produce a full 100-fold crop.

> In the vineyard an expert pruner applies his skills in four specific ways: to remove the growth that is dead or dying; to make sure sunlight can get to all fruit-baring branches; to increase the size and quality of the fruit; and to encourage new fruit development. Our Father the vinedresser is guided by similar principles.... His plan for pruning is anything but random, and He works in every life uniquely.... Discipline is about sin, pruning is about self. In pruning, God asks you to let go of things that keep you from His kingdom purposes and your ultimate good.[9]

The Lord has tended to the garden of the believer's heart as she has rested in His presence. In the Song, verses 4:14-15 the Lord lists the fruits that He finds in this garden of her life. Notice that there are nine fruits that are listed here and nine fruits of the spirit listed in Galatians 5:22. These fruits are love, joy, peace, patience, kindness, goodness, faithfulness, gentleness and self-control. Her life is beginning to show forth the abundance of the Lord. She is growing fully in the Spirit.

## The Wind of God

As the Lord is speaking to her, sharing with her all the fruit that He has planted and that is growing in her life, she bursts into the song again with a cry form her heart, *"Awake, north wind, and come, south wind! Blow on my garden, that its fragrance may spread abroad"* (Song 4:16). Just as the believer is recognizing that the Lord is a good, loving gardener who knows how and when to prune her life, she begins to understand that there are different seasons in life that are important to producing sweetness in that fruit. The times of discipline and pruning have taught her to trust in the dealings of the Lord, even though they may be painful.

She asks for the wind of God to come upon her life. The full revelation of what she is asking for has probably not dawned on her, but there is a desperation within her to go through whatever it takes to come to full maturity. The words for wind in both the Old and New Testament can also mean breath or spirit. She is asking for the breath of God to blow upon her heart. Symbolically, *The Dictionary of Biblical Imagery* tells us, "The winds can be a picture of God's supremacy, his authority over his creation, and the very spirit that breaths new life into the human soul…. Only by His authority do the winds emerge and blow where He sends them."[10] This is not a quaint little prayer; she is asking for God to do amazing things in her life. She is asking for a touch from God that is beyond anything she has yet known.

She asks for two specific winds to blow upon her: the north

wind and the south wind. It is from the north that God's glory emanates[11] and from which the turbulent whirlwinds of God come,[12] and it is the north wind that brings rain and cold. Metaphorically, it stands for the discipline of God. In this calling forth of the winds of God, she is crying out for the buffeting storms of the Lord to come upon her.

The south wind is a warmer wind that brings the end to winter and brings visible signs of growth. Metaphorically the south wind stands for wisdom. She is asking for the divine hand of discipline to come upon her life, for from discipline comes wisdom, and both of these come from the very heart of God.

The believer is asking for the winds of winter that send us into a season of seeming dormancy and the winds of summer that are dry and arid and oppressive. But she is not asking for the trials of this world; she is asking for the winds of the kingdom of heaven that bring life.

In Ezekiel 37, Ezekiel the prophet is brought to a barren valley in the wilderness. There he sees dry bones strewn throughout. As he looks upon the bones, the word of the Lord comes to him and commands him to speak to the bones and call them to life.

*"Then He said to me, 'Prophesy to the breath; prophesy, son of man, and say to it, "This is what the Sovereign Lord says: Come from the four winds, O breath, and breathe into these slain, that they may live." ' So I prophesied as He commanded me, and breath entered them; they came to life and stood up on their feet—a vast army."*[13]

As the winds of God blew on the dead bones and brought forth life, so God breathes on the dead places of our lives and brings them to life again. This is what the believer greatly desires.

The disciples, too, experienced these winds on the day of Pentecost, as they were together in an upper room, meditating and praying through the night in the tradition of the feast of Pentecost. Suddenly a rushing violent wind came upon them, with what looked like tongues of fire. Here we see both the hot breezes of the south wind (tongues of fire) and the cool breezes of the north (rushing violent wind) coming together. The Lord sends these two winds together on the day of Pentecost. And what is the result? The Scriptures say the disciples were filled with the Spirit; with boldness they proclaimed the word of the Lord, and 3,000 were added to them in that day. They were touched by the winds of God, and they became fruitful. Ultimately the result of the winds of God is life.

What the believer is asking for can only come as a result of a growing trust in her heart. For she is not asking that everything be comfortable and that life be easy. Brennan Manning writes in his book *Ruthless Trust*,

> Unwavering trust is a rare and precious thing because it often demands a degree of courage that borders on heroic. When the shadows of Jesus' cross falls across our lives in the form of failure, rejection, abandonment, betrayal... when we are deaf to everything but the shriek of our pain; when the world around us suddenly seems a hostile, menacing place.... It requires heroic courage to trust the love of God no matter what happens to us.... Our trust does not bring final clarity on this earth. It does not still the chaos or dull the pain or provide a crutch. When all else is unclear,

the heart of trust says, as Jesus did on the cross, "Into your hands I commit my spirit" (Luke 23:46).... The basic premise for biblical trust is the conviction that God wants us to grow, to unfold, and to experience fullness of life.[14]

When we ask for the winds or breath of God we are in fact telling the Lord we trust Him completely to bring whatever is needed to produce maturity in our lives.

Again this call for the winds to blow is where the two voices in the duet sing together. The Lord is speaking to the winds to come into His private garden, her soul, to temper the fruit, but also to begin to waft the fragrance of God in her life over the garden walls. The Lord had told her in verse 4:12 that she is an enclosed garden; no one but the King has access. But the Lord can hint to those outside what's inside. Can you remember ever going outside on a beautiful spring day, when a breeze blows, and on that breeze rides the sweet fragrance of the flowers that are in bloom? On such days the fragrance often catches my attention, and I begin to look around for the origin of the scent. If I see some flowers, I will often go to them and smell them up close to see if they are the ones. This is a beautiful picture of what the Lord wants to do for this believer. He is calling the winds to blow and spread her fragrance to others, not to call attention to her but to the Lord who is radiating out of her. Not all will think this fragrance is beautiful – for to some it will be the smell of death; to others it will be the sweet fragrance of life.[15] But nonetheless they all will smell it.

Selah

Stop for a moment. Ask the Lord to speak praises into your heart. Listen, for He will speak. Write them down. Will you dare to believe them? If you are willing to believe them, they will make your heart soar, and you will be able to take on the tasks that the Lord calls you to do. Are you willing to believe in His love for you?

Do you trust that it is at the heights of the mountain that you will win in the spiritual battles? What battles are you experiencing right now? Are you trusting the Lord to take you to the heights of the mountain of God from which you can see the battle being fought and won from the heavenly perspective?

Will you believe that the "yes" in your heart can captivate the heart of the almighty God? What is it that He is asking you to say "yes" to? What about works? Is He saying this to you because of what you have done? Are you still wrestling with the "doing"? If so, can you put aside the "doing" and just be with Him? Will you set aside a season to be and not to do? Will you press in and take the kingdom by force?

What fruits do you see growing in your garden? Have you locked your garden for only the Lord? Can you dare to believe that there is fruitfulness in you? What stage is your garden in: planting, cultivating, pruning, harvest? Ask the Lord to show you what he sees growing. Is the breath of God blowing? Is it the north wind or the south?

## Further Reading

*Costly Anointing* by Laurie Wilke

*Ruthless Trust* by Brennan Manning

*Secrets of the Vine* by Bruce Wilkinson

Thrones of the Soul by Paul Keith Davis

## 11th Movement
# The Midnight Hour

*You have found your seat again in the auditorium. The music begins to fill the room again with calming notes of serenity. When the curtain went down, before intermission, the Maiden was asleep in her bed, night had fallen and peace permeated her heart as well as yours. As the curtain rises the music takes you back to that place of rest, and once again you picture the Maiden asleep in her bed, the music filling you with the sounds of night.*

*Your mind scans the room the Maiden is sleeping in. She is prepared. The light burns in the window and there are extra oil jars sitting beside her lantern. There is a sense of anticipation even though she is at rest; you know that she is waiting for the King.*

*Suddenly there is a knock at the door. The Maiden instantly stirs, sitting upright in her bed. The knocking comes again with urgency. Then the voice of the King rings clearly through the door. "Oh My darling, My bride. Come open the door for Me. I must show you something about Myself that you do not yet know."*

*He is still speaking to her through the door as she lifts the already-lit lamp from its resting place on the window and tries to figure what she should wear for such an occasion. She had thought of this often, going through the many beautiful garments He had given her. But now that He is here, she isn't sure. He seems to be inviting her someplace she had not been before. Oh, what would He desire her to clothe herself in for this occasion? As she looks through the garments she hears His voice come again, "My darling, I have been out here a long time. This has been a night of agony for Me. I must share this with you. You must share this night with Me. You must understand what I went through the night before I came and paid the Taskmaster for you. I knew that the price he would demand would cost me everything. I knew that he would ridicule, mock and beat Me. I knew that he would imprison Me. I knew all this before My father sent Me to walk as a commoner in the kingdoms of fear and hatred. But I came.*

*The night before I paid for you I went into the garden on the hill – the one I've taken you to before, and there I pleaded with My Father to find another way, but I knew, We both knew, there was no other way – not if I wanted you to be truly free; not if I wanted you to be on the throne beside Me. And I did so want that, so I agreed to follow our plan.*

*I know you know much of this, My beloved. But what you need to know is that I went freely for you. I chose the way of death. The pain that was the deepest to Me was the separation from My Father. You see, in order to free you, I had to become all that was wrong and ugly and unthinkable. Oh, it was such a heavy load. The most pain came when My Father looked away, when He said I must feel what you would feel for all eternity if I did not pay this price. Oh, the darkness. The loneliness. When He looked away I felt My heart rip in two. It was a pain too deep for words."* The pain can still be heard in His voice.

Something begins to stir within the Maiden's heart; a pain she has never known before begins to grow.

As He speaks, the fragrance of the burial spices begins to waft through the air. "But I knew that you would be free to be with Me if you chose." His voice continues: "That was what gave Me the strength to go on. And I knew that I would see My Father again. If you are to be My bride, to reign with Me you must experience what I did. I must have a bride who has gone to the depths that I have gone. We must be like-minded. Just as I needed to live in the kingdom of fear and hatred to experience your experiences so that I would know first hand what your life has been, so you must experience the suffering that I went through. For, when you do you will then experience the power of My Father. Once you have experienced His power you will be able to rule in His kingdom and never be open to the treachery the taskmaster succumbed to when he became prideful and set himself against My Father. But you must be willing. You must do this of your own free will. Will you come? Will you walk the path of solemn promise that I have walked? Will you freely walk the path of blood?"

As she listens to the words of the King, determination and courage grow within her – an overwhelming desire to do whatever it takes to please Him, and to know Him as He is describing. But this determination is so foreign to her; she knows that it could only come through His touch on her life. "My heart is pounding within me. I will come, but you must give me your strength," she says as she grabs whatever coat she can find; for now how she looked doesn't seem to matter. All that seems to matter is the time; she feels an urgency to respond quickly to this call from her Lover.

"I cannot walk this path in my own strength. You must show me the very places you set your feet; I do not want to step anywhere that you have not," she says as she reaches for the door.

His scent is in the air. It comes to her like a hand of comfort on her shoulder. As she reaches for the door she notices that His servant has put the burial spices on her hands. With every move toward the door, His servant pours more of the precious oil over her. Her hands are so full of the oil that she finds it difficult to turn the lock and open the door. His servant comes to her assistance.

As the door is finally opened the bride is met with a horrifying sight. **He is gone.** The King has left without her. She knows she has to find Him. She knows she must walk the path alone. As she walks out the door she thinks. "My heart will surely break in two. I must find Him."

"My beloved King, where are You?" she calls. "I have answered your call. Was I too slow, was I not prepared? O, my King, I love you, come back." Yet there is a peace in her heart. She remembers His words, "I will never leave you. I will never forsake you. For I am with you always."

She thinks that He has either gone to the slums or to the garden. The path to both is through the middle of the city. She will search through all the monuments and castles on her way.

As she walks through the city the Noble guards find her. "What are you doing here? How did you get in the city at this time of night?" "I am looking for the King," she answers, somewhat surprised by the anger in their voices.

"You are a liar," they spit back. "The King would never be out at this time of night. You have come here to rob our monuments. You don't want the King. You just want the treasures He has given us." Their anger grows with each word, and they begin to mock her. "I bet you think He loves you. You probably think that you could be His queen. Are you better then we are? Do you think you know more about Him then we do? Who are you to speak to us this way? You insolent little upstart, we'll teach you a lesson!"

As their anger grows they begin to vent it with their fists as well as their words. A crowd has formed as the insults come with loud voices. There seems to be something in the nature of man that we want to see what the King does not. The crowd closes in around her; they are surrounding her; there is nowhere she can turn. Many in the crowd join in the jeering. Some of the onlookers pick up rocks and begin to throw them at her. Some say they are just watching so that they can give an accurate report to the King. Others sit silent, afraid to get involved, afraid that the fury would fall on them. So they watch, not doing a thing.

"You have no place among us. We have always wondered about you. There is nothing truthful or honest about you," says another. "You have such a holier-than-thou attitude. Who do you think you are? You don't even know the King. I bet you think you could tell me things that I don't know about Him," says another.

"You have a wicked spirit. You are a Jezebel leading the people astray," sneers someone else. Ripples of agreement went through the crowd.

She looks at the Noblemen and women who are speaking so violently to her. They are her friends. She knows them; she had shared her heart with them, and they had eaten together at the King's table. This is a pain too deep for words, to be accused so by those she had thought were her friends. She looks from one face to another, but there is not one look of understanding, just sheer hatred and anger.

"You think you hear from Him. You think you are some kind of a prophet – then tell us who hit you." And with that rocks begin to be hurled at her.

They continue to beat her, to strip her, to accuse her. It goes on and on until she is barely recognizable. Blood pours from the cuts on her face. But the physical pain is nothing compared to the pain of her heart. "What have I done to them? Why have they turned on me?" she wonders.

"My God," she prays within,
"My beloved, where are You?
My God, why have You
forsaken me?"

Selah

*chapter eleven*
# DARK NIGHT OF THE SOUL

Song 5:2-5:7

At the close of chapter 4 of the Song, we watched as the believer and the Lord have just had another time of intimacy. Intimacy with God, just as intimacy with our spouse, is not a one-time thing; it must continually happen for love to grow and mature. As that season ended, there was such an eruption of trust within the believer's heart that she asked for the full manifestation of God's love to come upon her; she asked that He would blow the breath of life upon her, bringing whatever He deemed necessary to produce perfection within her (Song 4:16).

Their time of intimacy brought her to a place of deep rest. As we said earlier, this is not a bad thing, but actually a fulfillment of the promises of God.[1] It is a gift from the very hand of God. Once again, as in 2:8, we find her alone with the Lord outside her place of comfort knocking on the door. Again, her rest is disturbed and she says, *"Listen...."* And again, the call of the Lord comes to her. But there is a marked difference this time in their interaction. This time she tells us that although she was in a place of rest, she wasn't fully asleep; oblivious to everything around her, she says, *"I slept, but my heart was awake. Listen! My Lover is knocking..."*

(Song 5:2). She was waiting, anticipating His arrival, even while being in a state of rest.

Earlier in the song in verse 2:8 when the Lord came to her, He revealed Himself to her in super-human terms, leaping over mountains and hills. But as the Lord comes to her in Chapter 5, it is with a new revelation of who He is and what He has done for her. This time He comes to reveal to her the agony of the garden of Gethsemane. He comes to her with His *"hair dripping with dew, He is covered with the dampness of the night"* (Song 5:2).

### Friendship with God

Jesus is looking for a friend, someone with whom He can share the trials and triumphs of His life. She has cried out for the deep things of God; she has cried out to know Him in every way. As their love has grown, the Lord recognizes that she is now ready to experience a deeper revelation of His heart, to see the agony that He went through as the *"Lamb that was slain."* There is a transformation that happens in our ability to love when we truly understand, by experience, what someone else has gone through; when we walk the path that they have walked, our love becomes deeper.

John, Jesus' disciple, is described as *"the one that Jesus loved."*[2] John was a friend of God and the only disciple who is recorded in the Gospels as being at the cross watching the agony of his beloved friend. Years later, John was imprisoned on the Island of Patmos, and there he had a new revelation of Jesus as the slain lamb.[3] John saw Jesus on the cross, but there was something new that was revealed to John's heart as he experienced in prison what Jesus experienced on the earth. The same is now true for the believer; she has feasted at His table, contemplating the sacrifice that He made, but there is something much deeper the Lord is about to reveal to her. Paul calls it the *"fellowship of his sufferings."*[4] Jesus is coming to her as a friend, revealing the pain He experienced so that intimacy can be deepened, and asking her to walk the same path so that His power can be made manifest through her.

I remember about five years into our marriage, a friend called from out of state thinking about us. He felt like the Lord impressed upon him that around Easter time Steve and I were going into a season of deeper intimacy. Well being married, we were expecting a new "honeymoon" of sorts. But the reality was much different. It was just a few weeks before Easter that we went to The Family Life Marriage conference. Those nights stirred up for us some unresolved issues in our marriage. We had a great, healthy marriage – but there were still issues, still things in our hearts that had never been revealed to one another – places of hurt and offense that we had not yet been able to bring to the light. And so we did go into a deeper time of intimacy, but not physical intimacy; rather, it was a deep emotional and spiritual intimacy that has had far greater impact on our marriage than a season of being physically close. Intimacy took on a whole new meaning as the Lord began to uncover our hearts and reveal where we were not living in love and unity.

It is the same in our relationship with the Lord; there are seasons when the intimacy will be on a manifestation level, feeling close to Him, times when we can sense Him in very real ways. Then there are those times when the Lord asks you to come out of that place of comfort and come with Him to the deeper places of intimacy – the places that sometimes don't feel so good, but that can have a far reaching impact on your relationship. I picture it like massaging a muscle cramp. The muscle is tight and frozen up. You begin to work on it and it hurts. You stop and it still hurts. But in the hours that pass, the pain lessens, and there is a greater range of motion (or emotion) than you ever thought possible. What is built in this season is a trust and security that only dealing with the heart issues can. It is in this time you experience the kindness of the Lord that leads you to repentance.[5]

### I Am Not Dressed

As the believer responds to the knock on the door she says, *"I have taken off my robe...I have washed my feet..."* (Song 5:3). The maiden's response to the call is not one of rebellion, but rather, I think, one of surprise. The fact that she has no robe or shoes on indicates that she has been expecting something quite different. In 5:1 the Lord told her – His bride – that He had come into His garden. He was gathering her sweetness and fragrance. So her natural inclination was to prepare herself for intimacy in the inner chamber of her heart as she had known it before.

The believer says to the Lord, *"I have taken off my robe; must I put it on again?"* Robes are representative of our personhood. Her garments speak of her deeds or acts.[6] This is a reference to her deeds in contrast to His deeds. His garments are garments of righteousness, whereas our garments are as filthy rags. Here I see the believer looking to the Lord in bewilderment, saying,

"Wait a minute, Lord, I gave You my filthy rags. I gave you all those gifts and talents. I laid down my desires. I threw my crowns at Your feet. I have given it all to You – how can I take it back again? Isn't it sin to take these back from Your hands? How can I touch what belongs to You? How can I put on those things that once kept me from You? They were things – giftings, talents, desires that I placed before You. The gifts, the crowns are not what is sinful. It is the place I gave them; they became more important than You. I committed idolatry and adultery with those gifts. Will they come between us again? I have taken all off, I stand before you naked and unashamed. I don't want to be covered before you any more."

She goes on to say, *"I have washed my feet...."* This speaks of Jesus' daily cleansing of our lives. Our feet get dirty through our contact with the fallen world in our endeavors to serve God. Jesus told Peter that he was clean; however, he still needed his feet cleansed.[8] Washing the feet meant a fresh cleansing from spiritual defilement. She wants to know how could she purposefully defile them again. This was not a statement of refusal to obey but a commitment to avoid defilement. Jesus called her *"perfect, undefiled"* in 5:2. How can she defile herself in the light of so great a love from Jesus? She is saying, "My feet were dirty by my own walk, but now they have been cleansed by God." It is a cry like the cry of Jesus in the garden: *"Pass this cup from me, but not my will but yours."*[9] Jesus was perfect, without sin; yet on the cross He became the very sin and defilement that He had kept himself from as He walked on the earth.

## Obedience

As the maiden is contemplating the new call that God has given her, trying to figure out what it is that He is really asking of her, suddenly the Lord breaks in and causes her heart to be ravished (captured by force) by Him. *"My lover thrust his hand through the opening of the door"* (Song 5:4). The Lord moves on her heart in such a way that in her love and adoration she obeys, even though to do so means certain death. Her actions show her response as, "There is an opening in my heart for only You. You have stuck your hand in like a surgeon massaging my heart back to life with Your very hands. I can feel the life start to pulse through my veins again. I can feel Your life surge through my very soul – what I thought was dead is back to life, but now in purity."

"Now these things are in their proper place because what makes my heart beat faster is Your touch – not my hopes and dreams – for You have become my hopes and dreams. You have become my all in all. I will put on that which I've laid at Your feet, because I can now pick it up in Your strength not my own. When I pick these up in Your strength, they remain Yours. They remain in their rightful place. They can now enhance our relationship and not come between us. I remain exposed to You, but covered as I go out into the world to do Your work."

## He Was Gone

With great trust and resolve the believer opens the door for the Lord. Yet something terrifying happens when she opens it: He is gone. This has led many to believe that she was disobedient to the call of God. But her response was to open to the

Lord. When He called before, she sent Him away; she said, "No, You go." She did not say no this time, so why was He gone? Why would He not be there?

As was stated in our discussion on the Song chapter 3, the Lord will never leave you or forsake you; however, He will lift the feelings of His presence. Once again the manifest presence of the Lord is temporarily taken from her life. But this time it is not out of discipline because of disobedience, but the pruning of self. It is the calling her out to greater depths. You see, if the Lord were to keep His presence near to us in our current place of growth we would stagnate. Why would we ever venture beyond what we know when He is pouring out His presence upon us in our current place. Who would want to go elsewhere?

Madam Guyon describes this time in her book, *Spiritual Torrents*,

> If you were to ask the believer about his present experience, he would surely tell you that he has reached the very center of God and that he is so tranquil and delighted with his Lord he is sure he has reached some ultimate pinnacle. He sees nothing more to do but enjoy the state he is in.... There are Christians who never reach beyond this experience in their lives.[10]

God wants us to go into new and deeper realms within Him. Ephesians 3 says that the love of God is beyond comprehension. It says it is deep and wide and long and high. Why would we search out the deeper of things of God if we are being touched by Him where we are? "If necessary, [God] will risk our misunderstanding of His methods and motives. His purpose is for you to cut away immature commitments and lesser priorities to make room for even greater abundance of His glory."[11] God wants us to know more about Him, so He withdraws His manifest presence, causing us to hunger and thirst for more of Him. "Hungering and thirsting for more disturbs complacency, induces a blessed state of disquiet, and propels our unending exploration into the Mysteries of God in Christ Jesus."[12] This is exactly what God is doing. He is disturbing her complacency, causing her to explore the mysteries of God. Oh, what a wonderful God we have, who refuses to let us settle for anything less than all of Him.

### The Sifting Of Our Hearts

The Lord hides himself because there are things in our lives that we need to face head-on, issues that if we are content and comfortable we will never face. If the Lord's presence were to remain strong and manifest, we would hide behind His grace and mercy. So the Lord hides Himself; He gets out of the way so that those things that have separated you from Him can be dealt with once and for all. Like the veil that separated the people from the Holy of Holies, there are still veils that we hide behind. The Lord wants nothing better than to rip them from top to bottom. He wants you in His presence without hindrance.

As the believer opens the door of her heart wider to the Lord and discovers He is not there, the lovesickness in her heart overwhelms her, and she runs into the city to find Him once more. The believer goes to what she has known before. As she does so, she runs into the watchmen (noblemen) again, but this time something unexpected happens; this time *"they beat me; they bruised me; they took away my cloak, those watchmen on the walls"* (Song 5:7).

This is a very hard thing. Our understanding of a loving God is so different than this. In our minds a truly loving God would not allow His children to be beaten and abused. But the Lord **does** allow hardship to come on the righteous. He does allow them to be persecuted, which can come in many different forms. The Lord sees things from a perspective that we do not. And He allows sifting and shaking to come into our lives to uncover our hearts in ways that nothing else can.

The whole book of Job is the story of one man's heart being sifted before the Lord. In Job 1:8, the Lord is addressing Satan and asks him, *"Have you considered my servant, Job?"* Scripture says that Job is a righteous man, yet God himself says to Satan, "Look at this man," and gives him permission to sift him. Why? Because as the story unfolds, it is revealed that there were things in Job's heart that needed to be brought into the light. There were areas in Job's life that were not wholly given unto the Lord. Job says himself in verse 3:25, *"That which I greatly feared is come upon me, and that of which I was afraid is come unto me."*[13] Fear is not of God. Job had a hidden fear in his heart that needed to be exposed – several in fact – so the Lord allowed outside pressure to come into his life to reveal his heart and purify him.

In Luke 22:31 Jesus is speaking to Simon Peter and tells him, *"Simon, Satan has asked to sift you like wheat. But I have prayed for you, that your faith may not fail. And when you have turned back, strengthen your brothers."*

Peter has had a revelation that Jesus is the Son of God. And yet even with that revelation, there is a sifting that must come to the heart of Peter. The Lord does not address him here by his new name, Peter – the rock – but rather by his old name, Simon. The Lord is getting his attention. "Listen, man. Satan is coming after you. I know that you will make it through this in the end, because I have prayed. But...when you come back...." Now there is a statement. The Lord tells Peter here and in the following verses that he will fall away, that he will deny Him. But he also tells Peter that he will be back and he will bring the stability of a rock into the community of believers. You see, it is the same with all of us. We often see ourselves so differently than we are. Our perceptions tend to be skewed by the years living outside of God. So God brings correction like a loving father into our lives. But it's not just about correction but strength training. It's the process of learning trust and learning to lean on Jesus alone. It is through this process that we come to say, *"I can do all things through Him who strengthens me."*[14]

Not only did Job and Peter go through this, but Jesus Himself did as well. Hebrews 5:8 says, *"Though He was the son of God, yet He learned obedience by the things He suffered; being made perfect...."* What a mystery. Jesus, the Son of the Most High, had to go through suffering to be made perfect. "Wasn't He already perfect?" you ask. Jesus came as fully man, putting aside His divinity. As a man there was something that He had to experience for Him to come into the fullness of who He is for eternity. Suffering was the vehicle. I have heard it explained this way: "An acorn is complete, but when it dies and rises up an oak tree it is perfected." Jesus became perfected, *"a planting of the Lord for the display of His splendor"*[15] by the things He suffered. That is what God is after – our perfection which displays His splendor.

Why does the Lord allow you to go through this? Why does He allow them to beat and bruise you? And why does He allow you to go through this seemingly alone? Because He loves you. Because He loves you too much to allow you to stay trapped by your fears, insecurities and lies. So He lets the battle ensue. He calls you out to what the mystics have called "the dark night of the soul," the place where you come to the end of yourself and say, *"Not my will, Lord, but Yours."*[16]

## The Enemy

There are two ways in which we can enter this season of the dark night of the soul: willingly or unwillingly. And there are two directions from which the battle lines are drawn: internally and externally. Facing the enemies within very often comes through our willingness to become whole. Then there are times when, even in our willingness, God must use outside pressures and people in authority to press in on us and reveal our hearts.

Jesus said that He came that we might have life and have it more abundantly.[17] This is not just to be obtained on the other side of glory. It is to be obtained now – here on earth – in this lifetime. But in order to gain it we must fight for it. It is our promised land that we must conquer. The inheritance of the Promised Land isn't just heaven. The Israelites had to fight the giants to obtain their Promised Land. There are no giants we must face in heaven. The inheritance that we must fight for is our eternal destiny that begins here on earth. And the giants we must face are not the establishment, the leadership or other of God's people.

In his letter to the Ephesians, Paul says, *"For we **wrestle** not against **flesh and blood**, but against principalities, against powers, against the rulers of the darkness of this world, against spiritual wickedness in high [places]."*[18]

The giants we must face are those taunting fears and lies of the enemy that have kept us from the fullness of our destiny. These are the watchmen of our souls.

## The Internal Watchmen

For a long time I knew that this battle would come. I knew that I would have to face the watchmen. I knew that they would beat me and abuse me and take away my covering. I knew this because I had studied this song and seen that this is what we must go through to be like Jesus. Jesus had to face the dark night of the soul in the garden of Gethsemane. And He had to face the cross, alone.

The first time the call came to me, it came in a way that I was not expecting. I thought that it would come from the outside. Going through false accusation and slander. Being even chastised from the church, that my authority would be stripped away. (That came later.) First, the Lord began to allow circumstances to arise that offended my mind. I didn't like some of the choices that people were making around me and the effects that those would have on me. When I began to search the Lord about my responses, He began to reveal to me what was really inside my heart. I knew He was asking me to willingly enter this battle. What I expected to come from the outside didn't need to. My worst enemies abide within. My worst enemies are the very things that I have allowed to stay between the Lord and myself.

The Lord in His mercy led me into a time of very deep healing. It was a time to face my past and to come to terms with some of the things that had been done to me and the things I had done to others. Looking at these deep wounds is incredibly painful, and in light of others', mine were relatively minor. But the devil doesn't care how minor the scrape; he will use anything he can to cause infection to fester in our hearts.

Earlier I shared part of a picture I felt the Lord had given me about the condition of my heart. The picture was that of a war-torn city with half-walls which I would hide behind. As I watched the scene unfold in my mind's-eye, I saw myself at various stages of my life and various parts of who I am. The different parts of me would venture occasionally to look out over the walls. As I dared to expose myself, sniper fire would come in upon me and I would duck behind the walls again for protection.

As I began to seek the Lord regarding this picture, the Lord began to reveal to me that those snipers were the watchmen of my soul. They are such things as the vows we make, the things we say and do to protect ourselves, things like, "I'll never allow that to happen again." "I'll never be like that." "I'll never get that close again." "I won't remember the past." And they are the lies of the enemy that we have believed for too many years to count: "You're not good enough." "You'll never measure up." "You'll never change," The walls – of what are they made? Fear, anger, bitterness, unforgiveness, lack of trust, self-reliance; the list could go on and on. These are the things that separate us from God and others.

You see that by facing these fears which so easily entangle us, we realize their true power and we realize God's true power. First, the battle exposes these lies that have been in residence for so long that you didn't even know they were there. As we begin to move in closer to the Lord, the enemies within get scared and they get angry. They know their time is limited, so they pull out every last-ditch effort to keep us from moving into the truth. The battle brings us to the place of knowing that all these things that we have held dear or have allowed to keep us captives now have little power in the face of the call of God on our lives and blood of Jesus covering us.

The battle may hurt us a little; it may take away things we hold dear. It may even kill the flesh in us. But in the end we realize that these watchmen were just a façade of protection, because the only real place of protection is with the Lord, stripped of all our flesh. It is at this point that we declare war on the self-protective mechanism. Loneliness, anger, resentment, fear and rage may be natural responses to rejection and abandonment, as well as just plain being hurt, but they are not from God. Over the years they may even have received the title of "necessary evils," but when we live in God no evil is necessary. These sentiments must be confronted. It is only by the guidance of the Holy Spirit that we can go deep within our hearts and fire the watchmen and dismantle the walls so that we become one – so that we become whole. You see, the watchmen have been there so long that when you begin to stand up to them, they get angry, and they assault you. They try to beat you into submission to them again. But if you stay the course, if you cling to Jesus, if you remind yourself of the truth of God, they will eventually leave. I encourage you, as God leads you to this place, look for another believer around you to help you through it. They can't go through it for you, and they may not even understand, but they can pray.

## External Watchman

The Lord will also use outside forces to test, try and purify our hearts. We can enter this battle either knowingly or unknowingly. He allows people who are hurt and broken to spew accusation and insult on us to reveal what is really in our hearts. Outside pressure reveals a great deal about inside character. And so He allows people, leadership within the body of Christ, even close friends to rise up against us. This should not surprise us, for who were the ones who judged Jesus? The leaders of the temple. And who were the ones who betrayed him? His friends, the disciples.

Although I do not relish this season, I do understand its place. The experience is incredibly painful. The first time I experienced the beating of the external watchman was several years ago. While I was praying one day, the Lord began to speak to me about a storm coming against the leadership of the ministry that I was involved in. He spoke clearly to me that it would be a storm of false accusation. Oh, my mind went to all kinds of places, trying to imagine what the accusation could be and which person it would come against. I shared it with the rest of the leadership team, knowing that God in His mercy was allowing us to be prepared for what was coming. Never once did I imagine that this storm would come against me personally. I knew the Song of Solomon intellectually, and I knew that one day there would be leadership that would rise up against me, for if it happened to Jesus, how could it not happen to me? But I didn't think it was my turn yet.

The Lord allowed the pain and offense in one individual to come boiling to the surface so that it would put pressure on me to expose and deal with issues of my own heart, as well as coming to a deeper confidence, trust and intimacy with the Lord. I was not in a place of disobedience or sin. I was growing and moving with the Lord. Because of that growth, the Lord saw that it was time to prune. And so I went through the wounding; I experienced the beating of false accusation. In a very, very small way I experienced the sufferings of Christ and the dark night of the soul.

I wish that I could say that things like this only happen once in our lives, but the truth is, it will happen over and over again to varying degrees and in varying ways. I wish that I could say that this will never come in the form of physical persecution, but believers are being tortured and killed around the world today for their belief in Jesus. In Western culture, it is only coming in the emotional forms. I wish, too, that I could say that it will only come from those that know you from a distance. But I can tell you from experience that it will come from friends and people you hold dear. Proverbs 27:6 tells us that *"faithful are the wounds of a friend."* Jesus was persecuted by the leaders who knew Him from a distance and betrayed by the kiss of a friend.

The Lord is not satisfied with anything but complete conformity to the person of His Son, and just as He had to learn obedience from the things He suffered, so must we.

## To Die Is Christ

Paul says, *"To die is Christ, to live is gain."*[19] Jesus told us in Matthew 10:28, that we should not fear the one that could hurt our body but worry about the one who can destroy our soul. Joseph was sold into slavery and was falsely accused, which ended in a prison sentence. Daniel was thrown into a pit of hungry lions. Hebrews 11, the great "faith chapter," says,

> *I do not have time to tell about [all the exploits of God's people]. Others were tortured and refused to be released, so that they might gain a better resurrection. Some faced jeers and flogging, while still others were chained and put in prison. They were stoned; they were sawed in two; they were put to death by the sword. They went about in sheepskins and goatskins, destitute, persecuted and mistreated —* **the world was not worthy of them.**[20]

"The world was not worthy of them." What a statement! We want to escape the pain of persecution; we are made to protect ourselves; it is innate within us. But in His wisdom, God knows that the trials of persecution are needed to refine us and to prepare us as the pure, radiant bride. Jesus loves us as we are, but loves us too much to leave us that way. So, the watchmen from within and the watchmen from without – the winter and spring winds – blow and buffet us so that we can be one with Christ. For again, *"If we share in the fellowship of his sufferings we will indeed share in the resurrection power."* And so it is through this experience that what is deep within the heart of the believer is exposed. She becomes one of whom it is written,

*"And they overcame him by the blood of the Lamb, and by the word of their testimony; and they loved not their lives unto the death."*[21]

## Selah

Have you experienced the beating of the watchmen? Did you recognize it as the sifting of the Lord? Have you been angry and resentful of those times? Have you run from God? Running doesn't just mean leaving the church, but it can mean withholding your heart. So I ask again – have you run from God? Have you allowed the watchmen to reveal the true state of your heart?

## Further Reading

*Shattering Your Strongholds* by Liberty Servard

*Don't Waste Your Sorrows* by Paul Billheimer

*Envy: The Enemy Within* by Bob Sorge

*Spiritual Torrents* by Jeanne Guyon

*The Heavenly Man* by Brother Yun

## 12th Movement
# Beauty of the King

*The music whirls with fury around you, and just when you think that the musicians cannot keep the pace of the driving refrains much longer, the sounds begin to ebb and calm. A stunned silence envelops the room. Your mind returns to the vision of the young Maiden, her appearance marred beyond recognition.*

*Once the crowd vented all their fury and hatred on her, the beatings begin to lessen. The taunting finally comes to a stop as well. Some just look at her in disgust; others begin to turn and walk away, shaking their heads. They have seen this before; they know what is coming next – they will leave her there to die. Another "casualty of war," they will call her. The Nobles will justify it as cleansing and part of the battle.*

*"Please." She speaks in barely more than a whisper. Everyone stops. She is still alive; what would the Nobles do?*

*Her eyes search the crowd for any who would understand, for any who would help. "Please. You do not understand. Please.... If you see Him...tell Him...." Strength begins to grow in her as she manages to stand to her feet. The crowd gasps in astonishment. They lean forward to see what she will say. At the first plea they thought she was begging for help, but that was not it. What did she want? "Please, tell Him...I love Him." Her words stun the crowd. They stand in gaping astonishment that one would go through such a beating and still proclaim her love for the very One who had caused this* beating. She begins to limp away. Her movements are slow and her breathing labored, every fiber of her being hurt. Then someone yells from the crowd, half mockingly, "Who is this King you serve, oh so beautiful Maiden? How is He so much better than the one we serve? How do you dare to make such a request of us?"

The voices in the crowd begin to echo the question. "Yea. Who is He?"

The bride turns to look at them. "Do you really want to know?" A look of love spreads across her face. Even the mere thought of Him begins to bring strength back to her being.

"I will tell you of Him. He is glorious. He stands above them all. He is sovereign, He is divine. He is completely dedicated to His Father. He is one of infinite knowledge and wisdom. The nations will fall at His feet. His throne will last forever. He rules with righteousness and justice. He sees things in their reality, not as we see them. He sees things we cannot. Oh, He is lovely beyond description. He is too beautiful for words. I wish that I could convey to you who He is. His voice is the sound of rushing waters, soothing and powerful at the same time. When He speaks, His voice reaches to the very core of your being until you become transformed.

Everything He does has meaning. Everything He does is for a purpose. Everything He does is filled with grace and beauty. He is so lovely to look upon. If you gaze upon Him, you will become like Him; you will become a reflection of His beauty. His ways are glorious and stately. When He moves it is like a spring wind that brings on it a heavenly fragrance.

## The Gospel of Love

*He is joyful and happy. Oh, when He speaks to me, He speaks words too intimate to repeat; they delight me more than words can say. There are not words enough to describe His beauty and His wonder. He is altogether lovely. He is my Lover! He is my Friend." She speaks with great strength and courage. Her heart overflows with love and adoration. Through the blood and the tears, her face is becoming radiant.*

*The crowd looks on at her in stunned amazement. Some even have tears streaming down their faces. Then someone breaks the hush that had fallen. "Where is this Lover of yours?" comes a whisper. "Yes, where has He gone?" asks another. "We can see the beauty in your face as you speak of Him. Even as you have spoken to us of Him your face has changed – there is a glow about you. Can you help us find Him? Can you show us how to know Him the way you do? Your words have pierced our hearts. Is it possible that there is more to Him than we have known before? Is it possible that these feelings deep within aren't wrong? Could this love be for us as well?"*

*The bride listens to the questioning crowd. First she is amazed, but then she remembers the words of the King. "If I am lifted up, I will draw all men unto Me." "Love is truly the banner of the Lord." She thinks. "For when the banner is unfurled for all to see they come and rally around it. It is His call to His people." And she remembers the words she had spoken herself: "You cannot arouse or awaken love until it so desires."*

*"Where can you find the Lover of my soul?" she answers. "Where He always is." And somehow she knows right where He was; the search is over. He is within her. "My Lover is in the garden of delights. He*

## UNQUENCHABLE FIRE

is within each heart tending to the ones who love Him. He can also be found working in the fields. Look for Him with the poor and the broken. Look for Him among the lowly. Look for Him among those who have never heard His name."

"You are beautiful, My darling," comes the voice of the King. The crowd stares in awe. No one has seen Him enter the crowd: no one knows where He had come from or how long He had been there, yet here He is speaking of the beauty of this Maiden for all to hear. "You are more beautiful than the victorious army returning from battle, more lovely than the city of My dwelling," He says as He looks deep within her eyes. His words once again are washing her clean and purifying her. Holding her close, He speaks in not more than a whisper, words that are for her ears only: "Turn your eyes from me, for I am overwhelmed." Tears are freely flowing from both of their eyes now.

Then the King begins to speak words of affirmation to her, loudly enough for the crowd to hear. "You have given yourself to only Me, you have been prepared as the Bride. You have matured and are capable of taking in the depth of My thoughts. Your thoughts are pure and set on Me." And then, holding her at a distance, the King begins to proclaim in a loud voice,"If there were 60 queens, or 80 lovers in My harem, or young women without number in My kingdom, you My darling, My beautiful one, you alone have reached a place within My heart that none of them could. You have surpassed them all!"

- *Selah*

*chapter twelve*
# THE GOSPEL OF LOVE

Song 5:8-6:9

We spoke earlier of how God allows the siftings in our life to show us what is truly in our hearts. It's a test. These are tests that we will all take. The wonderful news about the tests of the Lord is that you can't fail them. You get to keep taking them over and over again until you get them 100% right. The believer has just been publicly humiliated, verbally abused and physically beaten. As the beatings stop and the voices quiet, a plea comes from the heart of the believer. She calls out to those around her, *"If you find my lover...tell him I am faint with love"* (Song 5:8). She is not faint from the beatings; she is faint because she is lovesick. She has passed the test.

When trying situations come our way, we have ultimately two responses – we can run *from* God or we can run *to* Him. The believer has chosen the latter. In the midst of her pain and suffering, her eyes did not deter her from seeking the Lord. Here these angry carnal people have just beaten her to a pulp, yet her response is not one of retaliation or self-pity. She doesn't shake her fist at God and blame Him, either. Rather, her response is one of love for God. She has gotten to the point of being able to say, *"What could you possibly do to separate me from the love I have for Christ? Shall tribulation, or distress, or persecu-*

*tion, or famine, or nakedness, or peril, or sword? For your sake I am killed all the day long"* (Romans 8:35-36 paraphrased). Nothing can kill this love she has. It has just been proven. What more could she go through? She has gone through boredom and burnout, which is where she was when our story started. She has experienced discipline and she has experienced the desert season. Now, finally, she has experienced persecution and the dark night of the soul. Yet the love within her heart has grown, not died. And she proclaims to all, "I am lovesick! I know this is not normal behavior, but I am in love with an extraordinary God."

Now please remember what I talked about at the very beginning of the book. These events are not one-time occurrences in our lives. We won't go through the dark night of the soul only once. We will continue to go through it until there is nothing of self left. God, in His mercy, does not deal with all of our flesh at one time. For if He were to do so, we would be utterly destroyed. The purpose of these times is not destruction, but growth. Pruning will constantly happen in our lives, not because we are immature, but because we are maturing, and God will have a mature bride who is pure and undefiled. He will use the dark night of the soul as many times as needed for us to stay strong and pure.

## Rising Desire

Because of her response of lovesickness, there is a curiosity that has arisen in these spiritually dull people that are hurling insults at her. And even though they continue to treat her with contempt and disdain, they see something different in her.

There is something within each one of us that longs for something to believe in so deeply that we would willingly die for it. The issue that provoked the crowd to ask about God was the bride's deep love for Jesus, not her wisdom or giftedness. They saw Jesus as the One she loved insatiably.

These people are perplexed and amazed by her response of being lovesick. They see her unusual affection for Jesus and conclude she must know something about Him they do not. A.W. Tozer says, "There is a yearning to know Who cannot be known, to comprehend the Incomprehensible, to touch and taste the Unapproachable, arising from the image of God in the nature of man.... The soul senses its origin and longs to return to its source."[1] These people who just beat her couldn't imagine responding to Jesus with such passion. They could only wonder, "What is He more than a good job, a nice home or security? What is He more than the good things we have? We are satisfied and content; we are saved, isn't that enough?" They may well be in the system of grace, but they have not yet known Him intimately. And that is what they saw as different.

And so they ask her, "OK, explain this one to us. You think you know it all. Tell us something we don't know about God, oh most beautiful." I still hear a bit of an attitude in their question when I read verse 5:9. In essence they are still trying to beat her up and belittle her, disguising the rising desire in their hearts. They are asking, "How can you be so devoted to Jesus when He has seemingly treated you so harshly?" This question shows that something is beginning to awaken in these believers. Many believers know Jesus enough to be saved, but His majestic splendor is unknown to them. In essence the daughters are asking her the question that Jesus asked the disciples: "Who do you say that I am?"[2]

## The Beauty of the King

The Lord has revealed Himself to the believer in a unique way. She sees Him in a way few through the centuries have. Like Moses, she is seeing Him face to face. He has revealed Himself to her in this depth because she loves His commandments and is seeking Him with her whole heart. Through the discipline of the Holy Spirit, the maiden now has a larger capacity to behold the glory of God. It is she that no longer lives, but Christ who lives in her.[3]

The believer answers their question with one of the most powerful descriptions of Jesus and one of the most outstanding expressions of worship in the word of God. She has overcome her self-focus and is now consumed with Him and His majesty. She does not answer them with what He has done for her but with a description of who He is.

The Holy Spirit once again uses poetry in verses 5:10 - 5:16 to convey the deeper description of who Jesus is. The believer begins inflaming the hearts of those who just came against her. She uses words like *radiant, outstanding, pure gold,* and *precious gems* to describe His beauty. Even without dissecting the meaning of each word, what we get is a glimpse of a God who is magnificent, beautiful and wonderful, a God who is completely other than.

## Radiant

She starts her description by saying, *"My lover is radiant and*

The Gospel of Love

*ruddy. Outstanding among ten thousand"* (Song 5:10). Oh, I love that. *Radiant* means *emanating rays of heat or light; beaming with kindness or love; the quality of being shiny.* The believer here is starting her description of the Lord as the one that is enthroned on high. She is seeing Him as Isaiah did, as Ezekiel did and as John did.

I wish that I had the space to go through each and every word, but that would be a book in and of itself. For that reason let me paraphrase for you this incredible description the bride gives of the Lover of her soul in verses 5:10 - 5:15.

*"My lover is radiant and ruddy. Outstanding among ten thousand."* (Song 5:10) My lover is dazzling white, His face shines like the sun. His garments are white as light. His countenance flashes with brilliant lightning, and He is my sun and my shield. From the center of the throne, in the midst of the dazzling white light, God's glory emanates red like shining jewels – the brilliance of His passion and blood. My Lover is the Alpha and the Omega, the First and the Last. He is the one who sits on the throne divinely and righteously established. He Was and Is and Is to come. (Song 5:10)

My Lover is the Lord of hosts. He is a banner lifted up; when He is lifted up all men will be drawn unto Him. He is the Champion and the Deliverer. His eyes are flames of fire. He is the Head of the church. He is divine and Holy in His leadership. There is no flaw in Him. His thoughts are consistent with the Father's. (Song 5:10)

He never wavered from what the Father said or did. He was perfect although tempted as a man. A crown with many diadems is on His head – He is crowned Lord of all, Priest in the order of Melchizedek, and Bridegroom. He is the complete fullness of the God-head. He lived His life completely consecrated unto the Lord. He is holy, innocent, undefiled and exalted above the heavens. In humility and self-control He covers Himself so that we can come near the throne of grace with boldness. (Song 5:11)

He is singular in His vision. His eyes are deep pools of living water flowing from the throne of God, giving life, healing and wholeness. He looks towards the righteous, His Bride, forever. (Song 5:12)

My lover is not ashamed or disgraced. He emptied Himself to the point of death. Seeing the passion of the Lord creates desire in me for more of Him. His speech and His words are fragrant and intoxicating. (Song 5:13a)

## Words of Life

Here I must take a moment to do more than just paraphrase the verse. In verse 5:13b she says, *"His lips are like lilies, dripping with myrrh."* Lilies are a huge symbol in the scriptures and worth our looking at more in depth.

The lily motif was used to decorate the temple of Solomon. One of the many places they were used in the temple was the "brazen sea," which was the main receptacle for the ceremonial water in which the priests would wash themselves. It held three thousand baths. The sea was a handbreadth in thickness, and looked like a lily blossom.[4] Ephesians 5:26 says that Jesus sanctifies and cleanses the church "by the washing of the water of the word." The believer is telling us that Jesus' lips are like the sea in the temple that held the water to cleanse the priests. We are all priests before God, and it is His lips that speak forth the cleansing words.

In the believer's description, the lily lips of the Lord are not dripping with water but with myrrh. Remember that I shared earlier that myrrh was an embalming spice and the principal ingredient in holy anointing oil. It had preserving qualities, and it was used in cosmetics because it took away wrinkles and made the skin shiny and smooth. Jesus' lips, His words, anoint us with life and bring about a "radiant church, without stain or wrinkle or any other blemish."[5]

### His Body – The Church

Thus far the maiden has described the Lord as the all-glorious Leader in verses 5:10-13. Each aspect of His character has been related to His position as head through all things, as she described His head, His hair, His eyes, His cheeks and His lips. The remainder of the revelation speaks of His body, which is the Church. It speaks of the many-membered man, the sons of God, who have grown up unto the measure and stature of the fullness of Christ. Jesus cannot be separated from His body, which is the fullness of Him who fills all in all.

This is really amazing to think about. It is the very ones who have just beaten and abused the believer who she begins to describe as beautiful. She is now seeing things from a heavenly perspective, seeing things as they will be, not as they are. She says to them:

> The divine activity of the Lord is purposeful and beautiful. His body (the church – which is you) is pure and clean and lovely to look upon. His will in action, His authority and rule are through the lives of those who trust Him. And He desires to rule now through us in the earth – in the midst of His enemy. Through the fullness of testing, the new creation will be completed and will go forth in resurrection power, bringing eternal, never-ending life. The desire of the Bride is to be the dwelling place of the Most High. They are consumed with burning desire and passion for God alone. With Christ on the throne in their hearts, the believers are like lions – fearless, righteous and holy, strong and mighty. In the latter days, the Lord will have a people that have become so pure from the fire of His abiding presence within that they will all be consumed by zeal for His house. (Song 5:14)

> His walk and administration, the way He fulfills His purposes, are strong, lovely, permanent, established and orderly. They are founded on the divine nature of the Father. His ways are glorious, stately and fragrant. It is the Word of God, His plans, His counsel and His covenant on which the Body of Christ stands. They are sure and steadfast; they are unalterable; they cannot be broken. His overall appearance is the savior clothed in human flesh. He is the last Adam – the first-born of a new generation. For by His flesh, He

overcame the world and the evil one. It is His image that the Bride is destined to bear before all the world. (Song 5:15)

Jesus is the desire of all the nations. In Him all the prophecies of the centuries and the hopes of all creation are contained. The Bride proclaims Him in His entirety. "Here He is!" she says, "Hosanna to the son of David! He is my Lover! He is my Friend!" (Song 5:16)

What more can I say? In just six short sentences, by utilizing poetic verse, the Bride sums up the glory of the Lord. It is by no means exhaustive, for that will take all eternity to discover and recount. But it is exhilarating, and her words cause the hearts of all who hear her to beat faster and long to know God in the way she does.

## Where Is He

Who would not love someone they knew in the way the believer has just described? The very ones who just mocked her and teased her are now asking, "Who is this guy?" Now they long to know what she knows. There is something about watching someone go through a very difficult time in their life and seeing him come out more mature and less self-centered that causes others to stop and wonder, to want to know what he knows. Her description of the Lord has whet their appetite. She has been salt to them and has made them thirsty. So now, instead of teasing, they ask with all sincerity, "Where is He? Oh, will you show us the way? We want to know what you know" Song 6:1.

Suddenly they feel a desire welling up within them. "Who is this that has made you look so? But more importantly – where is He? If He can transform you, we want Him. We want the encounter that you have had; we don't want to just hear about it. For we can see that this encounter has changed you from an angry, war driven person into a passionate lover. We want Him."

The time has come that the believer's life looks different than what the other believers expected. They thought that she would turn and run, that she would lash out, that she would react in a fleshly manner to their beating and abusing, and when she doesn't, they see that there has been a difference in her life. This new look that the believers see is startling to them. Oh, if we could get a hold of this. The cross is not just about what it does to us, but about what it will do for others. Jesus learned obedience by the things He suffered, and we received salvation.

Bob Sorge writes in his book, *Envy: The Enemy Within*, on this very subject. And although he is relating the cross to the specific sin of envy, the words are true regardless of the reason you are crucified.

In his chapter entitled "The Cross: Death to Envy," he explains,

> Jesus' cross was the implement that empowered Jesus' brothers to overcome their envy. Up until His crucifixion, Jesus' four natural half-brothers were simply incapable of rising above their envy and putting their faith in their older brother.... Envy was literally keeping them from eternal life

(John 7:3-8). So God's answer was the cross....

When they beheld Jesus on the cross everything changed for them. The torment of His sufferings, and the dignity with which He bore it made their mark in their hearts. They saw the suffering that surpassed comprehension. How could they gaze upon this crucified form, which didn't even resemble a man because of its gruesomeness (Isa. 52:14), and continue to envy Him? As their envy melted at the foot of the cross, the sprouting seeds of faith were finally given opportunity within their hearts to rise....

The cross was the catalyst that empowered Jesus' brothers to overcome their envy and transition over into faith.... This is still how God deals with envy among the brothers. He crucifies the brother whom He has selected for honor...the crucible that dissipates the brother's envy also promotes the chosen one into spiritual fatherhood.

God protects power with problems. That is, when He grants spiritual power to a vessel, He protects His investment in that vessel by keeping him or her humble and dependent through resistance and hassles.[6]

A wise man said to me as I was going through the midst of a dark night season, "You must be getting ready for a promotion."

You see, as the believer is crucified and as she responds with dignity and love, something changes in the heart of her accusers and brings them to a place of believing. In Revelation 12, when John shares about the saints who did not love their lives as unto death, he states, right before that, in verse 12:10: *"For the accuser of our brethren is cast down, which accused them before our God day and night."* What was one of the causes of the accuser's being cast down? John says, *"They overcame him by the blood of the Lamb, and by the word of their testimony; and they loved not their lives unto the death."* I believe as we embrace the cross we will have onlookers who are watching to see how we deal with it. When we deal with it with lovesick hearts, trusting that God knows what He is doing, it breaks down their walls and causes the accusations to be cast to the foot of the cross, which enables them to receive the revelation of God's love for themselves. It becomes an on-ramp for them into truly knowing God.

In the Song 5:9 the accusers ask, "Who is this man?" And then after watching her response, after hearing the Gospel of truth, they ask with all sincerity, *"Where is He? Which way did He go that we may look for Him with you?"* (Song 6:1) What a startling turn of events! They not only want to know this man Christ Jesus as she does; they want to go on the journey with her.

### To His Garden

It is interesting that this whole episode started as she went about the city searching for the Lord. After her time of abuse she tells them, "If you find Him first...." Now they ask her where He is. And, somehow within her heart, she knows exactly where He is and what He is doing. She knows where to send

## The Gospel of Love

them. Why? How? Because she has walked the road they are now searching for. She asked the Lord this very same question in verse 1:7: "Tell me, You whom I love, where You graze Your flock...."

In verse 6:2 she says, (my paraphrase)

*Where has my Lover gone? I will tell you. He is with those who are cultivating a passionate life for Him and those who are broken and desperate for Him. He is close to those who are close to Him. He has come down onto the earth to be among those who love Him. He is gathering together those who look and smell like Him, those who are fragrant with the presence and desire of the Lord.*

She is giving them the same encouragement the Lord gave her – find those who know the Lord; there you will find Him in their midst.

It's almost as if this answer is as startling for her as it is for them, for she adds, *"I am my Lover's and He is mine!"* (Song 6:3) Something profound has happened in the heart of the believer, and suddenly the light dawns within her, "I know who I am. No longer is there a question about my identity. They took everything of this world away from me, everything that I thought gave me worth. And do you know what I found out? That wasn't who I was at all. It was what I liked to **do**. But who I am is **a lover of God**! And nothing and no one can take that away from me. I know why I am here; I know why I was created and I know who and whose I am."

## The Lord Breaks In

Suddenly, without warning, the voice of the Lord breaks in. The maiden was not searching for the Lord. She had stopped her search in order to proclaim the gospel to her abusers. And in so doing, the Lord suddenly comes to her. As He breaks in upon her he speaks more amazing words of love and affection. *"You are beautiful, my darling, as Tirzah, lovely as Jerusalem, majestic as troops with banners"* (Song 6:4). Here are those words of beauty again. I am sure she didn't look too beautiful at the moment. She was battered and bloody and torn. But in the eyes of Jesus she was exquisite.

He calls her Tirzah, which means *pleasantness; she will delight*. It was a city named for its beauty. He likens her to Jerusalem, the city of peace. It is called the "Holy City," the most important city of the earth, the city that will go on for eternity and that will be built out of the living stones of the Bride of Christ.[7] It was the very site at which redemption was accomplished. Jesus is affirming her place in eternity.

## "I Am Overwhelmed"

As if all these words of affirmation are not enough, the Lord declares, *"Turn your eyes from Me; they overwhelm Me."* (Song 6:5) The father turned his eyes while Jesus was on the cross. Could it be that He turned His head because He could not bear to look at the eyes of His Son? Jesus' eyes were set on the Father, single in vision and purpose with a look, a gaze, that overwhelmed the Father. Needing to see the purpose of redemption fulfilled, the Father had to turn His eyes so that the crucifixion, in its fullness, would be finished.

The Gospel of Love

The crosses we endure cause such love to rise up in the Father's heart that He proclaims, "Turn your eyes from Me, for like Jesus on the cross, even in your abuse, you have not run away from Me. If you do not look away, then I may come for you before the fullness of time, before all is complete in you." Oh, it is an amazing thing that we can overwhelm the very being of the Godhead.

### There Is No One Like You

The Lord finishes His description of the believer with a comparison. He compares her to 60 queens, 80 concubines and virgins without number (Song 6:8). Solomon, who is the human writer of this book and a type of the Lord, was known to be very familiar with women. In 1 Kings 11:3 we are told that he had 700 wives and 300 concubines. Who knows how many virgins were waiting in his harem? But, here Solomon writes, "You stand out above them all." With all these women what would set one apart from the rest? Nothing less than a heart of love and devotion. He could have any woman he desired, and in fact did, but this one stands out above them all (Song 6:9).

In the life of Jesus we can see this played out. *Virgins* in scripture stand for God's people. There were those who went to the wilderness to hear Jesus speak and follow Him. These were the virgins beyond number. But of those multitudes that came to hear Him, only 12 followed Him closely. The disciples were close and intimate; they were known personally by the Lord. These were like the 80 concubines. Then there were those who were His closest friends: John, Peter and James. These three stood on the mountain and saw the transfiguration of the Lord.

They were able to see Him in His glory. These were the three He took closer into the garden with Him the night He was betrayed. These are like the 60 queens. But there was only one who leaned his head on Jesus' breast the night that He was betrayed – John, the disciple whom Jesus loved, His best friend. John is the one disciple whom we are told in the Scripture accounts that actually stood at the foot of the cross and experienced the fellowship of His sufferings first hand. John then was asked to care for Jesus' own mother. John was one who saw it all, the one who endured with Jesus, the one who stood out from the rest. John represents the perfect one.

Being numbered among the 80, 60 or 1 is not about salvation. No, this is about our position before the Lord. There are those who will just be satisfied with knowing Jesus, with receiving heaven as their inheritance, with living at a distance (the 80). Then there are those who will be satisfied with knowing that they live in a different place with the Lord; they have experienced the touch of God on their lives. They know the joy of ministering to the Lord and being in fellowship with Him (the 60). But there are even fewer who will not stop at merely gazing upon the Lord, but will die to everything in order to receive the fullness of God. Like John they will experience the fellowship of His sufferings, and they will also experience the resurrection power. It has been my prayer for some time that I not have a mansion in heaven, or a throne; what I desire is to sit on the lap of God. A bold prayer, but one that states my desire to be as close to God as I can.

One of the amazing things about God is that He does have favorites. But His love is so unfathomable that we can all be

His favorite. What does it take to be called the "one whom Jesus loves"? An unoffended heart that says, "No matter what happens in life, I will love you forever. And I will die for you."

I want to caution you here just in case pride wants to raise up its head. Don't try to look at others and place them among the queens, concubines and virgins. You cannot always see in others where they are. They may have the dove's eyes and the heart that says "yes" but have not had the time to move forward. He knows our deepest desires even more than we. Don't try to look and guess where others are. Concern yourself with your own heart before Him. And if He has laid another on your heart, pray that they would become so lovesick and ravished by the Lord that they would be those who would lay their lives down for Him. For the Lord says, "Many are called, but few are chosen." This position, this place that John had leaning on the breast of the Savior, is available to all. God is no respector of persons, that only a certain race, denomination or social status can attain this place. If we become like little children, and come to Him believing that His word is true, then we too can stand in that place and be called "the one whom Jesus loves!"

## Selah

How have you responded to the dark night? Is your life causing others to stop and listen? How can you give an account of the beauty of the Lord? Do others want to know God the way you do? Are there others you have watched that are causing deeper desire to arise within you? Would you consider yourself one of the virgins without number, the 80 or the 60?

What about being "the one" that stands out above the rest? Do you realize that you are God's favorite?

## Further Reading

*The Knowledge of the Holy* by A.W. Tozer

*Understanding Types and Symbols* by Kevin Conner

*Preparation for the Bride* by Bob and Rose Weiner

*Fairest among Ten Thousand* by Gary Wiens (tape series)

*Envy: The Enemy Within* by Bob Sorge

## 13th Movement
# The Vision Unfolds

*The music is of such beauty now that a silent awe rests over the audience. Never have you heard such melodies. They seem to pierce your very heart.*

*As you listen you can see the Maiden in the arms of the King, with the onlookers standing in amazement, hardly able to believe their ears. The King had called this Maiden "beautiful – special – surpassing all others." As the King speaks to the Maiden loudly enough for all to hear, a sense of conviction begins to spread through the crowd. Those who still have stones drop them as they begin to realize their own sin. Those with insults on their lips are silent as the deceitfulness in their own hearts is unearthed. Though the words are not spoken, many hear a voice within saying, "If you are without sin, throw your stone, speak your insult."*

*Before the eyes of all, the words of the King perform a miracle. The crowd watches as the Maiden goes from beaten and bruised, nearly beyond recognition, to being radiant. She is gloriously beautiful, beyond what they had ever seen before. A ripple begins to spread through the onlookers, "Who is this?" "She looks as if she is glowing," says another in awe. "What majesty, grace and beauty she exudes," adds still another.*

*The King turns again to the Maiden, confirming to her where He had been. He says, "I was in the gardens, as you said. I was checking on those we had spoken to last week. I was looking to see if there were more who were ready to come into the Kingdom of Life. Before I knew what was happening, I found myself among this throng of people. Your words about Me put such desire in their hearts that I was instantly drawn in among them. You have done well today, My love. Go now and rest."* The King points to a carriage outside the pressing crowd.

The Maiden now sees the carriage that the King brought for her. She walks into it, tired but content, knowing that she has experienced the fellowship of His sufferings and the power of resurrection that He had spoken about to her. She knows that she has passed the test.

As she is climbing into the carriage, she hears the crowd calling, "Come back, come back! We want to look upon your beauty." Her heart breaks a little, realizing that they do not yet completely understand — it is not her that they should look upon, but the King.

She hears the King respond, *"Why do you want to look upon her, as if she is the only one who can dance with the armies of heaven? Yes, she is beautiful. But the beauty she possesses can be yours as well. She is prepared with the good news of peace of the Kingdom of Life. She stands with dignity and grace. From her being flows streams of living water and the bread of life. She has matured enough that she can reproduce and nurse the young. Oh, she is stunning, this bride of Mine! Her will is set on Mine, her eyes are only on Me. I have crowned her with wisdom and understanding. She holds Me captivated by her dedication. Oh, men and women, hear Me — this can be you as well."*

## The Dance

*He calls after the Maiden, "Your love is like the best of wine; you have intoxicated Me!" The Maiden smiles with a joy so deep that it is indescribable. She answers back, "May my love flow into Your heart bringing You joy forever." Then she says to herself, "I am His and He loves me. It doesn't get any better than this."*

*Leaning out the window of the carriage she calls, "Come, my Lord, let us be about the business of the Kingdom. I am ready to go where You go, to do what You do. Take me with You; let us go swiftly."*

*The King walks to the carriage and climbs in beside the Maiden, eyes of love blazing with passion. Taking His hand, the Maiden speaks: "I wish You were my brother and I could openly show my affections for You. I want all to know how I feel about You. I would share the truth with them about Your tender love and affection and they would understand. Oh, then I could bring them all to the place of worship and there the wine of love could flow."*

*The King embraces the Maiden, holding her and bringing comfort and peace to any pain that is left. The Maiden lifts her voice again to the crowd, "Oh, sons and daughters of the Kingdom, I charge you, do not travel down this road of love until you cannot bear it any longer, for it is not what you think, but it is worth it all!"*

*The orchestra begins to play the familiar sounds, repeating bars from earlier in the song. You remember the vision of the carriage that the Lord had shown the Maiden earlier. Now it has become a reality. For there she is, sitting in the very carriage of the King, the King sitting beside her, the carriage surrounded with valiant soldiers each carry-*

ing their swords, all prepared for whatever would come, all willing for the day of battle.

The conversations begin to emerge in the crowd as the carriage slowly moves through the city, the onlookers following in parade. "Who is this Maiden? How could she go through all that she just went through? What is it about her that is so different? Who is this one leaning on the King?"

The music turns into a triumphant processional as you envision the carriage of the royal couple moving through the streets of the city, a picture reminiscent of the European royal weddings. A joy unspeakable has risen in your heart as the music sweeps over you.

*Selah*

*chapter thirteen*
# THE DANCE

Song 6:10-8:4

Let me take a moment to recap the events that have just taken place in this believer's life. The Lord knocked on the door, and she answered Him in verse 5:2. But upon going to the door, He was gone. Desperate for His presence, she went back to where she had found Him the first time this happened – to the city, to the watchmen. This time her run-in with the leaders turned violent. They insulted her and removed her from any role she might have filled. They expected to find her bitter and angry, cowering before them; they instead met someone who was so completely lovesick that it didn't matter what they did to her. She declared that the things she was doing were insignificant in the light of knowing Jesus.

With her confession of being lovesick, the Lord suddenly appeared again. The first time this scene was played out in the Song of Solomon, in chapter 3:1-4, the Lord spoke to her privately; however, now He speaks of her virtue for all to hear.

Who Is This?

As Jesus finishes telling the believer how He feels about her in the hearing of her accusers, the ones who have just beaten her begin to see her with the eyes of the Spirit. They proclaim,

"Who are you? You look like Jesus!" She has become the exact representation of Jesus, just as Jesus is the exact representation of the Father. The crowd proclaims, *"Who is this that appears like the dawn, fair as the moon, bright as the sun, majestic as the stars in procession?"* (Song 6:10) Their description of the believer is that of the moon, stars and sun. It is a description of light. Just as Jesus is the exact representation of the Father who is The Unapproachable LIGHT, now this believer is the representation of Jesus, the Light of the World.[1]

The closer we draw to God, the more we will shine for Him on this earth. God uses us to show forth His glory and His love. Like Moses, who had to hide his face behind a veil because of the glory of God that shone from it, people will be able to see the glory brightness on our faces. Jesus told those that followed Him not to put their light under a bushel. In other words – don't cover the light of God that shines out of you into the spiritual darkness.

In 2 Corinthians 4:6-7 we are told, *"For God, who said, 'Let light shine out of the darkness,' made his light to shine in our hearts to give us the light of the knowledge of the glory of God in the face of Christ. But we have this treasure in jars of clay to show that this all-surpassing power is from God not from us."*

The problem is that when the glory is within the jars of clay, it is often concealed. Most of us hide our light, and our enemy will do anything he can to cover the glory of God within us. So God in His love and mercy moves circumstances in our lives to break open the jars of clay and let the light shine before men.

In Judges chapters 6 and 7 we are given a vivid example of how God reveals the light within us, jars of clay. The story is of

## The Dance

the cowardly hero, Gideon. Gideon is fighting the battle for Israel against their enemies, the Midianites. He surrounds their camp in the darkness of night and arms his solders with just two things: a shofar (a ram's horn trumpet) and an empty jar with a torch inside. When Gideon gave the signal, his army of just 300 blew their trumpets and smashed their jars, causing the torches to blaze out. The enemy horde, who were too many to be counted, was so overcome by the light and the sound that they turned and destroyed one another. Israel did not have to raise a sword. The battle was won with the light of God. You see, darkness cannot overcome the light.

Just as Gideon armed his troops with torches of light, the Lord gives us His fiery passionate love within our hearts, but that light must shine out. And how is that light revealed?

In 2 Corinthians 4:8-10 we are told, *"We are pressed in on every side, but not crushed; perplexed, but not in despair; persecuted, but not abandoned; struck down, but not destroyed."*

Just as it was with Gideon's army, the jars of clay must be smashed. It is through experiences like what the believer in the Song has just gone through – she was pressed in on every side, perplexed, persecuted and struck down – that we, jars of clay, are broken and show forth the glory of God within. When that happens all can see it, and like a moth drawn to a flame, so all are drawn to the light that shines from us.

### Why Would You Gaze on Her?

The glory of God that is shining out of this radiant believer is causing the crowd to turn. Where once they had been angry with her and hateful, now they find her beautiful and desirable.

In the Song verse 6:13, the crowd calls out to her, *"Come back, come back! That we may gaze upon you."* Exactly where the bride is going is unclear in the song, but that she is taking her leave is quite evident. They are so drawn to her beauty that they want her with them, so they ask her to come back. Why? Verse 13 tells us – so they can gaze on her.

This is a problem and one of the key reasons that we all must have our jars broken. Our jars are our egos, our self-centered wills that are more interested in our glory than God's. I have heard it said that there are three things that have killed revivals of the past – the gold, the girls and the glory. Those leading the revivals have not been totally broken, so they begin to set their affections on either the money (the gold), the affections of others (the girls), or the admiration of man (the glory), receiving their gaze. If we are not completely broken and dead to our flesh then we will take the glory that belongs to God, not necessarily because we ask for it, but because people will give it to us. People are naturally drawn to light. Because God is invisible it becomes easy to pour out our affections on the visible, on men and women who are showing forth His glory. But when the one who carries the glory is broken, their hearts remain pure; therefore the light remains bright and pure. And the things that man thinks – both good and bad – don't affect them.

## Mahanaim

In response to the request of the crowd the Lord speaks up, asking, *"Why would you gaze on her as on the dance of the Mahaniam?"* (Song 6:13) This is quite an interesting question the Lord is asking.

# The Dance

In order to answer the question we must understand it. It is really a loaded question with many layers. One is, "Why would you set your gaze on any other than Me?" Another is, "Why are you watching this dance in surprise?"

We have covered the first part of this question in the previous section. Let's take a deeper look at the second part. The word *Mahanaim* means *double camp*. The first reference to this is in Genesis 32:2. If you will remember back in chapter 7 when we discussed the maidens first experience with the discipline of the Lord we talked about this chapter in Genesis. This is the story of Jacob's return home and his wrestling with God. Just before Jacob spent the night taking on God head-to-head he first had an amazing angelic encounter. He had just parted company with his father-in-law; as Jacob turned to go his way, lo and behold the angels of God came to meet him. So, we are told, he named the place "Mahanaim – the place of the double camp." Jacob had come to a place where the veil between the seen and the unseen realms was rent. He saw into the reality of eternity and saw the armies of heaven. Like Elisha who prayed for his servant's eyes to be opened to see the armies of heaven that were with them, Jacob saw he was not really alone.[2]

As Jacob encountered the heavenly host he sends his family on ahead of him and prepares to spend the night in prayer. As he does so, a man appears, and the scriptures tell us that *"a man wrestled with [Jacob] till the break of day."*[3]

Coming to the place in his life where Jacob had to face his past, he spends the night wrestling. In order for him to walk in the full inheritance of the promises of God, he had to go back and face the things he was running from. It wasn't until he had come to the border of his own country, sent word that he was on his way and heard that his brother was coming to meet him that he personally met the God of his father. You see Jacob still referred to God as "the God of his father."[4] In the wrestling match that ensues through the night, God becomes real and personal to him. For those watching from a distance it could very well have looked like a dance.

God is amazing in His love and kindness to us. He has told us He will never leave us or forsake us. Yet, sometimes we are unaware of who is standing with us in the unseen realm.

On the night that Jesus was betrayed He went to His favorite place and withdrew from His friends to pray. His prayer was that the cup of betrayal that He was about to partake would be removed; that there would be some other way than the cross. Through His time of prayer Jesus came to the place of laying down His will and picking up fully the will of the Father. Immediately after He did this an amazing thing happened. Luke 22:43 says, *"An angel from heaven appeared to [Jesus] and strengthened Him."* Jesus was dancing the dance of the Mahanaim. Jesus encountered the armies of heaven. To what purpose? They strengthened Him in His dark night of the soul.

Jesus and Jacob were not left alone to go through their dark night, neither was the maiden and neither are we. Yet sometimes we do not have someone like Elisha with us to pray for our eyes to be open that we can see the armies of heaven at our side. Most often this we know only by faith. But this faith is credited to us as righteousness. The believer has learned a new way to walk, she is so lovesick that her walk looks like a dance and the onlookers are staring in amazement and bewilderment.

## The Dance of Heaven

The believer's persecutors have just witnessed her wrestling through the dark night of the soul. And they are also witnessing her resurrection. She is not coming out of this place the same. She is coming out of this beautifully clothed as the bride of the King, leaning on her Beloved. Again, I think that within the question of verse 6:13 lies more. I think that the Lord is asking them, "What do you see in her? Do you want what she has? She has learned to move with the Spirit, to function in the realm of eternity while walking on the earth. It's available to you, too. Do you want it?"

The Lord calls it a dance. The carnal believers are watching this maiden very closely because they recognize that she has something that they do not. But they think it is her in one camp and God in the other. They don't understand that the believer and the Lord are moving as one. So the Lord addresses this. "Why are you looking at the dance that we are doing – the movements of our feet – as if we do not belong together? You need to understand that she takes the very movements she uses from the movements of My feet. We are not dancing separately, but this is the dance of intimate love. We are touching and moving together, and I, the Lord, am leading. And she is a wonderful dance partner. She moves with much grace and beauty; she moves as I move her."

In a sense it is the difference between ballroom dancing and disco dancing. In disco a couple moves on the dance floor, and each does their own thing as they face each other; sometimes they are doing the same moves and are in sync, but they are not dancing as one. In ballroom dancing the couple holds to each other and moves in precise rhythm. The lead dancer gently moves the follower by a slight pressure on her back. The more they dance together the lighter his touch can be. Occasionally the lead will take the hand of his companion and swing her out in a beautiful spiral or pick her up in exhilaration, but the main body of their dance is precision. In fact, the more in sync and precise the couple is in a dance competition, the higher their score will be.

> The Lord of the dance doesn't want us worrying about our feet. He doesn't want us wondering about the steps ahead. He merely wants us to feel the music, fall into His arms and follow His lead.... There are places He wants to take us on the dance floor, things He wants to show us, feelings He want to share with us, words He wants to whisper in our ear. This is what the divine embrace is – an invitation to a more intimate relationship with Christ, one exhilarating, ennobling and uncertain step at a time.... We can dance. Or we can sit it out.8

The bride is dancing and those who have decided to sit this one out are watching in amazement.

## The Dancer

The Lord then speaks to the crowd of onlookers a description of the beauty of the maiden (Song 7:1-9). The Lord knows what it is we need to hear and when. And this time the description is not just for the believer's ears, but He says it to all who will hear, vindicating her before her accusers. In these next verses, the Lord begins to explain in detail what the onlookers are seeing. It's as if He says, "Alright! You are watching her very closely because she is moving outside your realm of understanding, so let me explain what it is you are gazing upon."

It is interesting because the first descriptions the Lord gives of her, in the beginning of the Song, concentrate on her face (Song 1:9-10). The face is the part of you that all see. With each description he adds more and more of her body (Song 4:1-5). The Lord starts out speaking about her at "face value," and then as she grows in maturity He tells her that her whole being is becoming like Him, that there is more to her than meets the eye.

The description here in verse 7:1-9 is similar to the one He gave to her privately in 6:4-10. But this time He adds a few things that He has never commented on before. He adds her feet and her legs. Feet are the symbols of proclaiming the gospel.[9] *"How beautiful on the mountains are the feet of those who bring good news, who proclaim peace, who bring good tidings, who proclaim salvation, who say to Zion, 'Your God reigns!'* "[10] As we set our feet on the paths of God we are given the promises of God, and we conquer our Promised Land.[11]

The Lord goes on to describe her legs. The legs are the things that support us, that upon which we make our stand. He says, *"Her legs are like jewels."* In essence she is making her stand on the clear and beautiful reflection of the light of the Father. Her goal is not to cause division or draw attention to herself, but like Jesus, to do as the Father is doing, to take her movements from His. She moves her feet and legs in the rhythm of the Father and goes to the nations with the peace of God. But remember, she walks with a limp, so sometimes her movements may not look very graceful.

He speaks of her entire countenance in verse 7:7, saying, *"Your stature is like that of the palm tree."* I know these are weird analogies to us, but there is meaning to them. Psalm 92:12-14 says, *"The [uncompromisingly] righteous shall flourish like the palm tree [be long-lived, stately, upright, useful, and fruitful]; he shall grow like a cedar in Lebanon [majestic, stable, durable, and incorruptible]. Planted in the house of the Lord, they shall flourish in the courts of our God."*[12] This is how the Lord summarizes the beauty of this lovesick worshiper. She is righteous and flourishing in the house of God.

### The Dance of Love

As the Lord finishes the description of the bride, He declares that her mouth and her words are like the best wine. If you will remember, in the very beginning of the Song the believer says to the Lord, *"I will extol your love more than wine"* (verse 1:4). In other words, "I proclaim that your love is better than any pleasure here on earth." And what does the Lord say of this radiant believer in this last description? He uses the same language that she used saying, *"Your mouth is like the best wine"* (Song 7:9). Or, in other words, "Your lips speak of heaven, where there are pleasures evermore." Wow, the very words that the maiden spoke to the Lord He now speaks back to her!

The believer then comes back into the duet with words of love for the King. Here we see a picture of the divine dance –

the movements of love flowing back and forth between the beloved and the Lord. She takes the movements of her feet from His, speaking words of love into the heart of the King. Back and forth they go, relishing the intoxication of love.

## The Song of the Lord

Zephaniah 3:17 says, *"The Lord will take great delight in you, He will quiet you with His love, He will rejoice over you with singing."* The Scriptures are full of wonderful descriptions of how God sees us and what He feels about us. These verses in the song encapsulate in poetry the vast expressions of the Lord that are found throughout scripture. As we close this chapter, I would like you to hear some of the words of the song that the Lord sings over you. As you read these words, feel the rhythm of the music and allow your heart to move in the dance. For, it is not just some mythical character that the Lord speaks to of her beauty, **but to you, the favorite one of God**.

## You Are the Lord's Splendor

*You, who with an unveiled face reflect the Lord's glory, are being transformed into His likeness with ever-increasing glory, which comes from the Lord, who is the Spirit.*[13] *For you also, like a living stone, are being built into a spiritual temple.*[14] *And you will be the dwelling place of God, coming down out of heaven, prepared as a bride beautifully dressed for her husband.*[15] *You will be His, and God Himself will be with you and be your God.*

*The Lord will build you with stones of turquoise, your foundations with sapphires. He will make your battlements of rubies, your gates of sparkling jewels, and all your walls of precious stones.*[17]

*The nations will see your righteousness, and all kings your glory; you will be called by a new name that the mouth of the Lord will bestow. You will be called "married and My delight."*[18] *You shine with the glory of God, and your brilliance will be like that of a very precious jewel,*[19] *for He has clothed you with garments of salvation and arrayed you in a robe of righteousness, as a bridegroom adorns his head like a priest, and as a bride adorns herself with her jewels.*[20] *He will bestow on you a crown of beauty, a bridal headdress, instead of ashes, [shame and filth].*[21] *The LORD Almighty Himself will be your glorious crown, a beautiful wreath for you, oh, bride.*[22]

*A wife of noble character who can find? She is worth far more than rubies. Her husband has full confidence in her and lacks nothing of value.*[23] *A wife of noble character is her husband's crown.*[24] *You are a crown of splendor in the Lord's hand, a royal diadem in the hand of your God.*[25]

*As a bridegroom rejoices over his bride, so I, the Lord, rejoice over you.*[26] *Come out [all the nations], and look at the King of Peace wearing the crown, the crown with which his mother crowned Him on the day of His wedding, the day His heart rejoiced.*[27]

*Let us rejoice and be glad and give Him glory! For the wedding of the Lamb has come, you, oh bride, are being made ready. You, My beloved, are radiant.*[28]

## Selah

Read again the words the Lord has spoken over you. Journal about them. Do you believe them? How does it make you feel? Read them again and again and let them saturate your soul. Write about them.

## Further Reading

*Bridal Intercession* by Gary Wiens

*Dangerous Duty of Delight* by John Piper

*Pleasures Evermore* by Sam Storms

*Pleasure of Loving God* by Mike Bickle

## Finale
# Blazing Love

*The music takes a turn once more. Still containing an air of triumph, it takes on a more romantic tone. The music brings visions of the Maiden and the King alone, holding each other within the confines of the carriage. Here you can see the King and the bride in intimate conversation.*

"Do you remember the time we met, in the forest?" asks the Maiden.

"How could I forget?" says the King with much joy. "It was there that our hearts began to beat as one." Looking at her intensely He adds, "Oh My bride, place My love as a seal over your heart and over your strength. For My love is a jealous love, an all-consuming love. It is unyielding, even as death itself is unyielding. My love blazes as a fire that cannot be put out. Nothing in heaven or on earth can ever quench My love. Nothing can even begin to put out this ardent love. You see, I gave all I had for you. I gave all I had for them. I became as nothing, setting aside My kingdom and My power to win the heart of My beloved. And though others may think it extravagant or a waste, I count it as nothing. For your love was worth it all." As the carriage moves slowly through the city streets, a young man approaches the window. "My Lord, may I ask You a question?" he says. Continuing with a nod from the King, "I have a younger sister. How do I prepare her for meeting You?"

"I know your sister," answers the bride, "I was once as she is. Help her to grow in her times alone with the King, then she will be one who can bring contentment to His heart. For He longs for a friend with whom He can share His heart and share in His work. It is in those secret times that their relationship and understanding will grow." She smiles at the King as He nods His approval of her answer.

"You see, our lives are like vineyards," she continues. "We can ask other people to tend them for us, but then they reap the harvest. It is not until we tend our own hearts that we can then reap the harvest of love and give it to the one we love. And now that my vineyard, my heart, is mine for me to give freely to the Lover of my soul, no amount of money, no nothing could get me to give it to another again."

"Oh, people, hear what the bride is saying," proclaims the King. "Take ownership of your hearts; don't give them to any but Me. For it is in the depth of your heart that I long for intimacy. Let Me hear you in our secret place, for it is sweetness to Me." The King looks with love into the eyes of the Maiden.

"Oh my King, you had promised to take me to the mountains," says the Maiden. "Is it time? I am ready to go. Come, my Lord, be who you are. Leap over the mountains; show yourself triumphant again."

With that the King gives the order and the carriage begins to move swiftly toward the beautiful mountains that surround the city. Now the adventure truly begins! The music takes its final turn, repeating the sounds that first assaulted you. Now the sounds don't startle; now they bring much comfort and you can hear what the author heard, and you begin to understand the song of creation, the beginning of love's awakening.

## Unquenchable Fire

*Listen to your heart –*
*You can hear the song*
*You can see the dance*
*You can hear your heart rising and falling*
*to the melody of love*

*Listen to the song of creation*
*A symphony of never-ending praise*
*Patiently waiting My redemption*
*Longing for the Desire of the Days*

*Can you not see?*
*Do you not understand?*
*The wind is My breath*
*The song is My hand*

*Let the music touch you*
*Let it reach your inner core*
*For there is none like Me*
*From now and evermore*

*My love is unending*
*sealing your heart*
*stronger than the death, eternally yours*
*It blazes, it burns, this unquenchable flame*
*Ravished love*
*never to be tamed*

*Selah*

*chapter fourteen*
# UNQUENCHABLE FIRE

Song 8:5-8:14

As the believer and the Lord enter into their dance, the onlookers begin to see the vision the believer was given in verse 3:6 coming to pass. If you will remember, it was at that time that the believer and the Lord were in a time of intimacy. The Lord let down a curtain before her and revealed to her a prophetic vision of the journey through the desert. As the vision began, the maiden asked, *"Who is this coming up from the desert?"* Now it is no longer a vision, but a reality. She has gone through the dark night of the soul; she has gone through the terrors of the night and journeyed through the dry and arid regions. And now others can see the outcome. As they look at her they begin to ask the same question, *"Who is this coming up from the desert..."* but they add, *"leaning on her Beloved?"* (Song 8:5) Her transformation has been so profound and her life so ruined by God[1] that she could do nothing but lean on her Beloved. He has become her only support. She has been so conformed to His image that the two are indistinguishable from each other.

## The Setting of the Lord

The two voices sing again in unison, *"Place me like a seal over your heart and like a seal over your arm"* (Song 8:6a). Seals and signets were made of metal or stone and often exquisitely engraved. They were worn on the hand as a ring, higher up on the arm as an amulet, or on a cord around the neck, resting on the chest. A seal served as a form of identification and was numbered among the person's most treasured possessions. Of deep symbolic significance, a seal stood for the owner's identity, honor and fate. A seal on the heart and arm implies belonging, physical closeness and intimacy.[2]

The Lord and the believer are requesting that intimacy be the thing that identifies them. It will be this very thing that will distinguish them from others. Jesus said others will know that we are His followers because of our love.[3] If that love is placed either on our arm representing our strength, or over our hearts, representing our affections, it is in a place that all can see and recognize. As others look upon our lives they will know whom we belong to because of our love.

As in other places of the Song, as the two voices sing out their duet, the same words are being spoken with two slightly different meanings. The meaning of these words is multi-dimensional; as the Lord sings He encapsulates the purpose and process for all that He has done in the believer's life. As stated above, seals are made of metal and stone and often intricately carved. We can see that the process that is used to prepare the amulet, one of mining, refining and carving, is the same process used to prepare us. As we come into relationship with Jesus He begins our beautification program. He does what needs to be done within our souls so that our hearts will have the capacity to feel all that He feels and love as He loves.

It's like a craftsman cutting a jewel so that it will shine its most brilliant. Jesus holds us in His hand and causes us to become sparkling, precious, rare jewels. This is one of the great mysteries of God. The Lord takes a handful of dust, fashions it into man and breathes His very breath into us. He creates us to be His image – His reflection. He declares, *"You will be a crown of splendor in the Lord's hand, a royal diadem in the hand of your God."*[4] We become as radiant as He is radiant. Spiritually this means maturing in God. The Lord explains that as we yield to this process, He sets us like a jeweler sets a stone, and then places us on His body for all to see, adorning the very God of the universe. We actually become a beautiful ornament for the Lord. Like beautiful jewels that show forth the glory of an earthly king, we show forth the glory of the King of kings.

Not only do these words portray how we beautify the King of kings but also what the seals and signets mean to us. Signet rings and seals were given by the kings to those he placed in authority to act in his stead. Here the Lord commands that love, His signature, be placed for all to see. In giving us His love, He is giving us His authority to move as His representatives on the earth. Jesus said, *"All authority in heaven and on earth has been given to Me. Go therefore*[5] *and heal the sick, raise the dead, cast out demons in My name.*[6] *Proclaim the kingdom of heaven is here."*[7] We can see that the disciples knew that they walked in His authority that was placed on them by fire on the Day of Pentecost, and the miraculous happened wherever they went. We too, if we have God's love, have His authority to act on His behalf bringing the Kingdom of Heaven to earth.

## A Royal Diadem

A diadem is a royal headpiece, a crown, that is set with gold and stones. Figuratively it speaks of power. Often the kings of the earth adorn their crowns with diamonds. To me, diamonds are one of the best examples of what the Lord does with us. Diamonds are one of our most precious stones, partly because they are rare. To us they are used to symbolize marriage as well as wealth and beauty. The name comes from the Greek word *adamas*, meaning *unconquerable*. Diamonds are made of carbon and are formed when the carbon is subjected to great heat and pressure. They are known for their fiery brilliance and are measured in quality by their color, clarity, cut and weight. They range in color from clear to yellow, brown, pink, green, and even red. And diamonds have a great ability to reflect light and break it into all the colors of the rainbow.

We, as humans, are carbon-based creatures. Like the diamond, the Lord allows great pressure to come into our lives, resulting in a beautiful countenance that reflects the fiery brilliance of God to the world around us. As we go through the formation process we become "unconquerable" to the enemy. And to God we become so beautiful that we can adorn His very person.

It is with this in mind that the Lord says, "I will set your love on My being for all to see, for you reflect My beauty" (Song 8:6 paraphrased). So the King of the universe takes us and places us, a royal diamond, in three places for the entire world to see.

First, as the King, He takes the jewels that He has made us to be and puts us in His crown, and we become part of the Royal Diadem.[8] We radiate from His head as His crown.[9] He gives us His glory, and we reflect Him and shine as a rainbow around Him.[10]

Second, as the great High Priest, He places us – precious jewels – into the breastpiece and carries us before the Throne of Grace. He places us like a seal over His heart (Song 8:6), and we show forth His love as we radiate from the very seat of His emotions.

Last, as Bridegroom and lover of our souls, He takes us – living rare gems – and fashions us into the Holy of Holies – the very throne room of the God Most High, and He comes into the midst of us.[11]

In Revelation 21:10–11, John describes how he is taken away to a high mountain and shown the bride of Christ. He describes the bride as a city called the New Jerusalem. *"Having the glory of God; her light was like unto a stone most precious, clear as crystal."*

In Jeremiah 31:22, the Lord is speaking to Israel and says, *"The Lord will create a new thing on the earth – a woman shall encompass a man."* The word for new thing can be translated simply as *fresh*. The word for *encompass* means *to turn about, go around, surround*. I believe that this can be translated, *"The Lord will create a fresh earth, and the bride shall envelop the God man, Jesus."* It is a description of what John saw in the heavenly Jerusalem. This is what happens as we become the bride and the Lord takes up residence within us. As we become His dwelling place, surrounding the throne of the Most High, His love blazes out through us; we act as a prism around Him, breaking down His pure white light into the colors of the rainbow. The Father told Noah that when he saw the rainbow in the sky it was to be a reminder of the eternal promises of God.

We become the very rainbow that encircles the throne – we become the radiance of His love, His beauty and His very being. We become a reminder of the promises of God. I believe that when John, in Revelation 4, and Isaiah, in Isaiah 6, saw the rainbow that encircled the throne, they saw the perfected bride surrounding her Bridegroom with eternal love.

## Power to Love

The believer has had a full revelation of the love of God. With the voice of the Lord, they proclaim together that *"love is a blazing fire, a mighty flame"* (Song 8:6). The word for flame here in Hebrew contains the name of God at the end. Although there is debate as to whether or not this actually is a reference to God, it seems to me very appropriate to think it is, since it is in keeping with the descriptions of God as light, as one of flaming brilliance, whose very eyes are described as *"flames of fire."*[12] Fire throughout Scripture is a description of God Himself. He appears to Moses in the form of fire on a bush.[13] He guides the Israelites through the wilderness as a pillar of fire,[14] and we are told in Deuteronomy 4:24, *"The Lord thy God [is] a **consuming fire**, [even] a jealous God."*

The believer is told to place the Lord over her heart, the seat of her affections, and over her arm, which represents her strength. But in and of ourselves we do not have the strength to love God. Paul, in his prayer for the Ephesians, writes, *"I pray that out of His glorious riches He may strengthen you with **power through His Spirit** in your inner being, so that Christ may dwell in your hearts through faith."*[15]  In other words, it takes God to love God. God's love is not like anything that we have ever known before, and in order to grasp it we must have the power of God manifest in our lives.

John the Baptist, the one who proclaimed himself the friend of the Bridegroom, declares, *"I baptize you with water for repentance. But after me will come one who is more powerful than I, whose sandals I am not fit to carry. He will baptize you with the Holy Spirit and with **fire**."*[16]

And like the prayer for the Ephesians, Jesus tells the disciples after His resurrection that there is a power that is still needed in them. These men were with Jesus for three years. They spent 40 days in His manifest presences after His resurrection, yet He tells them something more is needed, something more is coming. He says,

*"You will receive power when the Holy Spirit comes on you"*.[17]
A few days later that promise was fulfilled, *"When the day of Pentecost came, they were all together in one place. Suddenly a sound like the blowing of a violent wind came from heaven and filled the whole house where they were sitting. They saw what seemed to be **tongues of fire** that separated and came to rest on each of them. All of them were filled with the Holy Spirit and began to speak in other tongues as the Spirit enabled them.*[18]

On the day of Pentecost a new baptism that was two-fold, the Spirit and Fire, came upon them.

Fire and heat are words we use today to describe passion and love. God describes His own love as a burning, consuming flame. We have to realize that God is not a cold, unfeeling entity sitting in the heavens laughing as we struggle through life.

He is a passionate God who purposely has gotten involved with our lives so that we may know His abundant love on this side of heaven.

Passion is defined as *a powerful emotion, ardent adoring love.* Ardent means *glowing, flashing, hot as fire, burning.* I believe it was this ardent, passionate love that fell on the 120 in the upper room, enabling them to set aside their fears and go out of the locked doors and win 3,000 to the Lord in one day. For our *"God is a consuming fire,"*[19] and when He comes and falls on us He burns away impurities and enables us to burn for all to see. And this love is so all-consuming, so fiery hot, that nothings can extinguish its flame.

As the bride sings these words she is proclaiming that as she is placing the Lord on her heart and on her arm. She is declaring that she is clothing herself with Christ.[20] She is, in essence, putting on her armor.[21] In verse 4:8, the Lord had invited her to the mountains. She has now followed Him there and has experienced a transfiguration. As she has conquered the mountains in her life with the Spirit of the Lord; she has received her reward. She knows the truth of being seated with Christ in heavenly places and the enemy being made a footstool. She has been knighted with confirmed truth (Mt. Amana), given a coat of mail for protection under her armor (Mt. Senir) and has learned to use the divine weapons capable of pulling down strongholds (Mt. Hermon).

Here in verse 8:6, she is told to put on her armor, which is God's love. The rest of the Song verse 8:6 tells us, *"Love is as strong as death."* Love is stronger and more sure than anything. This is the key to the battles that lie ahead. *"Now these things remain: faith, hope and love. But the greatest of these is love."*[22] Nothing can conquer true love and devotion.

## Unquenchable Love

The voices, in unison, go on to describe this love. They sing, *"Many waters cannot quench love; rivers cannot wash it away. If one were to give all the wealth of his house for love, it would be utterly scorned"* (Song 8:7).

Paul said it this way in Romans 8:

> *Who shall separate us from the love of Christ? [Shall] tribulation, or distress, or persecution, or famine, or nakedness, or peril, or sword? For I am persuaded that neither death, nor life, nor angels, nor principalities, nor powers, nor things present, nor things to come, nor height, nor depth, nor any other creature, shall be able to separate us from the love of God, which is in Christ Jesus our Lord.*[23]

**Nothing**, absolutely nothing, can quench the fire of love once it is ignited.

Jesus felt the same way about us, the lover of His soul. *"[Jesus] stripped Himself of all privileges and rightful dignity so as to assume the place of a servant. And after He appeared in human form, He abased and humbled Himself still further and carried His obedience to the extreme of death, even death on the cross."*[24]

Jesus gave it all away. He humbled Himself, becoming a man, becoming our sin, bearing the scorn of the Father so that we could be one with Him. *"For the joy set before Him He endured the cross, scorning its shame."*[25] The word scorning here is the same concept of Song of Solomon 8:7. The word means *to disdain the cross or to look down on it, to consider it to be unworthy of notice.* Jesus had His eyes so set on the prize before Him that the cross was "unworthy of His notice." The prize set before Him was well worth the cost.

What was the prize that was set before Him? **YOU!** It was so that the ones He so passionately loves could come boldly and freely before His throne again. It was the knowledge that the veils of separation would be rent, and we could once again be united with God. The God of the universe considered nothing too high a price, not even brutal death. **You were worth it all!**

This is so hard for us to understand. Soren Kierkegaard, a Danish author from the mid-1800's, gives this wonderful description of what God did to win us in his writings titled *Disappointment with God*:

> Suppose there was a king who loved a humble maiden. The king was like no other king. Every statesman trembled before his power. No one dared breathe a word against him, for he had the strength to crush all opponents. And yet this mighty king was melted by love for a humble maiden. How could he declare his love for her? In an odd sort of way, his kingliness tied his hands. If he brought her to the palace and crowned her head with jewels and clothed her body with royal robes, she would surely not resist – no one dared to resist him, but would she love him?
>
> She would say she loved him, of course, but would she

truly? Or would she live with him in fear, nursing a private grief for the life she had left behind? Would she be happy at his side? How could he know? If he rode to her forest cottage in his royal carriage, with an armed escort waving bright banners, that too would overwhelm her. He did not want a cringing subject. He wanted a lover, an equal. He wanted her to forget that he was a king and she a humble maiden and to let shared love cross the gulf between them. For it is only in love that the unequal can be made equal.[26]

The king clothes himself as a beggar and renounces his throne in order to win the maiden's hand. This is what Jesus did for us. And He counted it as nothing.

### The Spirit and the Bride Say Come

The spirit calls out, *"You who dwell in the gardens with friends in attendance let me hear your voice!" (Song 8:13)* And the voices rise in answer, *"Come away, my lover!" (Song 8:14)* This beautiful song ends with the words that end the very Word of God. *"The Spirit and the bride say, 'Come!' Let him who hears say, 'Come!' Whoever is thirsty, let him come; and whoever wishes, let him take the free gift of the water of life.... Amen. Come Lord Jesus."*[27] The echo of the cry of love carries throughout eternity, beckoning the coming of the Lord.

*Oh Papa, my prayer is for all that read this book. I pray that their hearts will be stirred and convinced that there is more of You than we have ever dreamt possible – that even if we are walking in resurrection power and the fullness of your Spirit now, for all eternity we will get to learn more about You. Oh, what a profound mystery awaits us*

## UNQUENCHABLE FIRE

*to uncover. You are our Eternal Bridegroom. Capture our hearts. Ravish us with Your beauty today. And may we never be the same again.* Come, Lord Jesus, come!

Unquenchable Fire
My love is a consuming fire
Take my hand and let us walk together
into the flame of love
flames of fire
flames of fire
aflame with fire

Unquenchable flame burning within
the heart of the Savior
come take me again

Unquenchable flame
shining out your eyes
look upon me now
make me a living sacrifice
The spirit of burning is who You are
unyielding and jealous for your bride
strip me of all that is human and flesh
clothe me in You
the Splendor of Holiness

Unquenchable fire burning within
consume me, consume me, take me again
Unquenchable flame

my heart's one desire
consume me, consume me
set me on fire

Consume me, consume me
set me on fire
let the sparks from the flame lift us even higher
consume, consume,
in the flame of love
flames of fire
aflame with love

Selah

    Are there those that you can look on whom you would say, "They are indistinguishable from the Lord?" What do you think makes them so much like Him? Do you recognize the process that must take place for you to become like Jesus, to be conformed to His image? Are you able to yield to the process of the jeweler's chisel so that you can be the Glory of God?

    What do you think about the concept of you being the glory of God and representing His promises on the earth? Or what about the fact that you beautify the living God? How much of the power of God do you have? Could the lack of love be because you lack power, true power, to grasp the Love of God? Can you be courageous enough to pray that the power of God would come ignite you and making you a walking flame of Holy Fire? Imagine for a moment what your life would look like if you had the power to grasp the full passion of Jesus for you.

## Further Reading

*Fire Within* by Thomas Dubay

*Destined For the Throne* by Paul Billheimer

*The Sacred Romance* by Brent Curtis & John Eldredge

## Postlude
# A High and Lofty Wall

*I once sat on a high and lofty wall*
*I was only a child then and the sky was the limit.*
*I had no fear - I ran - I skipped - I jumped*
*on that high and lofty wall.*

*One day as I played, a stranger came along.*
*Friend or foe, I did not know, for he was so far below.*
*A watchman, near as I could tell.*

*He spoke,*
*a voice so soothing - so strong - so sure of himself*

*"Friend," he said,*
*"the wall is too high - take care lest you fall."*
*Suddenly I felt fear.*

*"Friend," he said,*
*"you cannot truly reach the sky - who do you think you are?"*
*Suddenly I felt doubt.*

*"Friend," he said,*
*"you should have known better- have you no common sense?"*
*Suddenly I felt shame.*

## UNQUENCHABLE FIRE

"Friend," he said,
"you are really quite homely - do you think any could
love you?"
Suddenly I felt loathsome and alone.

He told me many other things - that watchman of the wall,
of things that I had done so wrong,
that dreams were a waste of time.
Suddenly I lost hope.

His words were different than that of the King,
but he spoke as one who knew.
So I looked down from that high and lofty place.
And all that I feared came on me.

I fell to the ground below.
There I lay at the strangers feet
broken, shamed and dirty.
Cracked and unable to move.

The watchman laughed - he mocked and jeered.
He told me that "all the king's horses and all the king's men
can't put you back together again."
I felt something die within.
Then suddenly - I heard a rush of footsteps -
and the stranger fled away.

There at the foot of the high and lofty wall
came the lover of my soul.

## Postlude

"My Love," He said.
"why did you listen to him? Have no fear."
Fear gave way to peace.

"My Love," He said, "your sins are forgiven."
Shame gave way to love.

"My Love," He said,
"stay close to me and you will see
I have made the skies the limit. Dare to dream."
Hope sprang up within me.

"My love," He said,
"you are the apple of my eye - there is no flaw in you."
Suddenly - I felt beautiful!

My love whispered sacred secrets - things only for me
to hear,
and my heart was filled with joy!
Suddenly we were together
arm in arm
running - skipping - laughing - dancing
on that High and Lofty wall.

# End Notes

**Chapter one**

[1] Don Campbell, *The Mozart Effect*, Avon Books, 1997, p 2
[2] Sam Storms, *The Singing God*, Creations House, 1998, p 22
[3] John 1:1, *New International Version*, Zondervan
[4] Genesis 1:2, *New International Version*, Zondervan
[5] C.S. Lewis, *The Magician's Nephew*, Collier Books, 1952, p 98
[6] Isaiah 55:12, *New International Version*, Zondervan
[7] See Zephaniah 3:17
[8] Ken Gire, *The Divine Embrace*, Tyndale House Publishers Inc, 2003, p 81
[9] Deuteronomy 6:5, *New International Version*, Zondervan
[10] Bob and Rose Wiener, *Bible Studies for the Preparation for the Bride*, Maranatha Publications, 1980, p 1
[11] Brennan Manning, *Ruthless Trust*, Harper San Francisco, 2000, p 69
[12] Storms, *The Singing God*, Creation House, 1998, p 22
[13] See John 15
[14] Ephesians 3:17-19, *New International Version*, Zondervan

**Chapter two**

[1] Ken Gire, *The Divine Embrace*, p 81
[2] Mark 12:28, paraphrased
[3] James 4:8, *New American Standard Version*, Zondervan
[4] Acts 2:13, *New International Version*, Zondervan
[5] See Acts 2:3
[6] Ephesians 5:18, *New International Version*, Zondervan

[7] Don Nori, *His Manifest Presence*, Destiny Image Publishers, 1992
[8] Bob and Rose Weiner, *Bible Studies for the Preparation of the Bride*, Maranatha Publications, 1980, p 9

## Chapter three

[1] Luke 10:38-42, *New International Version*, Zondervan
[2] Psalm 27:4, *New International Version*, Zondervan
[3] Webster's 1828 Dictionary, www.cbtministries.org/resources/webster1828.htm
[4] Hebrews 4:14, *New International Version*, Zondervan
[5] *New International Version, New American Standard Bible, Amplified*
[6] *New King James Version, King James Version, Amplified*
[7] See Genesis 6: 1-16
[8] Isaiah 1:18, *New International Version*, Zondervan
[9] See 2 Chronicles 3:14
[10] See Revelation 19: 9
[11] See Isaiah 6
[12] 2 Corinthians 12:10, *New International Version*, Zondervan
[13] 1 John 1:5-10, *New International Version*, Zondervan
[14] 2 Corinthians 12:9-10, *New International Version*, Zondervan
[15] Philip Keller, *A Shepherd's Look at Psalm 23*, World Wide Publications, 1970, p 35
[16] Matthew 11:28, *New International Version*, Zondervan
[17] See Matthew 18:12
[18] See Isaiah 53:6
[19] See Esther 4:16
[20] See 2 Corinthians 4:7
[21] See Luke 17:21

# Endnotes

[22]*Amplified, New International Version*
[23]*New King James Version*
[24]*New American Standard Version*
[25]See Psalm 27:3
[26]See 2 Samuel 4:3-12
[27]Matthew 27:46, Mark 15:34, *New King James Version*, 1982, Thomas Nelson
[28]Numbers 13:33, paraphrased
[29]Numbers 13:30, paraphrased
[30]Exodus 33:11, *New International Version*, Zondervan
[31]John 4:34, *New International Version*, Zondervan

## Chapter four

[1] 1 Kings 4:22-23, New International Version, Zonervan Publishers
[2]See Ephesians 2:6
[3]Romans 14:17, New International Version, Zonervan Publishers
[4]John 6:43-59, New International Version, Zonervan Publishers
[5]See Ephesians 5:27
[6]See Genesis 3:8
[7]Exodus 19:16, New International Version, Zonervan Publishers
[8]Exodus 20:19, New International Version, Zonervan Publishers
[9]Exodus 20:20, New International Version, Zonervan Publishers
[10]1 Peter 2:9-10, New International Version, Zonervan Publishers
[11] John 15:15, New International Version, Zonervan Publishers
[12]Ryken, Wilhoit and Longman, Dictionary of Biblical Imagery, InterVarsity Press, 1998, p 309
[13]C.S. Lewis, The Lion, the Witch and the Wardrobe, Collier Books, 1952
[14] John 1:29, New International Version, Zonervan Publishers

UNQUENCHABLE FIRE

[15] See Exodus 12
[16] See John 19
[17] Acts 2:31, New International Version, Zonervan Publishers
[18] See 1 Corinthians 15:20 and John 12:24
[19] Brotman, Manny, The Fulfillment and Challenge of Passover, Messianic Jewish Movement International News Letter, March 1999
[20] See Deuteronomy16: 2
[21] See Matthew13, Mark 8, and Luke 12
[22] John. 2:13-16, New International Version, Zonervan Publishers
[23] See John 19:1; Isaiah 53:5; Psalm 22:6-7,17
[24] See Mathew 27:35
[25] See John 20:27
[26] See Psalm 22:14,16; John 19:19
[27] See John19:33; Mathew.27:35; Psalm. 22:18)
[28] John 19:30, New International Version, Zonervan Publishers
[29] Vander Laan, Ray, Why The Cross? Focus on the Family Magazine, March 1997
[30] Exodus 6:6, King James Version, www.blueletterbible.org
[31] Exodus 6:6, King James Version, www.blueletterbible.org
[32] See 2 Peter 3:9
[33] Exodus 6:6, King James Version, www.blueletterbible.org
[34] See 1 Corinthians 11:25,
[35] Vander Lann, Ray, His Body, His Blood, Focus on the Family Magazine, April 1999
[36] Exodus 6:7, King James Version, www.blueletterbible.org

## Chapter five
[1] 11 Corinthians 3:16

Endnotes

[2]Elmer Towns, My Father's Name, Regal Books, 1991, p 9
[3]See Revelation 2:1
[4]Isaiah 62:10, New International Version, Zondervan
[5]Revelation 3:12, New International Version, Zondervan
[6]Ariel and Chana Bloch, The Song of Songs: A New Translation, University of California Press, 1998, p 148
[7]Philippians 2:6-8, New International Version, Zondervan
[8]John 17:3, New International Version, Zondervan
[9]2 Samuel 6:21, New International Version, Zondervan
[10]Richard Booker, The Miracle of the Scarlet Thread, Destiny Image Publishers, 1981, pp 23-31
[11]See Jeremiah 18:1-7
[12]Jeanne Guyon, Song of the Bride, Whitker House 1997, p 54, original writing late 1600's

## Chapter six

[1]See Genesis 2:2
[2]Psalm 97:5, New International Version, Zondervan
[3]See 2 Chronicles 6:18
[4]Matthew 17:4, New King James Version, 1982, Thomas Nelson
[5]Ryken, Wilhoit, Longman, Dictionary of Biblical Imagery, Intervarsity Press, 1998, Rock, p732-733
[6]Psalm 18:2, New International Version, Zondervan
[7]See John 19
[8]See Colossians 3:3
[9]See John 12
[10]Genesis 2:18, New International Version, Zondervan
[11]see Genesis 2:5

[12]see 1 Corinthians 15
[13]Proverbs 2:1-5, New International Version, Zondervan
[14]see Proverbs 25:2
[15]2 Corinthians 4:7-11, New International Version, Zondervan
[16]Psalm 139:23-24, King James Version, www.blueletterbible.org
[17]Isaiah 64:6, New King James Version, Thomas Nelson.1982
[18]Proverbs 24:16, New International Version, Zondervan

## Chapter seven

[1]Hebrews 12:5-6, New International Version, Zondervan
[2]See John 21:3
[3]Matthew 27:46, New International Version, Zondervan
[4]Guyon, Jeanne, Spiritual Torrents, The Seed Sowers Christian Books Publishing House, 1990, p34
[5]Deuteronomy 6:5, New International Version, Zondervan
[6]James 1:2-4, New American standard, Zondervan
[7]See Hebrews 11:8
[8]See John 15
[9]See 1 Corinthians 12:28
[10] James 4:6, New International Version, Zondervan
[11]New American Standard and Amplified
[12]Webster's 1928 Dictionary, online
[13]Genesis 32:28, New International Version, Zondervan
[14]1 Corinthians. 10:3-5, New International Version, Zondervan
[15]Isaiah 6:5, New International Version, Zondervan
[16]John 6:44, New International Version, Zondervan

## Chapter 8

[1] See Acts 10:9-16
[2] See Exodus 30:33
[3] 2 Corinthians 2:14-16, New International Version, Zondervan,
[4] Luke 20:17-18, New International Version, Zondervan
[5] See Judges 7:13-22
[6] 2 Corinthians 4:7, Amplified, Zondervan
[7] Matthew 26:6-13, New International Version, Zondervan
[8] John 20:11-17, New International Version, Zondervan
[9] Ryken, Wilhoit, Longman, Dictionary of Biblical Imagery, Intervarsity Press, 1998,
[10] Wilderness, pp948-950
[11] Mark 1:9, New International Version, Zondervan
[12] Thomas Merton, The Wisdom of the Desert, New Directions Books, 1960, p3
[13] Thomas Merton, The Wisdom of the Desert, New Directions Books, 1960, p 6-7
[14] Hannah Hurnard, Hinds Feet on High Places, Tyndale House Publishers, 1975, p208
[15] Hannah Hurnard, Hinds Feet on High Places, Tyndale House Publishers, 1975, p212
[16] See Mark 10:38
[17] Philippians 3:10, New King James Version, Thomas Nelson
[18] See John 11:43
[19] Isaiah 40:3, New International Version, Zondervan
[20] Luke 22:31, New International Version, Zondervan
[21] See Psalm 2:7-8
[22] See Psalm 110
[23] See John 12:24

## Chapter nine

[1] See John 11:13
[2] See John 11:21
[3] John 11:21, New International Version, Zondervan
[4] John 11:4, New International Version, Zondervan
[5] John 11:14-15, New International Version, Zondervan
[6] John 14:39, Amplified Version, Zondervan
[7] See John 11:39,
[8] 2 Corinthians. 2:14-17, New International Version, Zondervan
[9] Philippians 1:21, New International Version, Zondervan
[10] John Piper, Dangerous Duty of Delight, Multnomah Publishers Inc., 2001, p26
[11] See Hebrews 13:5
[12] See 2 Corinthians 12:9
[13] Hebrews 13:6-7, New International Version, Zondervan
[14] Ephesians 6:12, New International Version, Zondervan
[15] See Exodus. 17:10
[16] Isaiah 62:5), New International Version, Zondervan
[17] Revelation 19:6, New International Version, Zondervan
[18] Hosea 2 :19-20, New International Version, Zondervan
[19] John 3:29, New International Version, Zondervan
[20] 1 Corinthians 6:19-20, New International Version, Zondervan
[21] Genesis 29:15- 30,
[22] 1 Corinthians 11:25, New International Version, Zondervan
[23] Ephesians 5:25, New International Version, Zondervan
[24] Matthew 4:19, New International Version, Zondervan

## Chapter ten
[1] Webster's 1928 Dictionary, online
[2] See Matthew 13:3-8, Luke 8:5-15
[3] See Revelation 19:6-10
[4] Psalm 27:3, New International Version, Zondervan
[5] Matthew 11:12, King James Version, Zondervan
[6] See Ephesians 3:17
[7] Webster's 1928 Dictionary online, www.cbtministries.org/resources/webster1828.htm
[8] Ryken, Wilhoit, Longman, Dictionary of Biblical Imagery, Intervarsity Press, 1998, Pruning, p 683-684
[9] Wilkinson, Bruce, Secrets of The Vine, Multnomah Publishers, 2001, pp60-62
[10] Ryken, Wilhoit, Longman, Dictionary of Biblical Imagery, Intervarsity Press, 1998, Wind pp 951-952
[11] See Job 37:22
[12] See Ezekiel 1:4
[13] Ezekiel 37:9-10, New International Version, Zondervan
[14] Brennan Manning, Ruthless Trust, Harper San Francisco, 2000, pp4-6
[15] See 2 Corinthians 2:14-16

## Chapter eleven
[1] See Hebrews 4:1
[2] See John 13:23; 19:26
[3] See Revelation 5:6
[4] Philippians 3:10, New International Version, Zondervan
[5] See Romans 2:4

[6] See Revelation 19:9
[7] See Isaiah 64:6
[8] See John 13:6-14
[9] See Luke 22:42
[10] Jeanne Guyon, Spiritual Torrents, Seed Sowers, 1990, pg 27
[11] Bruce Wilkinson, Secrets of the Vine, Multnomah Publishers, Inc., 2001, p58
[12] Brennan Manning, Ruthless Trust, Harper San Francisco, 2000, p103
[13] Job 3:25, King James Version, Zondervan
[14] Philippians 4:13, New International Version, Zondervan
[15] Isaiah 61:3, New International Version, Zondervan
[16] See Luke 22:42
[17] See John 10:10
[18] Ephesians 6:12, King James Version, Zondervan
[19] Philepians1:2, New International Version, Zondervan
[20] Hebrews 11:32-38, New International Version, Zondervan
[21] Revelation 1

## Chapter twelve

[22] Tozer, A. W., The Knowledge of the Holy, Harper San Francisco, 1961, p 9
[23] Matthew 16:15, New International Version, Zondervan
[24] See Galatians 2:20
[25] See 2 Chronicles. 4:5
[26] See Ephesians 5:27
[27] Sorge, Bob, Envy, The Enemy Within, Regal Books, 2003, p 77-78

Endnotes

[28]See Revelation 21 & 22

## Chapter thirteen
[1]See John 1
[2]See 2 Kings 6:17
[3]See Genesis 32: 22-31
[4]See Genesis 32:9
[5] 1 Corinthians10:3-5, New International Version, Zondervan
[6]Genesis 24:30, New International Version, Zondervan
[7] 2 Corinthians 12:9, New International Version, Zondervan
[8]Ken Gire, The Divine Embrace, Tyndale House Publishers Inc, 2003, pg7
[9]See Ephesians 6:14
[10]Isaiah 52:7, New International Version, Zondervan
[11]See Joshua 14:9
[12]Psalm 92:12-14, Amplified, Zondervan
[13]2 Corinthians 3:18, New International Version, Zondervan
[14]1 Peter 2:5, New International Version, Zondervan
[15]Revelation 21:2, New International Version, Zondervan
[16]Revelation 21:22, New International Version, Zondervan
[17]Isaiah 54:11-12, New International Version, Zondervan
[18]Isaiah 62:2,4, New International Version, Zondervan
[19]Revelation 21:11, 19-20, Exodes 28:15-20, New International
[20]Version, Zondervan
[21]Isaiah 61:10, New International Version, Zondervan
[22]Isaiah 61:3-4, The Amplified Bible, Zondervan
[23]Isaiah 28:5, New International Version, Zondervan
[24]Proverbs 31:10-11, New International Version, Zondervan

[25] Proverbs 12:4, New International Version, Zondervan
[26] Isaiah 62:3, New International Version, Zondervan
[27] Isaiah 62:5, New International Version, Zondervan
[28] Song of Solomon, New International Version, Zondervan
[29] Revelations 19:7, New International Version, Zondervan

## Chapter fourteen

[1] See Isaiah 6:5
[2] Ariel & Chana Block, The Song of Songs; A New Translation, University of California Press, 1995, pg 212
[3] See John 13:35
[4] Isaiah 62:3, New International Version, Zondervan
[5] See Matthew 28:18
[6] Matthew 10:8, New International Version, Zondervan
[7] Matthew 10:7, New International Version, Zondervan
[8] Isaiah 62: 2 &3, New International Version, Zondervan
[9] Revelation 10:1, New International Version, Zondervan
[10] Ezekiel 1:28, New International Version, Zondervan
[11] Revelation 21 & 22, New International Version, Zondervan
[12] Revelation 19:12, New International Version, Zondervan
[13] Exodus 3:22, New International Version, Zondervan
[14] Exodus 13:12, New International Version, Zondervan
[15] Ephesians 3:16-20, New International Version, Zondervan
[16] Matthew 3:11, New International Version, Zondervan
[17] Acts 1:8, New International Version, Zondervan
[18] Acts 2:1-4, New International Version, Zondervan
[19] Hebrews 12:28, New International Version, Zondervan
[20] Romans 13:14, New International Version, Zondervan

# Endnotes

[21] 1 Thessalonians 5:8, New International Version, Zondervan
[22] 1 Corinthians 13:13, New International Version, Zondervan
[23] Romans 8:35,38-39, New International Version, Zondervan
[24] Philippians 2:7-8, The Amplified Bible, Zondervan
[25] Hebrews 12:2, New International Version, Zondervan
[26] Soren Kierkegaard, as quoted in Sacred Romance, Brent Curtis & John Eldredge, Thomas Nelson Publishers, 1997, p 80
[27] Revelation 22:17,20, New International Version, Zondervan

# TERESA EKLUND

Teresa has a passion to see all people come to a deeper understanding of their position before Jesus as His beloved bride of Christ. She desires the bride of Christ to understand there is a depth in God that can be experience here on earth. Having led numerous Bible studies, she also speaks on various topics, but her favorite one is passion for Jesus.

Teresa and her husband, Steve, have been actively involved in the Cincinnati House of Prayer since its foundation. Teresa prays with the passionate heart of God. A vibrant and engaging spokesperson, her depth and energy is a reflection of the time she spends seeking after God's heart and gazing into His face. Teresa and Steve have three children, Rachel, Zachary and Shiloh, who have been raised in an atmosphere of prayer and also actively participate with them in ministry.

*For more information, book orders and study helps please go to:*
**www.unquenchablefire.com.**